# MEGHAN MARKLE

The Feminist Wire Books
Connecting Feminisms, Race, and Social Justice



**Also in The Feminist Wire Books**

*We Gon' Be Alright: Resistance and Healing in Black Movement Spaces, 2012–2021*, by Stephanie M. Crumpton

*Betrayal U: The Politics of Belonging in Higher Education*, edited by Rebecca G. Martínez and Monica J. Casper

*Frontera Madre(hood): Brown Mothers Challenging Oppression and Transborder Violence at the U.S.-Mexico Border*, edited by Cynthia Bejarano and Maria Cristina Morales

*Black Women and da 'Rona: Community, Consciousness, and Ethics of Care*, edited by Julia S. Jordan-Zachery and Shamara Wyllie Alhassan

*Lavender Fields: Black Women Experiencing Fear, Agency, and Hope in the Time of COVID-19*, edited by Julia S. Jordan-Zachery

*A Love Letter to This Bridge Called My Back*, edited by gloria j. wilson, Joni B. Acuff, and Amelia M. Kraehe

*Black Girl Magic Beyond the Hashtag: Twenty-First-Century Acts of Self-Definition*, edited by Julia S. Jordan-Zachery and Duchess Harris

*The Chicana M(other)work Anthology*, edited by Cecilia Caballero, Yvette Martínez-Vu, Judith Pérez-Torres, Michelle Téllez, and Christine Vega

*Them Goon Rules: Fugitive Essays on Radical Black Feminism*, by Marquis Bey

# MEGHAN MARKLE

## Essays on Monarchy, Race, and Colonialism

**EDITED BY**
Duchess Harris and Julie Schwietert Collazo

THE UNIVERSITY OF ARIZONA PRESS
TUCSON

The University of Arizona Press
www.uapress.arizona.edu

We respectfully acknowledge the University of Arizona is on the land and territories of Indigenous peoples. Today, Arizona is home to twenty-two federally recognized tribes, with Tucson being home to the O'odham and the Yaqui. The university strives to build sustainable relationships with sovereign Native Nations and Indigenous communities through education offerings, partnerships, and community service.



ISBN-13: 978-0-8165-5739-4 (paperback)
ISBN-13: 978-0-8165-5740-0 (ebook)

Cover design by Leigh McDonald
Cover portrait of Meghan Markle by Tim O'Brien
Typeset by Sara Thaxton in 10.5/14 Warnock Pro with Headline Gothic ATF and Bebas Neue Pro

Library of Congress Cataloging-in-Publication Data
Names: Harris, Duchess editor | Collazo, Julie Schwietert editor
Title: Meghan Markle : essays on monarchy, race, and colonialism / edited by Duchess Harris and Julie Schwietert Collazo.
Other titles: Feminist wire books
Description: Tucson : University of Arizona Press, 2026. | Series: The feminist wire books | Includes bibliographical references and index.
Identifiers: LCCN 2025054810 (print) | LCCN 2025054811 (ebook) | ISBN 9780816557394 paperback | ISBN 9780816557400 ebook
Subjects: LCSH: Meghan, Duchess of Sussex, 1981– | LCGFT: Essays
Classification: LCC DA591.A45 M446 2026 (print) | LCC DA591.A45 (ebook)
LC record available at https://lccn.loc.gov/2025054810
LC ebook record available at https://lccn.loc.gov/2025054811

Printed in the United States of America
⊗ This paper meets the requirements of ANSI/NISO Z39.48-1992 (Permanence of Paper).

# CONTENTS

# MEGHAN MARKLE

# INTRODUCTION

DUCHESS HARRIS

On January 9, 2020, I flew to San Juan, Puerto Rico, to attend the Southern Political Science Association meeting. I'd be lying if I said that I was going for purely professional reasons. It was minus ten degrees in my home state, where I was surrounded by white snow, white people, and more responsibility than I wanted to embrace. I was a wife, mother of three, and a professor at a liberal arts college, where I had the privilege and dread of being the presiding officer of the faculty. I was craving a three-day respite in the sun with Black women who shared many of my experiences.

On Saturday night, seven of us went to dinner. Three days prior, Prince Harry and Meghan Markle, the Duchess of Sussex, had released a press statement, announcing on Instagram their decision to "step back as 'senior' members of the British royal family" (@sussexroyal, January 8, 2020). They would be dividing their time between the United Kingdom and North America, they wrote, and intended to become financially independent. The dinner conversation turned to this international news.

I had never been a royals watcher, but our conversation offered a Black feminist analysis that I found intriguing. My colleagues suggested that Markle's mother, Doria Ragland, had behaved in a way that we recognized. She had sent for her only child and grandchild to meet her in Canada; the racism that they were experiencing would not be tolerated. A few of us said, "We should write a book." I left the dinner, and then the conference, filled with sun and more intellectual stimulation than I had expected. I was poised to watch Ragland and Markle to see how these Black American women would navigate Buckingham Palace—even if (and precisely because) Markle was opting out of her formal role as a royal.

Two months later, the world was faced with its first global health pandemic in a hundred years. The president of my college sent us home for two weeks of spring break instead of one. Two weeks turned into eighteen months. With our lives turned upside down, no one could prioritize the book. Still, I stayed tuned in to developments about Markle. I was somewhat intrigued by Oprah Winfrey's March 2021 interview with Prince Harry and Markle, which probed the complicated emotional depths that had been stirred in Markle as the result of racism she experienced—both in the royal family and in the court of public opinion—after her May 2018 wedding to Prince Harry.[1] But at that time, I still wasn't in a place to do the deep thinking that is required to ask, "What is the global political meaning of the monarchy's rejection of this woman?"

When the worst of the pandemic began to wane, however, that very question started taking shape in my head, and I couldn't stop thinking about it. I was officially a royals watcher . . . though my watching was through a very specific lens and came freighted with heavy, uncomfortable questions. Often, I discussed these questions with colleagues, and as I did, the form of this book began to take shape. Many would say that using the treatment of Meghan Markle as a way to discuss colonialism is not an academic project of import. Not only do I disagree; I argue that her treatment is the *best* way to analyze and understand the empire, and the discomfort that many in the Commonwealth feel about the "Crown."

I began by looking back. Unlike my mother, who woke up at 6:30 a.m. to watch their wedding, I hadn't bothered to get up for Prince Harry's and Markle's 2018 nuptials. As I embarked on the task of shaping this book, I knew I'd need to examine that moment. Weddings have *always* been one of the primary interests of royals watchers, events where all the trappings of royalty and monarchy are made large, and where symbolism—overt and covert—sends coded messages to those who know what to look for. I knew that clues could be found there about the treatment of Markle and about her own negotiation of her identity as an outsider-turned-royal.

My first observation of the wedding was that it was subversive. Sure, the marriage was heteronormative, but multiple facets of Markle's identity—her nationality, the fact that she had been married previously, and, of course, her race—didn't exactly tick any of the monarchy's boxes for "preferred life partner characteristics." From the beginning, wedding planning was fraught. In his memoir, *Spare,* Prince Harry recounted that there was some debate around whether Markle would be allowed to wear a veil because she was a divorcée. Somehow, the veil prevailed. It would become a symbol, not only because of its transgressive statement about Markle's marital status but also because of the code quite literally sewn into it. Though Clare Waight Keller, the first female artistic director of the French luxury fashion house Givenchy and designer of the veil never says so in the Netflix series *Harry & Meghan,* Markle made her veil doubly subversive by having wildflowers from all fifty-three of the Commonwealth's countries (read: former and current colonies and territories) sewn on the organza veil and its nine-foot train.[2] These included the tropical orchid, Kenya's national flower; Bangladesh's white water lily; and Trinidad and Tobago's *chaconia,* among several dozen others.

"There it is," I thought. This was one of the first indicators that Markle was with the Commonwealth.

The transgressions didn't end there, even if Prince Harry and Markle acknowledged that then-Prince Charles (now king) was both aware and supportive of their unconventional choice to have a gospel choir—a nod to Markle's nonroyal roots—perform Ben E. King's secular song "Stand by Me." The Kingdom Choir, composed entirely of Black British singers, had been relatively obscure prior to the wedding. Its largest audience had been just two hundred people, and the group was even described by the *New York Times* as "a passion project for part-timers." Afterward, the choir's founder and lead singer, Karen Gibson, couldn't go out in public without being recognized and, often, thanked. The choir recorded its first album (titled—what else?—*Stand by Me*) with the Royal Philharmonic Orchestra. "And there it is again," I thought. Markle was using her newfound power to open paths and create opportunities for others.

I was here for it.

As we all know now, Prince Harry and Markle have continued to stand by each other, but the House of Windsor made clear immediately that it would not stand by them. With a near-endless amount of resources at their disposal—resources gained largely through colonialist enterprise—Buckingham Palace did nothing to intervene as domestic and international press and the court of public opinion picked apart Markle's past and her post-wedding self-presentation. They stood by idly, a fact that is all the more damning and unforgivable given that Prince Harry's own mother died tragically as a result of such unrelenting, unmitigated scrutiny.

The generous buffer and ample safety net that royalty should have conferred upon her simply did not exist for Markle. Though she had become a royal in title, she remained an outsider, and not—at least not initially—of her own choosing. In the absence of royal protection, Markle's own friends circled around her. Powerhouse tennis superstar Serena Williams pulled up, as did Markle's white girlfriends Lucy Fraser, Abigail Spencer, Lindsay Jill Roth, Ashleigh Hale, Silver Tree, and Jessica Mulroney. These women pulled a protective curtain around Markle, not just looking inward, but working to protect her outward image by having *People* do a special issue about her. When Markle learned she was pregnant, they were the ones who planned and hosted her baby shower.

But when it came to making home for Markle—"home" in both the literal and emotional, abstract sense of the word—it wasn't white people or the House of Windsor that rolled out the welcome mat. Instead, it was Black celebrity Tyler Perry who literally took her in.

Tyler Perry had never met Meghan Markle before she married Prince Harry, but he *had* gotten in touch with her. As he saw the media storm gathering—a biracial, divorced, American woman marrying into the royal family?!—he wrote Markle a letter, expressing empathy and solidarity with her. Two years later, when she and Prince Harry decided to distance themselves from their royal roles and from the prince's family, they went across the pond—to Canada. As COVID-19 closed in, the couple decided to cross into the United States before the border closed. They left Canada on March 14, 2020, to secretly flee to Los Angeles. How did they get to L.A. undetected? Markle remembered a line from Perry's letter, in which he extended his support to her should she ever need it.

And now, she needed it.

Markle called Perry to vent about what she was going through with the royal family. "I was just a wreck," Markle said. "I was just crying and crying. Sometimes it's easier to just open up to someone who knows nothing at all, and that was that moment with me and Tyler." Perry, moved, still hadn't met Markle in person, but he offered the couple the option of staying in his multimillion-dollar mansion. He commended them for stepping down from being senior working royals, and he provided them security for six weeks. Perry was later asked by the couple to be the godfather of their daughter, Lilibet.

Perry wasn't the only high-powered Black celebrity to show public support for the couple. Oprah Winfrey came through, too, giving them what everyone else in the world had denied them: the opportunity to define themselves, their relationship, and their decisions about royalty in their own words, to the world. Oprah, in the role of interviewer, hosted the couple in a two-hour prime-time special after they had been in the U.S. for one year. Though geographically distant from their troubles, the racist tentacles reached across the Atlantic. British tabloids, including the *Daily Mail*, terrorized the couple, with scintillating (and need we mention untrue?) stories. What *was* true, viewers of the Oprah interview learned—in the couple's own words—was that the royal family was going to strip their son, Archie, of his title and deny him a security detail. What's more, prior to his birth, they asked pointed questions about how dark the child's skin would be.

The stresses of *the* most institutionalized forms of racism and rejection were revealed by Markle as the conversation continued with Oprah. Sagging under the weight of it all, Markle had suffered a miscarriage and had fallen into a depression so deep that she had contemplated suicide.[3] Prince Harry's anguish of not being able to protect her from the vultures that made his wife want to kill herself was palpable, and every Black mother felt in her bones Doria Ragland's grief when, in the Netflix series, she cries with despair because she could not protect her child either.[4] Prince Harry's family, meanwhile, is more concerned about *accusations* of racism than the *acts* of racism that precipitated Markle's suicidal ideation. This tells us everything about white folks that we need to know: They'd rather see us try to kill ourselves than accept accountability for colonialism.

Prince Harry says it best: The royal family missed an opportunity with his wife. With 2.5 billion people in the Commonwealth, mostly Black and Brown, *Meghan Markle looks like the Commonwealth*. For those billions, Afua Hirsch says, Prince Harry's and Markle's "relationship represented the idea that Britain can change, that the most intractable parts of Britain can reform and evolve." And when it became clear that the royal family wouldn't reform and evolve, prompting the couple's physical departure from the family and the country itself, Hirsch adds "their departure felt like the death of a dream."[5]

* * *

So why *was* this opportunity for reform and evolution ignored entirely? More pointedly: Why was it tacitly—if silently—rejected? Follow the through line: If King Charles III or the House of Windsor denounced the tabloids for depicting Prince Harry and Markle's son, Archie, as a chimp, they might have to address Jamaica's request for reparations. In other words, acknowledging the very existence of racism and its devastating consequences might make the empire . . . accountable. And *that* would exact a very high cost indeed. Strategically, it was easier to sideline Markle and summarily ignore the press—easier, in fact, to sideline Prince Harry and focus instead on Prince William, his white wife, and their white children, who would raise no such possibilities of a racial reckoning—than to do the work necessary to bring Markle into the fold, protect her, and evolve the monarchy.

All these issues are complicated by Markle's own evolution, which includes a shifting definition of her identity. Markle, the daughter of a white father and a Black mother, did not identify as Black until she married into the royal family. "People are very aware of my race because they made it such an issue when I went to the U.K., but before that, most people didn't treat me like a 'Black woman,'" Markle explains in the Netflix series, and both she and her mother, Doria Ragland, acknowledge that they never had "the talk." "As a parent, in hindsight, absolutely I would like to go back and have that kind of real conversation about how the world sees you," Ragland says.[6]

And yet, had they had "the talk," it would have to have acknowledged, too, that the world did not—and still does not—see Markle the way it sees her mother. Ragland's experiences of racism—grocers mistaking her for Markle's nanny as just one example—are not Markle's experiences, evident in the fact that her own Hollywood agent did not realize initially that Markle is mixed race, but instead thought she was "sun-kissed California freckly."[7] Markle had what her mother did not: the luxury of not even having to think about race at all until the U.K. forced it upon her.

After Markle and Prince Harry left the U.K., they began to define themselves independently of the royal family, and in their own words, on their own terms. Markle scrutinized her own conceptualization of her identity and grappled with her questions and realizations publicly. In the second episode of the Netflix series, viewers see footage of Markle's acceptance speech upon receiving the 2022 NAACP President's Award. "People don't talk about what it's like to be mixed race. So much of my self-identification was trying to figure out where I fit in. And I think a lot of that is that you are not white enough and you are not Black enough. But I don't see the world that way," she tells the audience. The camera pans to her mother, Doria, who nods her braided head like a crown of Black American royalty. The scene then shifts to a one-on-one interview with Prince Harry, who declares that his children are mixed race and how proud he is of that.

Prince Harry has also had an awakening, one the public has been able to witness as well. Misan Harriman, an Afro-British friend, said that Prince Harry was in an echo chamber of absolute privilege before marrying Markle. Once Harry stepped out of the chamber, he realized there was a much bigger world. He admitted that where racial issues were concerned, he was "sleepwalking" through life. But as with Markle, once in their relationship, Prince Harry began immediately to think about race. It took only eight days after their engagement to issue a statement about how the British press was racializing his fiancée.

Sadly, that awakening is neither interesting to, nor shared by, his family, who has defended against it at all costs. If Prince Harry's awakening can be seen as an opportunity for the nation to change, then the public response to his marriage shows how far the nation has to go. British Nigerian historian David Olusoga reminds us that as hopeful as many millennial Brits were to see the possibility of a modern monarchy, the U.K. was mired in a culture war over its relationship to the European Union when the couple got engaged. If most Brits are invested in celebrating their abolishment of slavery without acknowledging that former slave owners were financially compensated by the British government for their losses, why would we expect Brits to see Markle as mixed race? Their twenty-first-century racial formations are no different than the eighteenth-century Confederate U.S.'s "one-drop" rule. Once on their soil, mixed-race Markle became Black.

Writer and activist Afua Hirsch reminds us that the U.K. enslaved more people than the U.S.; it's just that their enslavement was in the Caribbean.[8] Slavery fueled the early British Empire, and the first slave voyage for Great Britain was financed by Queen Elizabeth I. Over the last fifty to sixty years, there has been a call to reimagine the Commonwealth as racially inclusive. That reimagining has not occurred for most, but it *has* happened for Prince Harry. The Netflix series—aside from being important because it was a platform that allowed the couple to define themselves on their own terms rather than being defined through the dirty, distorted lens of tabloids and public opinion—was also important because it asserted that the U.K. (still) has an opportunity to follow Prince Harry's lead, to pop the bubble of white privilege. If he can change from wearing a Nazi uniform at age twenty to living in a mixed-race family at thirty-eight, it's not too late for a nation that led the global slave trade for hundreds of years to become a leading antiracist force in the world.

Can the British public wake up from the racist past that bred its racist present? Kehinde Andrews, who became the U.K.'s first Black studies professor—in 2021—argues that the Commonwealth is still an empire that promotes an economic relationship of intergenerational wealth. This wealth is built on the backs of intergenerational extraction from impoverished African, Indian, and Caribbean nations. Many Afro-Brits, like Prince Harry's friend Harriman, who once regarded the prince as racist, identified his speaking at the twenty-fifth-anniversary Stephen Lawrence memorial—twenty-six days before his wedding to Markle—as part of his antiracist journey.[9]

We will never know how the royal family really sees Markle. Before Queen Elizabeth II passed away, Barbados removed her as its head of state, on November 30, 2021, breaking its ties with the British royal family—and with it, one of the island's last remaining imperial bonds to the U.K. Charles, heir to the British throne, was in attendance as Barbados celebrated ending its formal links with his ninety-five-year-old mother. In the queen's absence, Charles has become king of fifteen other realms, including the U.K., Australia, Canada, and Jamaica. Prince Harry's transformation around race could lead to the U.K. reforming its colonial impact on other Caribbean nations.

If you watch the Netflix series, pause when David Olusoga asks, "Who dreamed that Britain would have a Black princess?"[10] Apparently, the significance of the moment hasn't been shared by all. The day the series was released, Tory member of Parliament Bob Seely revealed his preparation for a bill that would see Meghan Markle and Prince Harry stripped of their royal titles. Once the U.K. got its Black princess, the empire struck back.

## Notes

1. Sun Reporter, "Mark My Words."
2. Newbold, "Story Behind Meghan Markle's Givenchy Wedding Dress."
3. Sun Reporter, "Mark My Words."
4. Garbus and Sashin, *Harry & Meghan*, episode 2.
5. Garbus and Sashin, *Harry & Meghan*, episode 5.

6. Garbus and Sashin, *Harry & Meghan*, episode 2.
7. Garbus and Sashin, *Harry & Meghan*, episode 2.
8. Garbus and Sashin, *Harry & Meghan*, episode 3.
9. Stephen Lawrence was an eighteen-your-old Black British student who was murdered in a racist attack carried out in southeast London in 1993.
10. Garbus and Sashin, *Harry & Meghan*, episode 3.

## Works Referenced

Garbus, Liz, and Erica Sashin, dirs. *Harry & Meghan*. Aired December 2022 on Netflix. https://www.netflix.com/watch/81478159.

Sun Reporter. "Mark My Words: Meghan Markle Oprah Interview." *The Sun*, January 31, 2024. https://www.the-sun.com/news/2475583/meghan-markle-oprah-interview-full-transcript/.

Newbold, Alice. "The Story Behind Meghan Markle's Givenchy Wedding Dress—and Her 16-Foot Veil." *Vogue*, May 19, 2025. https://www.vogue.com/article/meghan-markle-wedding-dress.

## CHAPTER 1

# UNDER THE GAZE

## *Meghan Markle, Media Representation, and Blackness*

PORTIA OWUSU AND ARIANE TULLOCH

Prior to her marriage to Prince Harry, Meghan Markle's public appearances and speech were arguably race neutral: unmarked, inoffensive, and palatable to the public at large. The ease with which she appeared to occupy spaces such as the United Nations as a goodwill ambassador, the roles she played as an actress, and even her self-presentation on platforms such as Instagram all pointed to a woman who seemed to have evaded the limitations of race, particularly the unique burdens placed on Black women in the entertainment industry.[1] What changed, then, when she married Prince Harry and became the Duchess of Sussex? How did a woman seemingly acceptable to the mainstream media and the public become so vilified, even accused of collapsing the British monarchy?[2] We propose that the answer is because Markle dared to exercise her voice and agency, and in doing so, she moved from being raceless to raced. In sum, she became Black.

Historically, women who have married into the British royal family have survived and thrived in their roles either by being silent or by being silenced. Markle, a Black American woman, defied this code. In the overwhelmingly white space that is the palace, she talked back, and she talked Black. This was a problem. This chapter interrogates the shift in media perceptions of her from this standpoint. We argue that although in the past Markle may have performed race neutrality in professional and public settings, and hence, stayed silent on matters of race, politics, and social justice, this posture was impossible at the palace.[3] There, she was, in the words of Zora Neale Hurston, "thrown against a sharp white background" and thus hyper-visible.[4] There, she was forced to confront realities of Black womanhood that she, a light-skinned biracial woman, may have previously evaded. In this vein, central to our argument is the notion of the palace (a term used interchangeably throughout this essay for the royal family and the British monarchy as an institution) as a site of racial and cultural reckoning for Markle. Specifically, pitched against the whiteness of the palace, Markle *became* Black. That is, as argued by Stuart Hall, the shift in public perception of Markle and the ways in which she, after leaving Britain as a "working royal," now clearly aligns with the Black community on race matters and social justice attest to the notion that identity is not static.[5] It is a constant production of both being and becoming.

In this chapter, we have selected moments in the public lives of Markle and Prince Harry, loosely categorized under the labels of courtship, engagement, marriage, and life outside England. We analyze examples from these to show how Markle progressively *becomes* Black in media representations. As her relationship with the prince deepens, Blackness is publicly thrust upon her and she must decide either to embrace it or ignore it with the world watching.

## Courtship

To understand Markle's relationship with Prince Harry, and the many courses it has taken in the public eye, one needs to place Markle and her transition from an actress to a member of the royal family in historical context: Traditionally, there have been limited roles available to Black women in the public sphere, and Hollywood has been instrumental in ensuring this. As a commercialized entity, the film industry aided and abetted in cultural and discriminatory practices.[6] The image of Black and other nonwhite people suffered. The roles minorities occupied reinforced colonial and slave-era stereotypes, namely Black people as subordinate, marginalized, or subjugated individuals or criminals. The presence of Black and nonwhite people existed to bolster the presence of white people and to affirm white superiority as societal norm. Specifically in America, cinema became a space in which contested ideas about history, citizenship, and racial and gender identities were debated and solidified. David Wark (D. W.) Griffith's *The Birth of a Nation* (1915), the first feature-length film, tackled all these subjects, but from a particular viewpoint. On the surface, *Birth* is a narrative that is clichéd: Two families, geographically and politically opposed, one based in the slaveholding South and the other in the North, collide when their sons befriend each other at school. Griffith uses this simple narrative, however, to present a particular vision of American society that emphasizes racist ideologies and Black abnormality—for example, the inherent criminality of Black people and the uncontrollable sexual appetites of Black men that endanger white women. The popularity of Griffith's film—aided by its viewing at the White House on February 18, 1915, by then-president Woodrow Wilson—helped cement problematic Black presence in American cinema.

The roles ascribed to Black actors generally reflected colonial or slave-era stereotypes because they were subservient and only differentiated and colored by gender. For the Black male actor, the typecast was either the submissive older man ("boy") who served the white person/family, or the young, attractive, and agile man who, because the white woman was physically attracted to him, was typecast as a rapist.[7] Similarly, available to Black female actresses were two prevailing roles: the mammy, the older, domesticated Black presence in the white household, or the Jezebel, the attractive Black woman named after the biblical character who weaponized her sexuality to manipulate men and those in positions of authority.[8] As a prevailing image in antebellum America, the Jezebel was particularly unique because she was attractive to both Black and white men and because she was intentional in her malice: "[She] was the counter image of the mid-nineteenth-century ideal of the Victorian lady. She did not lead men and children to God; piety was foreign to her . . . [and] domesticity paled in importance before matters of the flesh."[9]

The trope of the Jezebel has been particularly harmful to young Black women in entertainment because it reduces them to their sexuality. However, this has not been as pronounced in Markle's professional career. Whereas the roles she took did not deny or undermine her physical attractiveness, they were not solely predicated on it. In fact, most of her major roles positioned her character as a professional woman. In *General Hospital,* she was a health-care worker; in *Dater's Handbook,* she was a marketing executive; and in *Suits,* she was a paralegal with aspirations of becoming a lawyer. In all these roles, Markle escaped the duality of playing either the mammy or the Jezebel. Additionally, because her career was limited to the small screen, she benefited from a level of privacy that other actresses have not enjoyed. This, in theory, should have afforded her opportunities to control her public image when she entered into a relationship with Prince Harry. However, when their relationship became public, coverage in tabloids and conservative media aligned Markle with the negative stereotypes of Black America.

The 2016 article "Harry's Girl Is (Almost) Straight Outta Compton," by Ruth Styles for the *Daily Mail,* particularly stands out. The article attempts to do what Markle seemed to have escaped in her career: racially typecast her. While some may read "Compton" as a reference to Markle's Californian roots, Markle actually grew up in the prestigious View Park–Windsor Hills and Hollywood areas. Thus, the reference, more truthfully, aligns Markle with a type of Blackness that is insurgent, violent, and antiestablishment. This is because Compton, a predominantly Black city in South Los Angeles, has historically been known for radical Black arts and politics. Gangster rap, a subgenre of hip-hop and rap known for its brutal depiction of social realities in the Black community, has particularly deep roots there. Renowned artists such as Dr. Dre, N.W.A., Snoop Dogg, Tupac Shakur, and Kendrick Lamar all have connections to Compton. Relatedly, radical Black thought, especially that steeped in 1960s and 1970s civil rights activism, was formulated and developed in California generally, and Compton specifically.[10] Compton's allusion to radical Blackness would have resounded even louder for contemporary readers because of the worldwide success of F. Gary Gray's 2015 biopic about N.W.A., *Straight Outta Compton.*

Styles thus uses Compton metonymically to describe the environment of Markle's childhood, which, according to Styles, was "plagued by crime and riddled with street gangs. . . . Other crimes noted over the past seven days include multiple drug-related misdemeanors, vehicle thefts, vandalism and disturbing the peace." Alongside descriptions of her supposed childhood environment are pictures depicting Markle's "run-down" and "crime-ridden" neighborhood. Styles juxtaposes this with descriptions of pristine and "palatial" Kensington Palace and Highgrove House, Prince Harry's childhood homes. Implicit in the article is the question of whether Markle is worthy of being with the prince. The article's extended use of Compton, a place to which Markle has no tangible connections, suggests an answer in the negative. Although readers in the comments section criticized Styles's racist and classist undertones, the article achieved what Markle had long resisted: being typecast. As a woman *almost straight outta Compton,* Markle is presented not just Black, but impoverished, insurgent, and unworthy of her newfound position.

Prince Harry disagreed. Less than a week after the publication, the prince, via his press secretary, released a statement that spoke directly to the article. He emphasized the racism, sexism, and classism implicit in Styles's reportage of his relationship with Markle. Speaking of the "hidden" and explicit abuse received by Markle from the press, Prince Harry asserted that he was "worried about Ms. Markle's safety" and "deeply disappointed." He added that "it [was] not right that a few months into [their] relationship," Markle had been subjected to abuse on account of him.[11] The statement positioned Prince Harry as a protector of Markle, his intimate partner, and positioned Markle as the public figure. The conciliatory tone of his statement appealed to the goodwill of the press. That the statement was released solely in the name of the prince allowed Markle to continue to present herself as feminine and nonthreatening. This was significant because, as articulated by bell hooks in *Talking Back: Thinking Feminist, Thinking Black,* racist and sexist stereotypes of Black females often characterize them as "loud, rude, overbearing, and in relationship to black males dominating and castrating."[12] By not speaking out, Markle defied this.

The significance of silence in Markle's public presentation of herself as the ideal woman continued as her relationship garnered more public interest. Shortly after Markle accompanied the prince to the wedding of Pippa Middleton (Prince William's sister-in-law) in 2016, she attended a script-reading event with her *Suits* castmates as part of the ATX Television Festival in Austin, Texas. There, in a Q&A with the audience, Markle was asked about the possibility of a future marriage to the prince. She simply smiled and giggled. Prior to that moment, she had acted confidently and professionally with the audience. While some may have read her response as that of a woman in love, or as safeguarding her private life, the significance of her response—or lack thereof—was not lost on royal correspondents and commentators. Author and journalist Robert Jobson noted that in addition to her reticence to publicly discuss the status of her relationship, Markle had also permanently shut down *The Tig,* a personal blog she created and had maintained for three years. All these, Jobson opined on *Good Morning America,* pointed to a deliberate effort of "angling herself to be more acceptable to the royal family."[13]

Markle's willingness and need to police public forms of expression to maintain her relationship with the prince, and to enter the royal family, implies, as Princess Diana once suggested, that historically the success and sustenance of women who marry into the royal family is predicated on their willingness to be silent and silenced.[14] This idea was cemented in February 2018, three months before her wedding. In London, Markle, alongside Prince William and Kate Middleton (then the Duke and Duchess of Cambridge) and her fiancé, appeared on stage to promote the Royal Foundation, a charity founded by the two princes to advance their philanthropy. In a roundtable-style discussion, Markle, dressed in a navy V-neck, sleeveless flare dress, sat sandwiched between her future husband and the heavily pregnant Middleton. After a keynote speech by Prince William, the interlocutor asked each person the focus of their philanthropy and reasons for it. Princes William and Harry replied that they were motivated to break taboos surrounding male mental health, particularly suicide, and youth violence. Middleton replied that her philanthropic focus was to support mothers and early-year health interventions, while Markle said her focus was on girls' and women's empowerment. Each person touched on their personal connections to the work they do, but Markle's answer distinguished her from the rest of the panel.

In expanding on her work championing the cause of women and girls, Markle remarked, "I hear a lot of people saying when speaking about girl empowerment . . . that you're helping women find their voice and I fundamentally disagree with that. [Because] women don't need to find a voice; they have a voice. They need to feel empowered to use it and people need to be encouraged to listen."[15] She then referenced the Me Too and Time's Up campaigns as exemplars of women being empowered to use their voice.

Markle's answer, though popular with the audience and young people, deviated from two unspoken rules governing public expressions by members of the royal family: Refrain from commenting on current and political affairs, and refrain from giving personal opinions, even when asked. Traditionally, and especially in the reign of Queen Elizabeth II, this has been the modus operandi of senior members of the family. Thus, whereas the rest of the panel was asked about their personal connections to their philanthropies, their answers, notably, focused on the *work* they do and the *people* they work with, rather than on themselves; essentially, it is *we* rather than *I*.

Markle's break from royal traditions did not go unnoticed. Coverage of the event—the gathering of the "Fab Four"—drew attention to her assertiveness and self-confidence. On social media, women, young people, and people of color especially applauded her willingness to confront issues of social injustice and inequality. But traditional media, especially print, were divided. Newspapers with traditionally left-leaning politics interpreted her words as signaling a new and modern era in the British monarchy. The U.K.'s *Guardian* covered the event with the headline "Meghan Markle Pledges to 'Shine a Light' on Women's Rights."[16] Similarly, an article from *Belfast Telegraph* listed eleven things "learned from the Fab Four's first engagement together," and attributed six of them to Markle, whom they described as "articulate . . . the most relaxed out of the group."[17]

For conservative outlets, however, Markle's centrality at the event was a sign of impending fragmentation within the group, particularly between Markle and Middleton.[18] Markle's answer was controversial because it presented three possibilities as to her future role in the family: a hypocrite, a challenger, or a detractor. For those who saw her as the first, her answer was tone deaf because it was unmindful of the accusations of abuse that women have waged against the royal family.[19] For those who viewed her as challenger, her answer was seen as a subversive acknowledgement of the view, rarely spoken in public, that the royal family is inseparable from historical injuries and injustices. The sum of these two opinions was that she was dangerous, a detractor, and someone entering the family to work against the establishment.

In a March 3, 2018, article for her *Daily Mail* column, Rachel Johnson, a sister of conservative politician Boris Johnson, gave voice to these fears. She likened Markle's deviation from the political neutrality adopted by the rest of the group to the band member who abandoned her group to go "solo," and opined, "as a nation, we certainly prefer royal women who don't really speak, like the Queen, or the Duchess of Cambridge."[20] Johnson's focus on Markle's inability to conform to British norms and royal femininity positioned Markle as an outsider and someone doomed to fail in her new role. If Markle, who was expected to acquire British citizenship once she married the prince, could not perform the most basic of British characteristics—impassivity (the stiff upper lip)—then how was she to succeed as a member of the highest echelons of British society?

Johnson's critique of Markle shows, as bell hooks contended, that "serious" talk is reserved for "grown folks," who are men and white. In a patriarchal and racist society, therefore, to be respectful and submissive to authority, is to be silent or, at best, to speak in ways that do not demand others listen—"the soliloquy, the talking into thin air, the talking to ears that do not hear you."[21] For Markle, a Californian and an actress, this could have possibly entailed adopting a happy-go-lucky or Valley girl persona, both predicated on innocence, triviality, and whiteness. When Markle speaks—and speaks "seriously"—it is significant because not only does she seem to be forgoing the performance of innocence, triviality, and whiteness that silence suggests, but, applying hooks's thinking, Markle's audacity to utilize her new stage to speak "seriously" signifies Blackness since "in black communities (and diverse ethnic communities) . . . [the] struggle has not been to emerge from silence into speech, but to change the nature and direction of our speech, to make a speech that compels listeners, one that is heard."[22]

## Engagement

Following the criticism of Markle's dominance during the "Fab Four" interview, which occurred in the "courting" phase of Markle's and the prince's relationship, the engagement phase offered an opportunity to rein in and *re*-present Markle as poised and self-controlled. In an interview following the official announcement of their engagement, the couple sat down with Mishal Husain of the BBC.[23] In response to the first question—how the prince proposed—Markle looked to the prince to answer. When he initiated a response, she interjected every now and then to add her perspective. Gleeful and bubbly throughout, Markle interrupted her fiancé several times, but in a way that was both forgivable and even endearing. The difference in the body language of the couple—the prince cautious in the display of his emotion, and Markle ebullient—notably played on cultural stereotypes of the reserved Briton and the gleeful Californian.

Likewise, their body language was telling: Markle's attentiveness to her fiancé as he initiated answers to questions, handholding (notably, her two hands were clasped around one of his), the shifting of her body toward him rather than toward interviewer, and the constant smile on her face all worked to present Markle as the submissive and affable wife-to-be. The prince, in turn, was the loving and protective future husband. There was a sense in which their interview represented a break from previous royal engagement interviews, notably the palpable way in which they physically displayed their affection for each other.[24] Nonetheless, for students of history, there was some resonance with the past: Markle's mannerisms—the fixed eyes on her fiancé, nodding and smiling at him as he spoke, and her two hands locked with his—were reminiscent of Princess Diana's gestures during her official engagement interview with then-Prince Charles in 1981. The key difference was that Prince Harry, unlike his father, was receptive and encouraging of Markle's affection throughout the interview.[25] The function of the interview, therefore, seemed to signal a healthy change for both the public and the royal family.

Husain, the interviewer, attempted to home in on the change that their relationship represented by specifically asking about the scrutiny over Markle's ethnicity. The future duchess asserted that it was "disheartening." She was "proud" of who she was, she said, adding that their focus was on their relationship, not on "that." Prince Harry reaffirmed her answer about the insignificance of race by saying that she was just like an "added member of the family." By asking a question about her ethnicity, Husain tried to turn the conversation to "serious" talk, but their answers, which undermined its importance, rejected this invitation. At this point in their relationship, it was clear that Markle, unlike her articulations during the Fab Four interview, stuck to the script and answered the question in a way that removed her from controversy. The pictures, released alongside their interview, functioned to reaffirm a public image of the couple predicated on Prince Harry as the traditional male protector, Markle's wholesomeness as a future royal wife, and race as insignificant in their relationship.

A month later, a brooch would challenge this narrative. At a luncheon at Buckingham Palace, Princess Michael of Kent, a distant relative of the queen, wore a "Blackamoor" brooch. Blackamoor figurines, a popular trope in classical and Renaissance art, depicted "the African" (or North African Arabs) with caricatured features, such as extremely dark skin and big red lips. As art pieces and accessories owned and worn by members of the upper class, Blackamoor brooches reflected the fetishization of the Black body in Europe. Today, however, their one-dimensional depiction of Blackness means that they are regarded as highly offensive and racist. Awam Amkpa, a curator and professor of Africana studies at New York University, asserts that given its history and the fact that Africans continue to face racism, discrimination, and questioned citizenship, wearing Blackamoors as art pieces opts for Blackness in the white imagination rather than the realities of contemporary Black life. Essentially, it is "to say that Africans are more acceptable as pieces of art than as fellow citizens."[26] The piece of jewelry worn mocked the palace's attempt to present Markle as aracial. Pictures of the princess leaving the palace wearing the brooch sparked debate about negative experiences of Black people in predominantly white spaces. On social media and traditional print media, criticism of the princess ranged from her being overtly racist to her choice of accessory exemplifying racial microaggression. The princess issued a statement apologizing for the offense caused, but it is notable that Markle and her fiancé remained silent on the matter. This may be because social media came to their defense or, arguably, five months before the wedding, their focus was on their future.

## Marriage

By simply wearing the brooch, Princess Michael communicated unspoken anxieties surrounding Markle as a nonwhite person entering an institution whose relationship with Blackness has always been one of ownership. The power of Princess Michael's brooch arguably rests in the quietness of its gesture. In *The Sovereignty of Quiet: Beyond Resistance in Black Culture*, Kevin Quashie argues that the most powerful and effective forms of protest are not always loud. Referencing the famous Black Power salute by Tommie Smith and John Carlos at the 1968 Mexico City Olympics, Quashie argues that the power of their protest is, of course, in its details—"the clenched fists, the black gloves, the shoeless feet," but more profoundly, the "sublime balance between their intentional political gesture and this sense of inwardness," the physical posture of Smith and Carlos, as if they are "in a moment of deep spirituality, in prayer, as vulnerable as they are aggressive, as pensive as they are solidly righteous . . . their humanity on display."[27] Quashie argues that this is an element of Black resistance that is often not acknowledged because Black culture is stereotyped as histrionic, loud, and violent.[28] Doria Ragland, Markle's mother, would display elements of such resistance at the wedding on May 19, 2018, at St. George's Chapel at Windsor Castle. Dressed in a mint-green dress with white flower trim and a matching beret, Ragland sat quietly by herself in a pew.

Ragland's presence—marked by her teary eyes, pulled-back dreadlocked hair, and a nose ring—can be read in two ways. The first reading is that of an affirmation of her daughter's Black ancestry and resisting attempts to characterize her daughter as unbefitting of her new position. That is, whereas there have been previous attempts to manage Markle's public image to present her as not Black, or unraced, at the wedding, her *biological* mother, who is visibly Black, upsets this narrative by attesting to her African ancestry. Specifically, because Ragland is so poised, regal in her posture, the Blackness she exudes directly contradicts the kind of Blackness—violent, loud, and underclass—that was pinned on Markle in the *Daily Mail*'s "Compton" article. The still, and yet powerful, posture of Ragland, can be read as a quiet protest that resisted stereotypes.

Simultaneously, however, Ragland's poised position could also be seen as collaborating with the palace's effort to acknowledge Markle's Black ancestry, but in a way that was palatable, recognizable, and nonthreatening. The Black guests and elements of Black culture at the wedding attested to this. The presence of Oprah Winfrey, Idris Elba, and Serena Williams, among others, helped cement the palace's effort to present Markle as unraced, if not racially malleable. This is because while Oprah, Elba, and Williams are visibly Black, in their professional lives and public images, they have transcended racial boundaries and "crossed over" to mainstream and global audiences.[29] The wedding presented Prince Harry, Markle, and the royal family in the same light—global, inclusive, and transcending racial boundaries.

The Google Doodle commemorating the couple's union on the day of their wedding communicated a similar message. It depicted Markle in a wedding dress, locked in arms with her husband, who is drawn with his recognizable red hair, as they marched toward Windsor Castle, waving to well-wishers. A notable feature of the image is the multicultural crowd lined up on each side of the couple: people of visibly different races, happily waving the British flag as the couple walks by.[30] Clearly this piece of art—which would have been visible to the millions of people who accessed Google search that day—was meant to celebrate the couple as a symbol of inclusivity and interracial and intercultural harmony in a changing Britain. The success of the wedding granted the couple a respite from negative discourses about race, especially from conservative outlets. But this respite would not last for long.

The couple's first major assignment, a tour of the Commonwealth as husband and wife, took them to Australasia. Their positive reception reflected the goodwill that their wedding generated globally. With an itinerary that emphasized the couple interacting with minority and Indigenous communities, the trip was reminiscent of Princess Diana and then-Prince Charles's visit to the region thirty-five years earlier. Like Princess Diana, Markle's charm quelled some of the dissenting voices questioning the role of the monarchy in modern Australia. The trip was so successful, and the couple so popular with Australians, that the news that they were expecting their first child was announced formally while they were there.

As the world media rejoiced at the news and the global public congratulated them, the tide of public opinion turned in Britain. There, Markle was accused by conservative media of capitalizing on her pregnancy for personal gains. As Markle's pregnancy began to show, she would be accused of using it as a prop to manage her public image. A November 2018 article in the *Daily Mail* by Siofra Brennan ran with the headline "Maternity Wear? Meghan's in a Mini Dress!"[31] In it, Brennan observes that Markle continued to dress in designer clothes, rather than traditional maternity wear. Soon thereafter, Latifa Yedroudj of *Express*, another U.K. tabloid newspaper, reinforced the emphasis on her clothing choice with the headline "Meghan CAN'T STOP Showing Off: Duchess Uses These SNEAKY Tricks to Flaunt Her Baby Bump."[32] This article, published in January 2019, explicitly accuses Markle of drawing attention to her pregnancy to showcase an "array of wardrobe and styling trick[s]." Implicitly, she is accused of being vain and financially irresponsible for spending money on designer outfits. In response to the scrutiny of Markle's appearance by the tabloid press, Suzanne Moore, a journalist at *The Guardian,* wrote in her column on February 3, 2019: "The Duchess of Sussex is public property as far as the media are concerned. . . . Meghan, who was 'welcomed' into the royal family in a mood of self-congratulatory 'tolerance' . . . has been shoved back into her place since she returned from honeymoon. She is uppity (ie non-white)."[33] Thus, as Moore asserts, the focus on Markle's physical appearance attested to the intense public scrutiny she has been under since her relationship with the prince became public. However, because it came during her pregnancy, a stage in which women are normally protected and celebrated, the unchecked negative attention on her physical appearance opened the door for other criticism, particularly centered on her race.

We propose that Markle's pregnancy marked a shift in public perception of her, and ultimately initiated the Sussexes' split from the royal family, because her unborn child, Archie, would be the incarnation of fears of Blackness invading the whiteness of the monarchy. Historically and culturally, on both sides of the Atlantic, there is a long-standing history of weariness and disgust toward interracial relationships. In the early days of the American republic, lawmakers of British or Anglo-Saxon backgrounds prohibited interracial relationships and codified them in legal systems.[34] The one-drop rule, a legal and cultural classification, marked the extent to which Blackness, or African ancestry, had "stained" the purity of white blood. Subcategories, denoted by terms such *mulatto, quadroon, octoroon,* and *quintroon,* provided the exact mathematical quantity of Black blood that ran in an individual's veins.[35]

Arguably, Britain did not have quite the same fixation on race. However, in the eighteenth and nineteenth centuries, Britain and its colonies denigrated "race mixing" in cultural and scholastic discourses. The eugenics movement, fronted by prominent "scientists" Karl Pearson and Francis Galton, held the view that the white race was superior and that inferior races had to be stopped from reproducing. In "Social Problems: Their Treatment, Past, Present, and Future," a lecture delivered at the Galton Laboratory for National Eugenics in 1912, Pearson proposed that a key solution to social problems was biological in character, namely to advance "the homogenous white race whose fertility shall markedly dominate that of the black [*sic*]." Although these ideas may be fallacious, because of Pearson's and his colleague's standing in society—as endowed professors at prestigious universities—their ideas gained cultural and political currency. The International Eugenics Congress in 1912, held at the University of London, is an example. Attendance at the conference included official delegations from France, Germany, and Italy. Prominent attendees included political, social, and religious leaders such as Winston Churchill, the chemist Sir William Ramsay, and the Right Reverend Charles Gore, who was then the lord bishop of Oxford. The setting of the conference and its attendees belied the validity of the problem that they were there to tackle. It also attests to the sophisticated medium through which racist discourses have been filtered historically in Britain. This, arguably, is different from the United States, where manifestations of racism—lynchings, Jim Crow laws, redlining, and microaggressions—are not cloaked in sophisticated intellectual discourse, but are instead visceral and embedded in everyday experience.

Even though racism's manifestations are different on each side of the Atlantic, the commonality is that the Black body in white society is a problem to be solved. W. E. B. Du Bois alluded to this in *The Souls of Black Folk* (1903) when he asserted that exempt from babyhood, society looks at the Black person with a looming question: "How does it feel to be a problem?"[36] As a "problem,"

Blackness threatens the purity of white society and thus, looms as an ever-present specter that is a source of white anxiety.

When Markle was pregnant, her unborn child symbolized a problem because it would be this child who testified to the union between Markle, a mixed-race woman, and Prince Harry, a white British royal. A child between the couple was a cause of anxiety for some people because it represented the idea that the royal family, one of the last bastions of whiteness in British society, had been invaded by the monstrosity of Blackness. The wedding may have caused anxiety for racists. A child, however, amplified those anxieties. The child—a physical and genetic culmination of that union—attested to the consummation of the union, defiantly mixing Black and white blood.[37]

This anxiety is historical and literary. In classic and contemporary narratives of racial passing, for example Nella Larsen's *Passing* (1929) and Brit Bennett's *The Vanishing Half* (2020), pregnancy between a light-skinned, or racially ambiguous, Black woman, and a white man evokes uncertainty, unease, and dread for the woman hiding her race. But Markle was not passing. Therefore, she was free to enjoy her pregnancy. However, because the child she was carrying was seen as public property, some sectors of the British public became obsessed with what her child would look like and how the child's physical features could change everything. In an interview with Oprah Winfrey, Markle would say that questions about her child's skin color were raised as topics of "concern" in "several conversations" by a member of the family when she was pregnant.[38] A child that looks phenotypically white would calm the fears of the public in a notable way: It would show that the white genes of his father have dominated the Black genes of his mother, and it would make it easier to see and respect him as a bona fide member of the royal family. When Markle did not participate in this narrative, and instead openly expressed joy at the impending birth, she became an affront to the public. Tabloid articles accusing her of "flaunting" her pregnancy thus betrayed this anxiety.[39]

The criticism that Markle received when pregnant informed the couple's break from traditions when the baby was born. Unlike previous royal babies, Archie was born at the Portland Hospital, and not St. Mary's Hospital, where both Princes Harry and William were born and where Kate Middleton gave birth to the Cambridges' children. The couple also rejected the traditional photograph of the nursing mother on the doorstep as she left the hospital and instead made an informal announcement to the media waiting at St. George's Chapel. In the absence of a clear photograph showing the baby's features, social media speculated about what the royal child looked like. Among harmless discourse of whether he would take the features of Markle or Prince Harry, Danny Baker, a British broadcaster, tweeted an image of a finely dressed couple holding the hands of a chimpanzee, with the caption "Royal baby leaves hospital."[40] Baker's tweet, contemptible as it was and condemned by many, expressed the unspoken unease people had about Archie—what he would look like and what his visible difference might mean for the future of the royal family. The couple did not address this and the lack of official photographs of the child shielded him from direct public speculation. However, a tour of southern Africa in autumn 2019 would provide a space for Markle to address the impact of negative media scrutiny on her health.

In South Africa, Markle returned to serious talk. During an audience with anti-apartheid activist Archbishop Desmond Tutu, they chose to show the full face of Archie, the couple's son, for the first time. It was also in South Africa that Markle, in an interview with Tom Bradby, was asked if she was OK, and replied "No." She elaborated: "Any woman . . . especially when they're pregnant, you're really vulnerable, and so that was made really challenging. And then, when you have a newborn . . . it's a lot, so you add *this* on top of just trying to be a new mom . . ." After this, Markle turned to the reporter and said, "Thank you for asking because not many have asked if I am OK, but it's a very real thing to be going through behind the scenes."[41]

During the same trip, Markle initiated another serious talk. In the presence of a dark-skinned female audience, she identified herself as "a mother, a wife, a woman of color, and [your] sister."[42] Her comments, like her response at the Fab Four event, would be seen as deviating from the neutral, "safe," and pedestrian answers typical of the royal family, particularly women. The public at large applauded her honesty, but conservative media and monarchists lambasted her. Journalist and broadcaster Piers Morgan said in an interview, "I think she's an actress whining too much. I say that with great respect. But the most successful members of the Royal family, the queen, the queen's mother, the most beloved always understood, you never explain, you never complain, you do your duty and everyone loves you. The moment you start yapping away moaning about everything, people go, 'Hang on, you're living at our expensive palaces, with servants.'"[43] Morgan's comments, just like those of Rachel Johnson of *Daily Mail*, compared Markle to female members of the royal family and found her wanting. But while conservative commentators criticized Markle for breaking royal protocols and "whining," her time in South Africa arguably proved to be an advantage for her.

Whether it was the space, the people, or the history, South Africa gave Markle the license, opportunity, and courage to be truthful about her experience in the royal family. The statements on her postpartum mental health and her identification as "a woman of color and [your] sister" drew a link among her negative experience within the palace and her gender and race. Markle's usage of "a woman of color" to identify her race *in* South Africa is not an accident. Though "person of color" is loosely understood as a nonwhite individual in many parts of the world, in South Africa, and specifically under apartheid racial categorizations, it refers to a mixed-race person. A *colored* person in apartheid South Africa held an ambiguous position in society: Their position was akin to purgatory in that they existed in the in-between space of whiteness and Blackness. Simply put, a *col-*

*ored* person denoted a crime, someone whose very presence was an affront to the legal and cultural codes forbidding miscegenation. Equally, by identifying herself as a "sister" in an audience of Black women, she solidified her membership in the Black community because a "sister" is, in both Africa and the diaspora, someone who is not necessarily kin but a female with whom one shares cultural and political experiences. In South Africa, therefore, Markle aligned with Blackness and broke from whiteness.

## Life Outside England

It was in South Africa that Markle became Black. Her Blackness was denoted by her refusal to be silenced, her willingness to speak truth to power, and her rejection of racial erasure as a condition for remaining in the palace. These factors culminated in the couple's decision to leave the United Kingdom soon after returning from Africa. It was reported that South Africa was the first choice for places the couple could emigrate to when they decided to leave Britain. When the couple emigrated to the U.S. instead, they took opportunities to continue with the work initiated in Africa, namely, affiliation with Black organizations and greater participation in movements for racial and social justice.

The year that they moved—2020—would prove to be particularly advantageous in allowing them to use their celebrity to champion these causes. In May of that year, George Floyd, an unarmed Black man, was murdered by four Minneapolis police officers. As the keynote speaker at the virtual graduation for Immaculate Heart, her former high school, Markle stressed racial justice. Directly aligning with the Black Lives Matter movement, she recalled the names of Black Americans murdered by law enforcement and said, "George Floyd's life mattered; Breonna Taylor's life mattered; Philando Castile's life mattered; Tamir Rice's life mattered and so do so many other people whose names we know and those we don't."[44] The focus on race in the graduation address showed the way in which Markle's experience in the royal family had marked her.

The graduation address signaled a new form of self-presentation for the couple, specifically Markle, that was direct, assertive, and unafraid to tackle social issues. It was in direct contrast to the "Don't explain, don't complain" mantra that she had had to live by as a member of the royal family.

The graduation speech was followed by a series of public engagements in which the couple explicitly confronted issues of race and racism. The most prominent of these was their sit-down interview with Oprah Winfrey in March 2021. In it, Markle detailed the trauma the couple endured as they started their new life in the U.S. The couple's grievances and line of reasoning for leaving the U.K. was presented as twofold: the unfair treatment by the press and the lack of the protection from the royal family. Prince Harry explained that historically, there has been an "invisible contract" between the family and the press corps, where the royal family has been able to influence press coverage. This privilege has been used in the past to protect members of the family, but he claimed that this was not so for him and his wife.

Furthermore, the couple accused the family of failing to take seriously the racial component that influenced the negative media representations of Markle. The prince pointed out that while seventy-two female members of the U.K. parliament wrote a letter to Markle showing support for her lawsuit against "outdated and colonial" representations of her, the royal family remained silent.[45] Therefore, the royal family, Prince Harry implied, were complicit in media harassment of his wife. Of greater significance to their decision to move, however, was a desire to protect Archie, their first child. In the same interview with Oprah, Markle and the prince recounted a conversation with an unnamed member of the royal family regarding "how dark" the unborn child would be. Concerns about the skin tone of her unborn child would be a cornerstone in Markle's reckoning with race: Questions about the phenotype of Archie (whose African ancestry would be even less than Markle's) would have, inevitably, communicated to Markle that in the palace, she could never be anything but Black. Whereas in her previous image, her race had been presented as both ambiguous and malleable, the historical whiteness of the palace would present her as Black. Rather than negating the experience of being denied the opportunity to choose one's racial identity, Markle embraced it. Visibly aligning herself with Black organizations—such as the NAACP—publicly empathizing with minority groups and causes, and speaking of her friendships with Black individuals, such as Serena Williams, Tyler Perry, and Gayle King, Markle became Black in the eyes of the public. It is a Blackness that allows her to be all that she is and unapologetically engage in conversations in which she is not silenced. At last, she can engage in serious talk.

## Notes

1. Consider the reception that visibly Black actresses have received by non-Black audiences, especially in remakes of classic films, for example Leslie Jones in *Ghostbusters* and Halle Bailey in *The Little Mermaid*. Both Jones and Bailey faced torrents of online abuse by fans who were unhappy that classic white characters had been reprised with Black actresses. Likewise, films featuring interracial relationships, especially between Black women and white men, have been the subject of significant criticism. For example, after the death of Whitney Houston, Kevin Costner reflected, "Some people weren't happy that I picked Whitney Houston to be my love interest in *The Bodyguard*" (*The Herald*). Similarly, Viola Davis said that to "have a dark-skinned woman with a big nose and wide lips and all of that and her natural hair kissing—romantically kissing a white man on screen" as an opening scene in *Widows*, provoked some audience members (Doty).
2. Conservative outlets and commentators have accused Markle of trying to undermine the British monarchy. See, for example, Rosenwald, "Meghan, Duchess of Sussex, Is Being Compared to Wallis Simpson."
3. By "race neutral," we refer to an individual who is racially (phenotypically) ambiguous and thus able to evade stereotypes assigned to specific racial groups.
4. Taken from Hurston's 1928's essay, "How It Feels to be Colored Me," 67.
5. Hall, "Cultural Identity and Diaspora."

6. Guerrero, *Framing Blackness*, 99–100.
7. Films such as *Driving Miss Daisy* (Beresford) and *To Kill a Mockingbird* (Mulligan) show this duality. In *Miss Daisy*, it is the affable older Black man serving white people; in *Mockingbird*, the young and attractive Black man is typecast as a rapist because of his close proximity to white women. The latter is reflective of historical realities, such as the 1955 murder of Emmett Till.
8. See, for example, *Imitation of Life* (Stahl) and *Gone with the Wind* (Fleming), in which Black women are typecast in subordinate roles. See 1 Kings 16:31 for the story of Jezebel.
9. White, *Ar'n't I a Woman?*, 49.
10. See Johnson, "How Compton Became a Citadel of Black Political Power."
11. Kensington Palace, "A Statement by the Communications Secretary to Prince Harry," press release, November 8, 2016, https://sussex royal.com/archival-statements/a-statement-by-the-communications -secretary-to-prince-harry/.
12. hooks, *Talking Back*, ix.
13. This conversation on *Good Morning America*, May 8, 2017, is archived at https://archive.org/details/KGO_20170508_140000_Good _Morning_America/start/4440/end/4500.
14. See Martin Bashir's Panorama Special interview with Princess Diana, initially aired November 20, 1995, on the BBC.
15. This conversation is archived in a Facebook post by the Female Lead, April 24, 2020, https://www.facebook.com/watch/?v=36401535787 0535.
16. Siddique, "Meghan Markle Pledges to 'Shine a Light.'"
17. *Belfast Telegraph*, "Things We Learned."
18. Seyfort, "'Very Quickly It Became Meghan Versus Kate.'"
19. See, for example, testimonies by Princess Diana and later accusations against Prince Andrew as part of the Jeffery Epstein case (Seal, "It Was Catastrophic;" Wigglesworth, "How Damaging to the Royal Family?").
20. Johnson, "The Royal Fab Four?"
21. hooks, *Talking Back*, 6.
22. hooks, *Talking Back*, 6.
23. *BBC News*, "FULL Interview."
24. While then-Prince Charles, Prince Andrew, and Prince William demonstrate affection to their spouses during their official engagement interviews in 1981, 1986, and 2010, respectively, it is muted. Both Princes Andrew and William, for example, maintain physical distance between themselves and their fiancées. This is unlike Prince Harry and Markle, whose hands are locked throughout the interview.

25. King Charles and Diana are physically close in their interview but his answer to the question "Are you in love?" to which he replied, "Whatever being in love means" hints at emotional distance between them.
26. Quoted in Rautenbach, "Gaudy, Sure—but Racist Too?"
27. Quashie, *Sovereignty of Quiet*, 1, 3.
28. Quashie, *Sovereignty of Quiet*, 3–4.
29. All three have global images that are tied to their nationalities. The *Oprah Winfrey Show* was arguably one of the most watched shows by the white middle class in America and one of America's biggest entertainment exports. Idris Elba is known all around the world as British to the extent that there was talk that he would play the next James Bond. Likewise, in 2018, he was voted "The Sexist Man Alive" by *People* magazine. Equally, Serena William's dominance in tennis, a white space, has made her a household name around the world.
30. See https://www.google.com/doodles/royal-wedding-2018.
31. Brennan, "Maternity Wear?"
32. Yedroudj, "Meghan CAN'T STOP Showing Off."
33. Moore, "Poison and the Papers."
34. *Loving v. Virginia* (1967) was landmark case that, finally, declared unconstitutional state laws that had made interracial marriage illegal.
35. *Mulatto* was a person of biracial ancestry; *quadroon*, an individual of one-quarter African ancestry; *octoroon*, an individual of one-eighth African ancestry; and *quintroon*, an individual of one-sixteenth African ancestry (Hickman, "The Devil and the One Drop Rule," 7–9, 14).
36. Du Bois, *Souls of Black Folk*, 1.
37. The concept of "Negrophobia" is steeped in the belief that people of African descent were closely related to primates, particularly the orangutan. See, for example, Thomas Jefferson's defense of these ideas in *Notes on the State of Virginia*. Thus, race mixing—particularly of Black and white—was akin to bestiality.
38. Sun Reporter, "Mark My Words."
39. See, for example, Jones, "Why Can't Meghan Markle Keep Her Hands off Her Bump?"
40. Reproduced by Simon Lancaster (@bespokespeeches), "Astonishing Danny Baker could think even for a second this tweet was ok." https://twitter.com/bespokespeeches/status/1126408674119958529?ref_src=twsrc%5Etfw%7Ctwcamp%5Etweetembed%7Ctwterm%5E1126408674119958529%7Ctwgr%5E0b00457d185df0dd7be5ff39c11d890a1ab4dd00%7Ctwcon%5Es1_&ref_url=https%3A%2F%2Fwww.newsweek.com%2Froyal-baby-archie-harrison-danny-baker-bbc-meghan-markle-prince-harry-1420702. Baker was later fired by the BBC, his employer.

41. *ITV News*, "Meghan Says 'Not Many People Have Asked if I'm OK.'"
42. *ITV News*, "Meghan Says 'Not Many People Have Asked if I'm OK.'"
43. *US Weekly*, "Piers Morgan Says Duchess Meghan 'Needs to Stop Whining.'"
44. *Inside Edition*, "Full Speech."
45. See letter on Holly Lynch's Twitter account (@HollyLynch 5, October 29, 2019): https://twitter.com/HollyLynch5/status/1189175248035483648?ref_src=twsrc%5Etfw%7Ctwcamp%5Etweetembed%7Ctwterm%5E1189175248035483648%7Ctwgr%5E034c69b5c073df19ff08e2534d8d7b1fc2a269f3%7Ctwcon%5Es1_&ref_url=https%3A%2F%2Fmashable.com%2Farticle%2Fmp-letter-meghan-markle.

## Works Referenced

Bashir, Martin. "Panorama Special—the Princess Diana Interview." Dailymotion video, 55:16. https://www.dailymotion.com/video/x9mukpk.

*BBC News*. "FULL Interview: Prince Harry and Meghan Markle." November 27, 2017. YouTube video, 20:25. https://www.youtube.com/watch?v=LQicq60aJaw.

*Belfast Telegraph*. "Things We Learned from the Fab Four's First Engagement Together." February 28, 2018. https://www.belfasttelegraph.co.uk/news/uk/things-we-learned-from-the-fab-fours-first-engagement-together/36654537.html.

Bennett, Brit. *The Vanishing Half*. New York: Riverhead Books, 2020.

Beresford, Bruce, dir. *Driving Miss Daisy*. Los Angeles: Zanuck Company, 1989.

Brennan, Siofra. "Maternity Wear? Meghan's in a Mini Dress!" *Daily Mail*, November 21, 2018. https://www.dailymail.co.uk/femail/article-6413681/Pregnant-Meghan-isnt-ready-embrace-maternity-wear-yet.html.

Doty, Meriah. "Viola Davis on Interracial Kiss with Liam Neeson in 'Widows': 'Elusive to Me Because of the Way I Look.'" *The Wrap*, November 17, 2018. https://www.thewrap.com/viola-davis-interracial-kiss-liam-neeson-widows-illusive-diversity-steve-mqueen/.

Du Bois, W. E. B. *The Souls of Black Folk*. Oxford University Press, 2007.

Fleming, Victor, dir. *Gone with the Wind*. Culver City, CA: Metro-Goldwyn-Mayer, 1939.

Griffith, D. W., dir. *Birth of a Nation*. Mamaroneck, NY: Epoch Producing Co, 1915.

Guerrero, Ed. *Framing Blackness: The African American Image in Film*. Philadelphia, Temple University Press, 1993.

Hall, Stuart. "Cultural Identity and Diaspora." In *Identity: Community, Culture, Difference*, edited by Jonathan Rutherford, 222–37. London: Lawrence & Wishart, 1990.

*The Herald*. "Kevin Costner: Some People Not Happy I Picked Whitney Houston for Bodyguard Role." February 14, 2017. https://www.heraldscotland.com/life_style/arts_ents/15090823.kevin-costner-people-not-happy-picked-whitney-houston-bodyguard-role/.

Hickman, Christine B. "The Devil and the One Drop Rule: Racial Categories, African Americans, and the U.S. Census Review Question." In *A Reader on Race, Civil Rights, and American Law: A Multiracial Approach*, edited by Timothy Davis, Kevin R. Johnson, and George A. Martínez, 7–19. Ann Arbor: University of Michigan, 2001.

hooks, bell. *Talking Back: Thinking Feminist, Thinking Black*. New York: Routledge, 2014.

Hurston, Zora Neale. "How It Feels to be Colored Me." Reproduced in *The Meaning of Martin Luther King Jr. Day: The American Calendar*, by Amy A. Kass and Leon R. Kass, 66–69. New York: What So Proudly We Hail, 2013.

*Inside Edition*. "Full Speech: Meghan Markle's Surprise Graduation Address to Her Old High School." June 4, 2020. YouTube video, 6:10. https://www.youtube.com/watch?v=FWstrgBr6Xg.

*ITV News*. "Meghan Says 'Not Many People Have Asked if I'm OK' amid Intense Media Spotlight | ITV News." October 18, 2019. YouTube video, 2:26. https://www.youtube.com/watch?v=Zo9G91QWMQs.

Jefferson, Thomas. *Notes on the State of Virginia*. N.p., 1785. https://tile.loc.gov/storage-services/service/gdc/lhbcb/04902/04902.pdf.

Johnson, Rachel. "The Royal Fab Four? I Fear Meghan's a Bit Out of Tune Already!" *The Daily Mail*, March 3, 2018. https://www.dailymail.co.uk/debate/article-5459067/RACHEL-JOHNSON-Royal-Fab-Four-fear-Meghans-bit-tune.html.

Johnson, Robert Lee. "How Compton Became a Citadel of Black Political Power." *PBS SoCal*, February 3, 2022. https://www.kcet.org/shows/artbound/when-compton-was-a-citadel-of-black-political-power.

Jones, Liz. "Why Can't Meghan Markle Keep Her Hands off Her Bump? Experts Tackle the Question That Has Got the Nation Talking: Is It Pride, Vanity, Acting—or a New Age Bonding Technique?" *Daily Mail*, January 26, 2019. https://www.dailymail.co.uk/news/article-6636233/Why-Meghan-Markle-hands-bump-Experts-tackle-question.html.

Larsen, Nella. *Passing*. New York: Alfred A. Knopf, 1929.

Moore, Suzanne. "Poison and the Papers: Why Tabloids Are Obsessed with Meghan 'Flaunting' Her Bump." *The Guardian*, February 3, 2019. https://www.theguardian.com/uk-news/shortcuts/2019/feb/03/poison-and-the-papers-why-tabloids-are-obsessed-with-meghan-flaunting-her-bump.

Mulligan, Robert, dir. *To Kill a Mockingbird.* Los Angeles: Universal Studios, 1962.

Pearson, Karl. "Social Problems: Their Treatment, Past, Present, and Future." Lecture delivered at the Galton Laboratory for National Eugenics, University College London, London, March 19, 1912.

Quashie, Kevin. 2012. *The Sovereignty of Quiet: Beyond Resistance in Black Culture.* New Brunswick, NJ: Rutgers University Press.

Rautenbach, Anneke. "Gaudy, Sure—but Racist Too? Unpacking Centuries of 'Blackamoor' Art." *NYU News,* July 31, 2015. New York University. https://www.nyu.edu/about/news-publications/news/2015/july/awam-amkpa-on-blackamoors-at-la-pietra.html.

Rosenwald, Michael S. "Meghan, Duchess of Sussex, Is Being Compared to Wallis Simpson, the Last American to Roil the Royal Family." *Washington Post,* January 9, 2020. https://www.washingtonpost.com/history/2020/01/09/wallis-simpson-meghan-markle/.

Seal, Mark. "'It Was Catastrophic': Inside Prince Andrew's Misguided Bid to Explain Away Epstein." *Vanity Fair,* January 27, 2022. https://www.vanityfair.com/style/2022/01/inside-prince-andrews-misguided-bid-to-explain-away-epstein.

Seyfort, Serena. "'Very Quickly It Became Meghan Versus Kate': Prince Harry Claims Media Created 'Fab Four.'" *Nine News,* January 9, 2023. https://www.9news.com.au/national/prince-harry-tv-interviews-book-release-memoir-airs-in-the-uk/5167fe22-20f2-4a17-9b59-53b2686bc237.

Siddique, Haroon. "Meghan Markle Pledges to 'Shine a Light' on Women's Rights." *The Guardian,* February 28, 2018. https://www.theguardian.com/world/2018/feb/28/meghan-markle-pledges-to-shine-a-light-on-womens-rights.

Stahl, John M., dir. *Imitation of Life.* Los Angeles: Universal Pictures, 1934.

Styles, Ruth. "Harry's Girl Is (Almost) Straight Outta Compton: Gang-Scarred Home of Her Mother Revealed—so Will He Be Dropping By for Tea?" *Daily Mail,* November 2, 2016. https://www.dailymail.co.uk/news/article-3896180/Prince-Harry-s-girlfriend-actress-Meghan-Markles.html.

Sun Reporter. "Mark My Words: Meghan Markle Oprah Interview." *The Sun,* January 31, 2024. https://www.the-sun.com/news/2475583/meghan-markle-oprah-interview-full-transcript/.

*US Weekly.* 2019. "Piers Morgan Says Duchess Meghan 'Needs to Stop Whining': 'You Do Your Duty and Everyone Loves You.'" October 28, 2019. https://www.usmagazine.com/celebrity-news/news/piers-morgan-duchess-meghan-needs-to-stop-whining/.

White, Deborah G. *Ar'n't I a Woman? Female Slaves in the Plantation South*. New York: W. W. Norton.

Wigglesworth, Kirsty. "How Damaging to the Royal Family Is the Scandal Surrounding Prince Andrew?" *The Conversation*, October 22, 2025. https://theconversation.com/how-damaging-to-the-royal-family-is-the-scandal-surrounding-prince-andrew-267983.

Yedroudj, Latifa. "Meghan CAN'T STOP Showing Off: Duchess Uses These SNEAKY Tricks to Flaunt Her Baby Bump." *Express*, January 26, 2019. https://www.express.co.uk/news/royal/1078127/meghan-markle-baby-bump-style-tricks-royal-family-news.

CHAPTER 2

# ARE YOU OK?

THERÍ A. PICKENS

This is about Meghan Markle. This is not about Meghan Markle.

This might be about you. It is certainly about me.

I begin in a place of relative safety. Well, as safe as one can be writing about depression and suicide. So I begin with validation. I take seriously the facts of depression and suicidal ideation. They are as much a part of human experience as anything else. I refuse shame and self-deprecation, not just because they are hurtful, but because they are unhelpful. How can anyone possibly deal with depression or a desire for death if it is buried under a mountain of silence and shame?

Yet that is just what we are asked to do. We are asked—as Meghan Markle was—not to speak of such things in polite company. Unfortunately, everywhere public, including the therapist's couch, is polite company. That maxim does not just apply to the royal family. I forget where I was when I heard that Meghan Markle had considered suicide. My outward reaction was probably an imperceptible quirk of my left brow. My inside reaction? *Same, girl. Same.*

I was twelve the first time I thought about killing myself. I had just been diagnosed with myasthenia gravis, an incurable neuromuscular disease. I did not know how my life would change. The doctor's diagnosis relieved me of not knowing why I suddenly couldn't walk as much as I used to, why I was tired all the time, why my mother had to spoon-feed me soup I could not swallow, why I was afraid to hold anything heavier than a pen. What his diagnosis did not do was give me any measure of hope.

First of all, he had to pull out a large reference book to test me. That hefty (burgundy? blue?) tome sat near my thigh, opened to the page on myasthenia. The pediatric neurologist, following the suggestion of an octogenarian ophthalmologist who had seen it all, ran his finger down the page and tested me for each symptom on the list. I passed. I failed. I was given pyridostigmine bromide, which only blocked symptoms for a few hours. It worked, until it failed. In my mother's best friend's kitchen, I took one of the chef's knives from its block and held it up in the moonlight. The glinting silver looked like a smile.

Suicidal ideation, when confessed, tends to be understood as a personal failing. People flinch away from you as if the thoughts are contagious, a disease passing on the breath. Of course, people are more afraid of suicide-as-contagion than they are of actual viral aerosols. It never occurred to me to disbelieve Meghan Markle. As someone who has considered suicide, I find it nearly impossible to lead with disbelief. The specter of shame feels too imposing (larger for someone in the business of mollifying the public) to start there. Telling is too great a risk to one's image. In this case, the risk concerned the reputation of one of the most recognizable families in the world.

But she did tell.

Meghan Markle told.

Watching *Harry & Meghan* on Netflix, I get the impression that the pair are trying to widen the narrative in contrast to the British tabloids' focus on the minutiae of fictitious "royal protocols," incremental changes in posture, and speculation about one's inner life. Each episode includes interviews with chosen family, friends, select family, and experts on Black British life. While the episodes trace the couple's private life, the docuseries takes care to depict what is happening in the public arena, including Brexit. Their story is also spliced with that of Harry's mother, Diana, Princess of Wales, and her treatment at the hands of the British press, a harassment that led to her death.

The docuseries begins with a reference to Nina Simone's rendition of "I Wish I Knew How It Would Feel to Be Free" as the preface to their love story, presented in the first episode. Then they move to Meghan Markle's backstory in the second episode, providing information about her childhood, youth activism, poetry and theater interests, now-defunct lifestyle blog, *The Tig*, and her career as an actress. The third episode pans outward to focus on the relationship between the British tabloids and the royal family, while also providing some of Harry's background, tracing his own antiracist journey. The fourth episode details the couple's wedding and the beginning of Meghan Markle's suicidal ideation and depression. She describes how she was prohibited from discussing it or asking for assistance. That episode ends with Lesley Gore's "You Don't Own Me." In the fifth episode, the docuseries goes behind the screen to help viewers understand social media and the British tabloids as a machine, churning out stories, with Samantha Markle (Meghan Markle's half sister) partially at the helm. Then the couple clarifies when and why they began to think about leaving. The final episode coincides with the beginning of the pandemic, detailing their rescue by Tyler Perry, and their Oprah interview. The Oprah interview is bookended by an encouraging text from Beyoncé Giselle Knowles-Carter, who writes that Meghan Markle was chosen to break generational curses.[1] *My God,* I thought, *how lonely.* As Beyoncé herself says—in a song that draws from a Warsan Shire poem—"What luck. What a fucking curse."[2]

I admit my scholarly fascination with Afua Hirsch, author of *Brit(ish),* and David Olusoga, author of *Black and British,* who assess how Meghan Markle, as a concept, functions within the British imagination. I balk a little at calling a human being a concept, but let's be real.[3] The British tabloids were not talking about *the real* Meghan Markle any more than the American tabloids talk about the real Megan Thee Stallion. Public figures are fundamentally and necessarily ineffable. They become palimpsests for national and global desires, dreams, ambitions, and nightmares. Black British conceptions of Meghan Markle remain tethered to the Crown's relationship with the Commonwealth and those hailing from countries within it. For a Black British public, Meghan Markle represents them. For a brief time, she symbolized the possibility of change and inclusion. Then, with the swiftness of London rain, the influx of white supremacist tabloid coverage indicated everyone was living inside the changing same.

Even though the first three episodes foreshadow a discussion of mental health, episodes 4 and 5 of *Harry & Meghan* delve more into Meghan Markle's depression and suicidal ideation. She clarifies her own thought process: all the drama about her presence, all the difficulty with her father, half sister, and niece, all the harassment—she found it, as anyone would, overwhelming. Harry talks about the racism in the tabloid coverage with barely controlled vehemence. Meghan Markle, for her part, thought, "All of this will stop if I'm not here" (episode 4). During overwhelm, one's thoughts can feel like a tape that plays over and over; they can also feel like a barrage. Either way, they are a kind of mental noise that feels both sporadically intrusive and constant. Suicidal ideation cuts through those thoughts with the sharp precision of a butcher's blade. The clarity of the thought may be one of the scariest aspects of the experience.

Most friends and advisers in the series comment on how low Meghan Markle gets, how obvious it was to them that she was not doing well. Harry laments that he became the institutional version of himself rather than the loving fiancé and husband. James Holt, their former PR spokesperson and current executive director of the Archewell Foundation, recounts, "People have asked me what the causes were. My view is, it doesn't matter. I think that [when] we start down a path of trying to get someone to justify why they feel depressed, that's a dangerous place for us to be. What you had was someone that was struggling and she needed more help" (episode 6).

On the one hand, Holt is absolutely correct, indicating the practice of seeking to understand the origins of depression in order to reframe one's own story about oneself. Holt's comment seeks to reroute that process toward taking the person at their word and getting them the professional assistance (if not the personal assistance) that they need. Holt's remarks also come with some degree of chagrin, embarrassed as he is about encouraging the couple to "play the game" for the British press. As a PR professional, his job was to advise them on their public image, a duty that comes into conflict with his knowledge of how much Meghan Markle's depression was augmented by said public image.

On the other hand, Holt's commentary assumes that suicidal ideation and suicide are personal phenomena. They are. They are not. They are social phenomena. Suicide is a consequence of social pressures and circumstances. In 1897, Émile Durkheim published a germinal sociological tome, *Suicide: A Study in Sociology*. Current sociology students encounter Durkheim's work primarily as a methodological text since his study indexes the underpinnings of sociology itself. Namely, the field takes for granted that society is not composed of individuals but of groups. Social groups.

Another reason why current sociologists only use Durkheim's work for methodological reasons is because the nineteenth-century text bases its ideas on wrongheaded assumptions regarding gender, race, class, and disability. Nevertheless, Durkheim's major point remains clear and salient: Suicide results from a set of personal reactions to social circumstances, specifically the influences of social integration (how well one fits into their society) and moral regulation (how well the society controls and channels human nature). Just in case anyone else is confused by the idea of moral regulation, I hasten to add that moral regulation encompasses religion but more broadly refers to social and cultural norms that influence the structures of society, including the economy, legislation, and the influence of social hierarchy. The four types of suicide correspond to failures of social integration and moral regulation: egoistic (not enough social integration), altruistic (too much social integration), anomic (not enough moral regulation), and fatalistic (too much moral regulation).

My second suicide attempt was a mix of egoistic and altruistic intentions. I was a sixteen-year-old, first-year student in college. My classes were challenging enough and my peers were nice enough. But their behavior indicated I was an anomaly. While I searched for the ramps to go to class, they hopped up the stairs. *They're faster. They're easier.* I followed behind the gaggle of backpacked Black students. I even took a picture of them this way. I wasn't invited to study sessions or parties or somewhere just to chill. The school year started to feel like one long pursuit of elusive friendships and the dawning realization that the best I could do as a disabled person was be invisible. In the wee hours of the morning, I contemplated lying in the middle of Washington Road, between Fine Hall and Schultz Laboratory. But in the middle of the night, there would not be any traffic. I deliberately drove my scooter into the cordoned-off area leading to Guyot Hall, letting the rope catch me by the throat. I lay there dazed, realizing my head had not hit the pavement. A botched self-stoning. When I told the senior I was "seeing," he giggled, spitting words in his California accent between laughs: *You got clotheslined!* I let the red in my cheeks say whatever it would have meant to him.

I expect Durkheim would be baffled by this vignette, since comprehending it relies on a complex understanding of Black collegiate social and psychosexual politics, structural and casual ableism, women's friendships, and structural and casual misogynoir. After all, he did write, "A woman's sexual needs have less of a mental character because, generally speaking, her mental life is less developed." Too bad he published this volume ten years after his marriage to Louise Dreyfus, with whom he had two children. I shudder to think what her intimate life was like. For me, though, Durkheim might reiterate a portion of his argument: "Society is not only something attracting the sentiments and activities of individuals with unequal force. It is also a power controlling them."[4] In the original text, these words sum up the nature of social integration forces and introduce the problems regarding moral regulation. Without pulling Durkheim's words too far out of context, I would suggest that they aptly characterize the imbricated nature of how well one fits in and how well one's impulses are controlled. That is, suicide and suicidal ideation are not solely a matter of how well one fits in, nor solely a matter of how well society allows for that fitting in. It is both. Always both.

Curious by nature and a researcher by trade, I turned to contemporary sociology and psychology to understand the study of suicide now. I encountered some limitations. Some of the literature indicated that it discussed Black people or African Americans, but the data set was composed only of Black or African American men. Other articles began with faulty assumptions based loosely on the infamous, woefully inaccurate Moynihan Report. Their biased questions were of little use. In addition, it became clear that social scientists have data sets of convenience. College students, for instance, are a particular segment of the population, especially in the United States, where traditional students' stage of development functions more like extended adolescence than young adulthood.

One review article aptly summarizes some of the other limitations of current lines of study related to suicide: There is not enough information on suicide completers, and current studies fail to differentiate among different kinds of Blackness. I would add, given the history of medical experimentation and state intervention in Black America, I am not sure any qualitative data would be accurate or ample enough to draw conclusions. These limitations stem from the prohibitions of the fields. Sociology collects information in aggregate; psychology collects it at the level of the individual. Both fields rely on the presumption that the researcher receives accurate information that can be extrapolated to explain social or psychological phenomena. When dealing with Blackness and disability (the broad umbrella category under which mental health falls), information acquisition hits several roadblocks, including shame, secrecy, and suspicion.

Certainly, social science has its uses here. Durkheim and others function in an anti-ableist way by removing suicide from the sphere of insanity or individual failure, into being a social phenomenon.[5] They crystallize the distinction many disability studies scholars make between impairment and disability. Specifically, impairment describes what happens in the body or mind (in this case, depression) and disability describes what happens when that impairment makes social meaning. The oft-used example still applies: A wheelchair user is not disabled until they enter a building where the only way in or up requires stairs. The same is true here: A person experiencing depression is not disabled until they are denied assistance or told they're "just sad."

Yet social science reaches its limitations when it encounters me and Meghan Markle, because race, gender, and disability cannot be reduced to variables. Moreover, history—both people's relationship to it and how it shapes people's daily lives—connives to distort whatever data attempts to perform such a reduction. The answer, as I understand it, lies in the bailiwick of poets and novelists. After all, the answer to "Are you OK?" requires narrative. Complicated. Messy. Unquantifiable. Nuanced. Narrative.

Meghan Markle's understanding of her own story—prior to Harry—requires some attention to history. I am not attempting to go down the road James Holt warns against, but I sit on my stack of degrees in asserting that we all sit inside history. The docuseries overtly references (usually through the mouth of Harry) how racist the stories were about Meghan Markle in the British press. Though this treatment was indeed unprecedented in its racism toward a member of the royal family, such treatment is not unprecedented in the U.S. Just as there are side-by-side comparisons of Kate Middleton and Meghan Markle, there are also side-by-side comparisons of white Hurricane Katrina "survivors" and Black Hurricane Katrina "refugees" or "looters," as well as similar comparisons of white basketball star Caitlin Clark as a "competitor" and Black basketball championship winner Angel Reese as "classless." These biased depictions are based in the U.S.'s long history of white supremacy. Meghan Markle's specific history, shaped as it is by race, gender, and nation, may explain why the British press's reaction was, to her, overwhelming and, based on her stated bewilderment, unexpected.

Meghan Markle's parents wed in 1979, just over a dozen years after *Loving v. Virginia,* the 1967 landmark U.S. Supreme Court case declaring interracial marriage to be legal. Meghan Markle was born two years later. Socially speaking, Meghan Markle is part of the Loving generation, a generation of mixed-race children whose parents' marriages were state sanctioned. She also belongs to the post-soul generation, those who grew up after the mid-twentieth-century civil rights struggle, when integration gave racism a flimsy makeover.

There is some mental gymnastics in those sentences. Let me explain.

I differentiate between state sanctioned and socially understood, not because one is more legitimate than the other but because the latter has a longer, uglier history. Mixed-race unions between Black women and white men have long been a feature of American sexual politics. American chattel slavery was a social, economic, and legal system that functioned for pleasure and profit. For some white male authority figures—enslavers, overseers, esteemed community members—pleasure coincided with profit, such that they raped enslaved women and continued to make money from their progeny. In the postbellum era, anti-Black racism required the production of cultural narratives that continued the social hierarchies of slavery: Paramount to this enterprise was the stereotype that Black people broadly, and

Black women in particular, were lascivious and sexually profligate. Such narratives allowed for the rampant lynching of Black men, supposedly because of their rape of white women. Ida B. Wells-Barnett's journalism in her 1895 book, *The Red Record*, exposes as a lie the idea that white womanhood was in jeopardy. Instead, lynching and the subsequent destruction of Black communities stemmed from white economic jealousy of thriving Black communities. These narratives about Black sexuality and the threat of white mob violence undergirded the relationship between Black domestic laborers and their white employers. Being a Black woman domestic in a white home put a Black woman at the mercy of her white male employer's sexual advances and her white woman employer's unfounded fears. (This is why *The Help* is bullshit.) In the wake of integration, the post-soul generation has had to wrestle with the same narratives even though their packaging changes. That is, white supremacy does not always surface in the spectacularity of an auction block, the use of racial insults, or a lynching. Sometimes it appears in the adverbs and adjectives used to describe your relationship to your baby bump. Sometimes it is a brooch. The same structural white supremacy and anti-Blackness remain even with the patina of happy multiculturalism.

This longer, uglier history is often erased in the triumphant love stories about the parents of the Loving generation. Even if those relationships end, those couples are understood as part of a vanguard who boldly followed the calling of their hearts. Unfortunately, romantic choices and sexual politics are more complex. Specifically, they cannot be cleaved from the economic, social, and political circumstances surrounding them. To be clear, I do not know the details of Doria Ragland's marriage to Thomas Markle. But I do know that the category of mixed race in the U.S. has a complicated social history given the history of interracial relationships. Let us not forget that parenting is difficult labor.

There are a slew of authors who, like Meghan Markle, are part of the Loving generation, and seek to understand their specific place in America's imaginary. In her 1998 satirical essay "Mulatto Millennium," Danzy Senna (b. 1970) zeroes in on the absurdity of race and the trendiness of mixed-race-ness in the multicultural-obsessed moment of the 1990s. She takes *Time* magazine to task for its 1993 cover story, "The New Face of America," pointing out that the computer-generated face of multicultural America already existed in Puerto Rico, Latin America, and Spanish Harlem. The reference to Latinidad is entirely apt given the long histories of race mixing through colonialism, enslavement, and economic oppression. For my part, I see similar versions and variations of that face everywhere I go. Because that face operates as a projected racial fantasy, depending on my makeup, my hair, and what language I speak, my face can sometimes be subject to scrutiny. There is a sober moment in the second section of Senna's essay when she writes, "With all due respect to the multiracial movement, I cannot tell a lie. I was a black girl. Not your ordinary black girl, if such a thing exists. But rather, a black girl with a Wasp mother and a black-Mexican father, and a face that harkens to Andalusia, not Africa. I was born in 1970, when 'black' described a people bonded not by shared complexion or hair texture but by shared history."[6]

Senna situated her Blackness within a specific time and space, Boston circa 1970s; yet her Blackness was not unique to that time and space. The institutional racism that gave us redlining kept on giving, all over the country, even in California. When the *Harry & Meghan* docuseries focuses on Meghan Markle's childhood, they take care to clarify that she was raised in Los Angeles, not Compton. The difference between zip codes is largely about race and the cultural imagination: In the early 1990s, Compton emerged as part of the map of Los Angeles in connection with the L.A. uprising and the rap group N.W.A., specifically a new subgenre of music, gangsta rap. Los Angeles, on the other hand, retained—and retains—its long reputation of glitz and glamour as the sleek cityscape of dreams. In the words of the vagrant (played by Abdul Salaam El Razzac) from *Pretty Woman* (1990), "Welcome to Hollywood! What's your dream?"[7]

For her part, Meghan Markle is fixated on the issue of accuracy. Her attention there struck me as an odd focal point, as Compton functions as proxy for the doxic seduction of believing Meghan Markle was from a place *like* Compton, the deindustrialized urban, inner-city landscape of Black poverty, abjection, and pathos. The British tabloids were not simply refusing to learn American geography; they understood Compton as synonymous with a particular kind of deviant and dangerous Blackness that threatened the pristine image of the monarchy. They refused to understand Meghan Markle as similar to other mixed-race stars and public figures like Halle Berry, Mariah Carey, Lenny Kravitz, Lisa Bonet, Jennifer Beals, Alicia Keys, Rosario Dawson, Paula Patton, Rashida Jones, Tracee Ellis Ross, Slash, Maya Rudolph, Zendaya, and Amandla Stenberg, among others.

There's an entire galaxy of mixed-race stars in Hollywood, but Meghan Markle does not situate herself among them. If I am honest, I found myself baffled by her sense of self. Noting that she was always treated as a biracial woman suggests that she, when examining the details of her life, does not view how Blackness operates in the public's perception of her. As a student of Black literature and culture, I did not (and still do not) understand how a young woman who lived among her maternal grandmother and uncle (from Ohio) did not or could not articulate how Blackness shaped her life. Interpersonal contact with Black members of one's family usually provides clear insight into the inner workings of structural racism.

The literary critic Barbara Christian is correct: Black people theorize in the everyday, including narrative forms like the stories we create, the play with language, and the dynamism of interaction. For that matter, interpersonal contact with one's white relatives would provide a distinct, but instructive, experience regarding whiteness and how it operates. In *Harry & Meghan*, Meghan Markle does not think through how she was tokenized at her school, Immaculate Heart, how her curly hair, darker skin, and "activism" were all read as an unobtrusive, palatable Blackness. After all, she advocated broadly for women in relation to household work, not for a change to the conditions that fueled the Los Angeles 1992 uprisings. That was not mixed-race-ness at work; that was Blackness, more specifically the anti-Blackness of tokenism, at work. Part of me suspects that the child and adolescent Meghan Markle prioritized her identity as a kid of divorce who simply wanted to belong. All other difficult aspects of the experience—including racial difference—were subsumed under that trauma. Perhaps her aloofness is a consequence of being numb.

I am also aware that Doria Ragland admits to not having explicit conversations with her daughter about race. My anger at Doria for missing that opportunity still simmers. How does one leave their child unprepared to encounter the world? I am reminded of Michelle Obama telling Kelly Rowland that there is no part of her that wants to be her children's friend, because "there's so much of parenting that has nothing to do with them liking you."[8] In my household, that included difficult conversations about who I was in the world and who people would perceive me to be. I want to sit in my discomfort with my anger at Meghan Markle as well. I bristle at her choices. Despite her closeness to her mother, perhaps seeing herself in her mother's smile, in the slope of her shoulders, quirk of her brow, and figure, her social life reflects very little engagement with Blackness: a white sorority (Kappa Kappa Gamma), a largely white friend group, few relationships (or articulated role models) among mixed-race or Black Hollywood, and what feels like a willful aloofness about race. I stiffen with my own consternation about these choices. As a child and young woman, I have felt the violence of being the "one Black friend." As a professor, I have seen how a cadre of white women can fail to support their "one Black friend," their "one mixed friend." In looking at Meghan Markle's sorority photos (I refuse to read the tabloid articles attached because they are so opportunistic), I cannot help but wonder whether she was safe then. Was she OK?

Once, I tried explaining David Foster Wallace's take on suicide to a white man I was dating. Wallace pointed out that hopelessness or conviction of life's difficulties or death-as-appealing are not the main reasons for suicidal ideation or suicide itself. Instead, "the person in whom *its* invisible agony reaches a certain unendurable level will kill herself the same way a trapped person will eventually jump from the window of a burning high-rise."[9] I was in the middle of the bit where Wallace talks about being in a burning building. All of a sudden, this man, with all of his six-foot frame, lifted his arms to chest height, his full wingspan and bird chest emphasized by the thin T-shirt he was wearing. *No! No! In that case, you run into the flames! Suicide is never the answer!* He pretty much crystallized what Wallace says about people on the ground: "Nobody down on the sidewalk, looking up and yelling 'Don't!' and 'Hang on!', can understand the jump. Not really. You'd have to have personally been trapped and felt flames to really understand a terror way beyond falling."[10] Instinctively, I sized him up, moving into a fighter's stance as my uncles had taught me. As physically weak as I was, I knew I could do no real damage. The gesture allowed me to announce to myself that I felt unsafe in his presence. I trusted myself enough to be sure that, in that moment, I was communicating something real about my experience, no matter how inconvenient to him. I was sure of myself, secure in my own knowledge of who I was. He ghosted me a few weeks later. I was relieved.

That surety in one's own identity tends to be slippery in narratives about mixed-race identity in the United States. The trope of the "tragic mulatto or mulatta" mobilizes the antiquated term for "mule" to devalue the identity of mixed-race people. In addition, that anti-Black literary and filmic trope requires that the mixed-race person die, since they supposedly cannot ever assimilate; the underlying premise is that Blackness is to blame for the outsider status of mixed-race individuals. An oft-repeated refrain for this trope continues into the present: "I do not fit in anywhere."

Meghan Markle voices this refrain in an article for *Elle*.[11] The article's stated purpose is to provide a window into Meghan Markle's experiences as a mixed-race woman. It is part personal story, part advertisement for *Suits*. She states that the writers and producers were looking for Rachel Zane, so Meghan Markle could perform Rachel without needing to fit into the narrow confines defined by race, hair color, height, weight, figure, and the like. (Who am I kidding? Rachel Zane was never going to be thick.) Meghan Markle's article provides anecdotes about people misunderstanding her or solely understanding her based on race. The questions "What are you?" and "Where are you from?" or, obstinately, "Where are you *really* from?" and "Where are your parents from?" are staples of mixed-race narratives. Meghan Markle's article is no different. She details several moments when she navigates the "verbal dance," as she terms it. The startling encounter with racial opprobrium is also a hallmark of mixed-race narratives. The *Elle* article is no different there either, except that for a lot of narratives, that encounter with racial slurs tends to occur much younger than Meghan Markle's college-aged encounter. At times, the encounter with racial slurs is not as spectacular as being publicly called the N-word. It can be as simple as noting the differences between one's own treatment as mixed race and that of one's putatively more racially legible kinfolk. It can also be the use of the N-word as an in-group term of endearment. Regardless, the mixed-race narrator tends to have a racial awakening at the moment of encounter and makes decisions about how legible they wish their body to be and how often they will speak for their body. Typically, the decision to speak for one's mixed-race self occurs around the area of box checking or choosing a parent or choosing a friend group. This part of the narrative generally points to the desire for self-determination.

Meghan Markle's *Elle* article includes a "box checking" moment in seventh grade (where she is told by a white woman to check "white"). She leaves the question blank. I wonder whether it was filled in for her later by some supposedly well-meaning adult. The article ends with her determination—she draws a straight line between herself and her formerly enslaved ancestors choosing last names—to forge her own path. I often receive these kinds of reflections on mixed race from students in my classes, ones that know enough to mobilize certain parts of history, but do not know enough to complicate how much, how often, and how intimately history caresses the present.

Let me return to Danzy Senna for a moment. Senna's work crystallizes how absurd racial categories are in the U.S., without dismissing or diminishing the history of how said categories come to me. Senna's second novel, *Symptomatic,* follows an unnamed narrator through her experiences with her first job. The novel deftly uses film noir techniques—an abundance of half-lights, low lights, shadows, doppelgängers, and spotlights—to pinpoint the absurdity of another mixed-race woman, the antagonist, who takes her understanding of her identity to a codependent and then homicidal extreme. Like other novels with unnamed narrators (I am thinking specifically of *Autobiography of an Ex-colored Man* by James Weldon Johnson), this protagonist allows for the seduction of the first-person narrative to permit readers to imagine themselves or someone they know in the main character's place. Moreover, the absurdity of the plot spotlights the absurdity of how race functions. This protagonist is not ignorant about American history, nor is she unaware of how whiteness functions as a currency, but she is exhausted from having to define and redefine herself for a public that voraciously reads her. Her solution? Go to California, specifically Los Angeles, where a multiracial and multiethnic friend group does not force her to choose.

Danzy Senna's work does not suggest that mixed-race people must choose. Instead, Senna's work catalogs what happens when one refuses to account for the brutality of how one is understood by others. In *Symptomatic*, the protagonist is certain about her own identity and understands the absurdity of race even as she laments how it shapes her social life. It is the antagonist, a villainous narrative foil, who cannot come to terms with the limited knowledge of the public, the uncomplicated, inaccurate stories people tell themselves about race. It is not only a matter how well she fits in. It is also a matter of how well society allows for her to fit in. It is both. Always both. The willful aloofness—because of cowardice, confusion, or coercion—results in rage borne of heartbreak. Like any good student of the social sciences, I refuse to assign causality to Meghan Markle's mixed-race identity as it relates to her suicidal ideation. I do see a correlation, though, between the British tabloids' white supremacist coverage and how ill prepared Meghan Markle was to face racial discourse.

I do not have a neat ending to this. I do not know if Meghan Markle still sometimes contemplates suicide. Perhaps, for her, as for me, the thoughts are like an echo, the sound decreasing the further away one gets from its origins. What I know for sure is that a few people will probably read this and think, *Same*. A few people will read this and put as much emotional distance between themselves and this writing as possible. Somebody might seek their own answers in history, fiction, or film. Somebody might get comfortable with there not being any satisfactory answers. As of this writing, it is spring, and there is nothing as beautiful and as terrible as a new beginning.

## Notes

1. Sun Reporter, "Mark My Words."
2. Beyoncé, "Pray You Catch Me." Spoken-word poetry in this song was written by Somali British writer Warsan Shire.
3. You may note that I use Meghan Markle's full name every time I mention her. This is because I want to remind readers that they do not know "Meghan" or "Meg." Just as Jason King ("Any Love"), scholar of celebrity, describes Luther Vandross, celebrity comprises a wide

variety of sources, but very few are intimate enough to give anything other than the veneer of intimacy or vulnerability.

4. Durkheim, *Suicide*, 235, 201.
5. There are other ableist aspects to Durkheim's work (as well as that of other social scientists studying suicide) but this premise itself is anti-ableist.
6. Senna, "Mulatto Millennium."
7. Marshall, *Pretty Woman*.
8. REVOLT Studios, "Michelle Obama" (time stamp 1:19).
9. Wallace, *Infinite Jest*, 696.
10. Wallace, *Infinite Jest*, 696–97.
11. Markle, "I'm More Than an 'Other.'"

## Works Referenced

Beyoncé. "Pray You Catch Me." Track 1 on *Lemonade*. Parkwood Entertainment and Columbia Records, 2016.

Christian, Barbara. "The Race for Theory." In *African American Literary Criticism*, edited by Winston Napier, 280–89. New York: New York University Press, 2001.

Durkheim, Émile. *Suicide: A Study in Sociology*. 2nd ed. London: Routledge, 2002.

Garbus, Liz, and Erica Sashin, dirs. *Harry & Meghan*. Aired December 2022 on Netflix. https://www.netflix.com/watch/81478159.

Hirsch, Afua. *Brit(ish): On Race, Identity and Belonging*. London: Vintage Books, 2018.

Johnson, James Weldon. *Autobiography of an Ex-colored Man*. New York: Penguin Classics, 1990.

King, Jason. "Any Love: Silence, Theft, and Rumor in the Work of Luther Vandross." In *The Greatest Taboo: Homosexuality in Black Communities*, edited by Delroy Constantine-Sims, 290–315. New York: Alyson Books, 2000.

Markle, Meghan. "Meghan Markle: I'm More Than an 'Other.'" *Elle*, updated December 22, 2016. https://www.elle.com/uk/life-and-culture/news/a26855/more-than-an-other/.

Marshall, Garry, dir. *Pretty Woman*. Burbank, CA: Touchstone Pictures 1990.

Olusoga, David. *Black and British: A Forgotten History*. London: Pan Books, 2017.

REVOLT Studios. "Michelle Obama: The Cross-Generational Conversation." December 14, 2022. YouTube video, 1:40:23. https://www.youtube.com/watch?v=Zo9G91QWMQs.

Senna, Danzy. "Mulatto Millennium." *Salon*, July 24, 1998. https://www.salon.com/1998/07/24/24feature_10/.

Senna, Danzy. *Symptomatic*. New York: Penguin, 2004.

Sun Reporter. "Mark My Words: Meghan Markle Oprah Interview." *The Sun*, January 31, 2024. https://www.the-sun.com/news/2475583/meghan-markle-oprah-interview-full-transcript/.

Wallace, David Foster. *Infinite Jest*. 10th anniversary edition. New York: Back Bay Books, 2006.

Wells-Barnett, Ida B. *The Red Record: Tabulated Statistics and Alleged Causes of Lynching in the United States*. Frankfurt: Outlook Verlag, 2018. Reproduction of original 1895 pamphlet.

CHAPTER 3

# MEGHAN MARKLE, RACE, AND FEMINISM IN POST-BREXIT BRITAIN

SHARON D. WRIGHT AUSTIN AND LUCCA RAMONE CARLSON

On May 19, 2018, Harry, Duke of Sussex (usually referred to as Prince Harry) married American actress Meghan Markle in an extravagant wedding ceremony. Meghan Markle's marriage not only transformed her into one of the most famous women in the world but also made her the target of immense scrutiny. For example, during a one-week period in March 2021, when the Duke and Duchess of Sussex participated in an interview with Oprah Winfrey, she was the subject of 25,894 online articles.[1]

Markle was not the kind of woman traditionally chosen to be the wife of a royal. She considered herself to be biracial, but to the British, she was simply a Black, American divorced actress who openly expressed feminist ideals.[2] Less than two full years later, on January 8, 2020, the couple announced their intention to "step back as senior members" of the royal family, gain financial independence, and move out of Britain.[3] Both had been the subjects of intense scrutiny during their marriage, but allegations of British media abuse of Markle surfaced. Several rationales were given for her alleged treatment, including her marriage to one of the world's most eligible bachelors, the British media's long history of abuses toward royal wives, her openly feminist views, and lastly, her race.

Their marriage and departure from their royal duties occurred during the post-Brexit period. On June 23, 2016, Britain voted to leave the European Union. As we will explain, the experiences of the Duchess of Sussex teach us important lessons about race and gender in the post-Brexit era. To many, the acceptance of the Duke and Duchess of Sussex's union was supposed to represent the modern monarchy's racial progressiveness. Because of the unlikelihood that a woman from this background could ever be a member of "the Firm,"[4] "this marriage," according to one study, "offered a sense of comfort to a racialized world, as it appeared that even one of the most conservative institutions, the House of Windsor, was opening its doors to 'others.'"[5] In addition, Markle was initially perceived as a "'royal feminist' who [modernized] the royal family and [made] the institution more progressive."[6] Because of her biracial, feminist, and humanitarian background, it was believed that the monarchy would benefit from her presence.[7]

The experiences of the Duke and Duchess of Sussex, in particular, reveal the complexities associated with racial identities in Britain. Markle has often referred to herself as a mixed-race or biracial woman rather than as a Black woman. On the *Harry & Meghan* Netflix special, she says, "I'd say now, people are very aware of my race because they made it such an issue when I went to the U.K. But before that, most people didn't treat me like a 'Black woman.' So that talk didn't happen for me."[8]

Markle, who once said, "I am proud to be a woman and a feminist," clearly takes her feminist activism very seriously.[9] However she self-identifies, a one-drop rule has always existed that defines men and women with any Black ancestry as Black, which means that she is a Black feminist rather than simply a feminist.[10] Also, when the word *feminist* is used, it usually refers to white women.[11] In this chapter, we question whether the negative coverage she has received from the British press results primarily from her feminist activism or from the perception the British public has of her as a Black feminist activist. To this end, we examine the question of whether the esteemed *The Times* newspaper devoted more derogatory coverage toward Markle when she addressed issues concerning race rather than gender.

## Data and Methods

We conducted a content analysis of *The Times*, which has been Britain's premiere newspaper since 1785. It is common knowledge that the royal family receives extensive coverage from broadcast, print (including tabloid), and social media sources. Several media outlets hire royal correspondents, whose sole responsibility is to report on the family's activities.[12] The relentless attacks by British tabloids on the royals is well known.[13] Both Prince Harry and Meghan Markle have won settlements against the British press because of what Markle once referred to as "deception, intimidation, and calculated attacks" against her.[14] The couple abandoned their roles as senior royals in large part because of the misogynoir (racist and sexist) media coverage of Markle.[15]

We chose *The Times* because of its reputation as "one of the most highly regarded resources for 18th-, 19th-, and 20th-century news coverage" in Britain.[16] We therefore wanted to examine coverage of Markle from a prestigious newspaper with a reputation for its "quality press" articles.[17]

In *The Times* digital archive, we searched Meghan Markle's name and the key words "race," "feminism," and "race and feminism." Gale North America publishes an extensive archive of *Times* articles published between 1785 and 2019. As a point of comparison, we also searched Kate Middleton's name and the same key words. Both women were nontraditional "commoners" who married into the royal family, and both discussed issues of women's empowerment, justice, and equity (although Markle has done so to a greater extent than Middleton).[18]

Our study seeks to determine whether the Duchess of Sussex (Markle) was treated as more or less harshly than the Princess of Wales (Middleton) by *The Times*. This comparison will allow readers to make inferences about the media's perceptions of a race-neutral form of feminist activism (as expressed by Middleton) versus a race-conscious form of Black feminist activism (as expressed by Markle). It will also reveal *The Times*'s perceptions of Markle's racialized and gendered statements.

## Immigration, Class, and Race in the Brexit and Post-Brexit Eras

This section of the chapter provides important context for our analysis of Meghan Markle. As an immigrant of color and a nontraditional royal wife, she entered the royal family during a difficult time in its history. Britain's racial climate during the eighteen months between her wedding to Prince Harry and their departure from their royal duties remained polarized. When Meghan Markle became the fiancée, and later the wife, of Prince Harry, the British monarchy was attempting to transform its image during the post-Brexit era. The 1970s and 1980s British antiracist movements resulted in a sense of optimism about improved race relations; however, that feeling was short lived. After these movements ended, an era of white nationalism soon followed.[19] A white, working-class electorate, commonly referred to as Leave voters, consisted of conservative citizens who led a backlash against multiculturalism.[20] Several studies have discussed these voters' unhappiness with their economic plight as well as their opposition to non-European immigration.[21] For example, a 2018 found that Leave voters blamed the nation's growing immigrant populations for their financial problems, especially during the post-2008 financial crises. Ethnographic interviews indicated that many Leave voters felt "left behind"—i.e., ignored by political figures they viewed as instead addressing the needs of immigrant families.[22] Most of these voters were described as being the "pensioners, low-skilled and less well-educated blue-collar workers and citizens who have been pushed to the margins."[23]

After interviewing Leave voters, researchers Patel and Connelly attributed their beliefs about immigration to feelings of "victimised whiteness" and an example of a new form of racism.[24] In fact, racism fared prominently in the events leading up to Brexit. White Leave voters heavily emphasized the need to leave the European Union as a way to "[reinstate] the sovereign will of the British people."[25] By using the slogan "Let's take back control," Brexit supporters communicated that they wanted the British government to enact more stringent immigration rules, including the implementation of quotas to strictly limit new immigrant authorizations.[26] According to the views of Leave voters (which were reinforced by some media depictions), immigrants posed serious economic threats, but also threatened national security.[27] By painting immigrants as threats to the nation's well-being, the post-Brexit era media contributed to the uptick in hate crimes that targeted them.[28] Within four weeks after the Brexit referendum, in which 52 percent of votes opted to leave the European Union, over six thousand racially motivated hate crimes were reported to the National Police Chiefs' Council.[29] Thus, immigrants of color became the new scapegoats for white Britons who blamed them for most of the economic and other ills of the white working class. Although the media portrayed the typical Leave voter as a member of the white working class, this was later found to be false. The average Leave voter was actually a white middle-class resident of southern Britain.[30] Thus, the stereotype that low-income white people were more hostile toward immigrants of color and also more likely to be Leave voters was a misrepresentation. White people from both disadvantaged and advantaged economic class sectors were Leave voters who disapproved of the presence of immigrants of color.

The discontented feelings of Leave voters were apparent in the years immediately before and after the Brexit era. Racism is seldom discussed in Britain, and Islamophobia is no different, despite a significant number of hate crimes toward Muslim people. Much of the hostile behavior is based on a negative connotation of the word *Muslim*. In Britain, conservatives have characterized people of the Muslim faith as being dangerous.[31] The United Kingdom has a troubled legacy of slavery, colonialism, and racism that long predates the recent anti-immigrant and Islamophobic climate.[32] Racist sentiments were apparent in Europe long before the mass arrivals of immigrants of color, and Britain's troubling colonial history is well documented. In the days following Queen Elizabeth II's death on September 8, 2022, some African residents refused to mourn because of British abuses that occurred during her reign.[33] Grievances ranged from the country's involvement in slavery to more recent human rights abuses.[34] From the seventeenth to the nineteenth century, the Church of England emphasized England's need to conquer other countries—many of which had large Black populations.[35] Certainly, widespread, systemic racism existed prior to the Brexit and post-Brexit anti-immigrant sentiments.

Britain had a complex racial history long before the influx of non-European immigrants. The earliest waves of Black immigrants, or "negroes" as they were called, lived in the "coloured quarter" of Britain.[36] In addition, Britain was plagued by "white race riots, gollywog jokes, and 'for rental' signs everywhere with the byline 'No Irish, No Blacks, No Dogs.'"[37] However, explicit public discussions of race have never occurred there on a frequent basis. Some surmise that the absence of open and honest discussions of race stems from the smaller Black populations in European nations.[38] For example, over 74 percent of the English and Welsh populations identified as white during the 2021 census.[39] While the media and some British residents focus on an imagined forgotten white working class, the stories of immigrants and people of color have gone untold. When their harassment does receive some attention, it is through police and policymaker frames, where the solution is always law and order.

Yet the racist political discourses driving the violence are never meaningfully addressed.[40]

Because of Britain's emphasis on whiteness and its denial of its historically racist practices, Meghan Markle, as an American citizen with an African American mother, was at a disadvantage from the very beginning of her entry into the royal family. The status of royalty is traditionally equated with "blood purity."[41] This emphasis on blood purity is so severe that "the idea of royals marrying people of mixed heritage [is] difficult to accept both by the public and by the press. Princesses are usually stereotyped as 'pale, blue-eyed and beautiful and anyone who is not is of a lesser status.'"[42] These were qualities that Meghan Markle—in the public's view—could not possibly have possessed. We next turn to our analysis of *Times* articles and the paper's coverage of Markle's racialized and gendered statements.

## Findings

In our search of articles published in *The Times* between 2016 and 2019, we found the following: four under the category of Meghan Markle and race, seven under feminism, and one under race and feminism. We found a May 19, 2018, article entitled "Thoroughly Modern Meghan Can Be the Royals' Biggest Asset or Greatest Danger," in our search of the "Markle" and "race" key words. It first refers to the monarchy's experiences with "outsiders" like Wallis Simpson, Princess Diana, and Markle. Authors Emma Duncan and Valentine Low then discuss the challenges Markle encountered as an actress and because of her biracial background. They write, "Her mixed-race parentage did not make her struggle any easier. She grew up in a mostly white neighbourhood at a time when being 'biracial,' as she calls it, was still rare." Even in the world of entertainment, her race was sometimes problematic. When the *Suits* writers decided to give her a Black father, the comments on Twitter included "Ew, she's black? I used to think she was hot."[43] In their commentary, the *Times* authors also observe, "Meghan will never be as popular as Diana, for she lacks the reckless fragility that made the princess so mesmerizing and dangerous."

We found that Meghan Markle received more negative media coverage when we searched the "feminism" key word than when we searched "race." The November 1, 2016, article "Meghan—oh How the Royal Family Need You" includes an interview with Markle and contains no negative language. In it, she discusses her earliest identification as a feminist and says, "I was 11 or 12 years old when I became a member of the National Organization for Women in the States. I've always been a young feminist, and looking back, I guess there are all kinds of pieces to that puzzle. It's always been important to me to be vocal about what I feel is right, whether that's as a woman, or being bi-racial. I think so much of it is when you can't find which box you can tick, or where you fit in. My dad always taught me to just make your own box."[44] Although the interview lacks derogatory language, the accompanying article, published on the same page, refers to a quote from Markle, who expresses her desire to "focus less on glass slippers and more on pushing through glass ceilings." The author of this article observes,

> Meghan: the royal family need you. They don't have form at assimilating feisty women and Americans, but it's 2016. We can hope that they've raised their game. Besides, a few weeks at Princess School should knock her into shape. Kate emerged with a posh voice, a debilitating grooming regimen and a keen awareness of the need to have your hands clasped demurely in front of you at all times. There's nothing to be done about Markle's accent, but she already looks a million dollars, so that just leaves the hand-clasping. Princess Meghan, over to you.[45]

On May 22, 2018, *The Times* published "Welcome to the Firm" with the subtitle "The new Duchess of Sussex has brought happiness to Harry and modernity to a royal family who needs it. But she needs to be wary of the pitfalls in her own role." In hindsight, this article seems to have predicted what eventually happened to Markle. Two years before her engagement to Prince Harry, Meghan Markle gave a speech to the United Nations in which she hailed the Rwandan parliament for its majority female membership and lamented the slow pace of progress toward gender equality everywhere else. Within two hours of the royal wedding on Saturday, a web page for the new Duchess of Sussex was added to the royal family's official site. It proclaims her pride in being "a woman and a feminist" and describes her activism on behalf of women, girls, and the poor since the age of twenty-one. Meghan was an unusually articulate and passionate UN women's advocate. The article continues:

> She will unquestionably enhance the royal family's appeal in Britain and abroad as an embodiment of diversity and modernity. . . . Even so, the judgments that the duchess will have to make as she settles into her new role will inevitably be hard. . . . Clearly she has no intention of giving up her activism and yet it carries clear risks. Activism strays easily into politics, and it is an iron law of the constitutional monarchy of which she is now a part that its members stay out of politics if they want to survive. The Queen has grasped this intuitively. So, apparently, do the Duke and Duchess of Cambridge. They manage to unite people from all walks of life in patriotism and affection for the monarchy by scrupulously offending no one. . . . In her new role she is a princess, not a politician. She will have to find a way to be content with that.[46]

On July 30, 2019, *The Times* published "Meghan's 'Woke' Vogue Is Shallow and Divisive," clear evidence that *The Times* was now shifting into negative coverage and had turned against Markle. Its author, Melanie Phillips, writes,

> Who knew that among her many accomplishments, the Duchess of Sussex would exhibit an unparalleled talent for excavation? When in a hold, she doesn't just keep digging, she keeps going until the earth caves in on top of her. The duchess, the former actress Meghan Markle, has been criticized for high-handedness and for failing to grasp that, as a member of the royal family, she needs to be apolitical and no longer make herself the center of the story. She has now guest-edited the September issue of British *Vogue*. The cover features 15 women she admires from the "frontline of fashion, film, tech and wellness" who are supposed to represent "the values, causes and people making impact in the world today." They were described by Buckingham Palace as "trailblazing changemakers, united by their fearlessness." The list, however, is beyond parody as reflecting the shallow aspirations of a social justice warrior. The only achievement of several of them is being famous, being the right non-white skin colour or, like the duchess, aspiring to making the world a kinder and gentler place. Oh, and some just happen to have connections with *Vogue* itself. . . . Alas, she still doesn't understand the complex and nuanced point that her new status precludes political statements. She still hasn't grasped that the role of the monarchy is to unite the country. For many of the 15 are associated with causes that are deeply divisive.[47]

When thinking about Meghan Markle's feminist expressions, it is noticeable that she does not discuss aspects of Black feminism. She has made several comments about women's empowerment, but we found none specifically about Black women's empowerment. This should not be surprising because researchers found that she often has discussed her mixed-race background, but "rarely exclusively aligned with Black culture and politics."[48] Yet despite her tendency to downplay her Black identity, British society perceived her as a Black woman. On this point, one observer remarked that her depictions of herself as a person of mixed-race origin sharply contrasted with British perceptions of her as a Black woman and said, "Seemingly, Markle always tried to exist as if she were colorless."[49]

In an article published in *Elle* magazine in 2015, she writes that she dreaded the inevitable question she was always asked: "What are you?" As an answer, she would say, "My dad is Caucasian and my mom is African American. I'm half black and half white."[50] But as Dahleen Glanton points out in a 2018 commentary, other people saw her differently: "She wasn't just the Duchess of Sussex. She was the Black duchess. That's how the royal family saw her and how the world defined her."[51]

A January 10, 2018, *Times* article, "Feminist Meghan Wears the Trousers," describes Markle and Prince Harry's visit to the predominantly Black Brixton community in South London to visit Reprezent, a youth radio station. Reprezent had been established in 2003 in response to rising crime rates in the nearby Peckham area and as a way to provide youth with a positive musical outlet. The focus of the article centers on Markle's feminist views rather than her and Prince Harry's outreach efforts and says, "When Adrian Newman, the station manager said he had a question for Harry, the prince promptly pointed at his fiancée and said: 'She answers the questions.' 'Yes, talking of gender equality,' Meghan quickly added with a smile."[52]

When examining articles using the "Markle" and "race" key words, we find that Meghan Markle and Prince Harry participated in symbolic efforts to address racial injustices. A May 21, 2018, *Times* article entitled "Who Is Michael Curry?" discusses the Reverend Michael Curry, who delivered an address at the couple's wedding ceremony and has repeatedly expressed his support for both social justice and feminist ideals. "Born in Chicago, Illinois, where Meghan Markle would go to college, the 65-year-old bishop is known for his opinions on social justice. His appointment in 2015 followed the Episcopal Church's decision to bless same-sex marriages. . . . This year, he added his voice of support to the #MeToo movement, saying that the church needed to investigate incidents of sexual abuse it had 'mishandled.'"[53]

In an April 23, 2018, article, "Racist Abuse at Lawrence Memorial," Richard Ford points out that racists shouted abuse at workers cleaning a memorial that had been defaced. It honored Stephen Lawrence, who was beaten and stabbed by a group of men while waiting at a bus stop in Eltham in southeast London in April 1991. Lawrence and his friend, Duwayne Brooks, both of whom were Black, were attacked in what was later confirmed as a racist hate crime. Only two of the group of up to six men were convicted for Lawrence's murder. Harry and Meghan attended a celebration of life memorial service in his honor.[54]

When searching the terms "race," "feminism," and "race and feminism" and "Kate Middleton," we found none for "race," four for "feminism," and one for "race and feminism." Three of the "feminism" articles focus on Kate—"Forget Our Designer Frocks," "Kate Is a Modern Girl," and "The Genuine Hair to Blair Strategy"—while a fourth, "Thoroughly Modern Meghan Can Be the Royals' Biggest Asset or Greatest Danger," has information on both Markle and Middleton. Most of the articles about Middleton deal with topics relating to the paparazzi, her hair, and her relationship with her husband. The fact that we found no articles including statements from her about gender discrimination, racial discrimination, or discrimination of any kind for that matter suggests that she understands her nonpolitical role. The lack of references makes it difficult to compare *The Times* coverage of her to that of Meghan Markle. According to a March 1, 2018, article, "Meghan Sets Out Her Stall as Feminist Figurehead," while Markle spoke openly about her feminist views when expressing support for the Me Too movement, Middleton expressed support without making overt references to feminism or to politics. The article points out that their first joint appearance revealed notable differences. "Her [Markle's] willingness to express feminist ideas was in contrast to the duchess, 36, who was criticized when she appeared at the Bafta Film Awards in a green dress rather than joining the stars by wearing black in support of the campaign against sexual harassment. Ms. Markle's performance contrasted with the duchess's, which seemed quieter and less confident."[55]

## Conclusion

Before, during, and immediately after the royal wedding, the media and the royal family strategically utilized Markle as a symbol of the monarchy's evolution during a difficult time in its history.[56] Although the monarchy's acceptance of Meghan Markle was supposed to represent their and Britain's willingness to embrace a person of color, that plan quickly fell apart. Prince Harry and Markle's relationship with the monarchy deteriorated to such an extent that the couple abandoned their royal duties and their country of residence. This was not surprising to many Black British citizens, who understood that Markle felt unwelcome. They, too, believed that they never gained acceptance in their country of residence.[57]

Our content analysis of *Times* articles finds harsher perceptions about Markle's feminism compared to her race. Despite troubled race relations in Britain that pertain to both racial and immigration statuses, commentaries in *The Times* more often criticized her for her feminist views. In fact, her stances on racial and social justice were seldom mentioned in *The Times*. This may have stemmed from the newspaper's desire to avoid being labeled as racist. Our findings provide evidence Markle was in a no-win situation. As a biracial woman with a long history of feminist and social justice activism, she felt compelled to take stands on certain issues. However, other royal wives, like Kate Middleton, have tended to avoid controversial topics (feminism, social justice, and others).[58] Instead, they have received attention for their fashion choices, parenting skills, and promotion of familiar values.

It remains to be seen whether the lives of Meghan Markle and Prince Harry will be better in the United States. They are no longer confined by the constraints associated with royal life. However, they relocated to America during difficult times—the height of the COVID-19 pandemic and a racial reckoning prompted by the murders of Ahmaud Arbery, George Floyd, and others; the prevalence of Black Lives Matter protests; and the polarized aftermath of the 2020 presidential election.[59] Despite troubles they might encounter in the U.S., both are probably relieved that they no longer have to grapple with the stresses resulting from the attacks leveled at the first woman of color in the monarchy's history.

## Notes

1. Taylor, Alex. 2021. "Harry and Meghan."
2. Dowler and Bartos, "Comfort Feminism"; Weidhase "Feminist Politics of Meghan Markle."
3. *BBC News*, "Prince Harry and Meghan to Step Back."
4. Clancy, *Running the Family Firm.*
5. Dowler and Bartos, "Comfort Feminism," PAGE NUMBER.
6. Weidhase, "Feminist Politics of Meghan Markle," PAGE NUMBER.
7. Pramaggiore and Kerrigan, "Brand Royal."
8. Garbus and Sashin, *Harry & Meghan*, episode 2.
9. Schwarz, "I'm Proud to Be a Woman and a Feminist."
10. Austin, *Caribbeanization of Black Politics.*
11. Schuller, *Trouble with White Women.*
12. Clancy, "If You Move in the Same Circles as the Royals."
13. Conboy, *Tabloid Britain*; Venäläinen, "Meghan Markle in the British Tabloid Press."
14. Davies, "Meghan Calls for Tabloid Industry Overhaul."
15. Bailey, *Misogynoir Transformed.*
16. "Times Digital Archive," Gale North America.
17. Agility PR, "Top 10 U.K. Newspapers."
18. Pramaggiore and Kerrigan, "Brand Royal."
19. Favell, "Crossing the Race Line."
20. Virdee and McGeever, "Racism, Crisis, Brexit."
21. Dorling and Tomlinson, *Rule Brittania.*
22. Virdee and McGeever, "Racism, Crisis, Brexit."

23. Goodwin and Heath, "Tale of Two Countries."
24. Patel and Connelly, "'Post-Race' Racisms."
25. Virdee and McGeever, "Racism, Crisis, Brexit."
26. Sobolewska and Ford, "British Culture Wars?"
27. Virdee and McGeever, "Racism, Crisis, Brexit."
28. Awan and Zempi, "You All Look the Same."
29. Virdee and McGeever, "Racism, Crisis, Brexit."
30. Dorling and Tomlinson, *Rule Brittania.*
31. Ahmad and Sardar, *Muslim in Britain.*
32. Morgan, *Slavery and the British Empire.*
33. Busari, "Cloud of Colonialism Hangs Over Queen Elizabeth's Legacy."
34. Elkins, *Legacy of Violence.*
35. Reddie, *Theologising Brexit.*
36. Favell, "Crossing the Race Line," 18.
37. Favell, "Crossing the Race Line," 5.
38. Adekoya, "Europe Needs to Talk About Race Too."
39. Office for National Statistics, "Ethnic Group, England and Wales: Census 2021," November 29, 2022, https://www.ons.gov.uk/peoplepopulationandcommunity/culturalidentity/ethnicity/bulletins/ethnicgroupenglandandwales/census2021.
40. Burnett, "Racial Violence and the Brexit State."
41. Mahfouz, "Representation of Meghan Markle in Facebook Posts," 247.
42. Mahfouz, "Representation of Meghan Markle in Facebook Posts," 247.
43. Cited in Duncan and Low, "Thoroughly Modern Meghan."
44. Rose, "Meghan—oh How the Royal Family Need You."
45. Rose, "Meghan—oh How the Royal Family Need You."
46. *Times*, "Welcome to the Firm."
47. Phillips, "Meghan's 'Woke' Vogue."
48. Woldemikael and Woldemikael, "From Suits to Royals."
49. Glanton, "Meghan Markle Saw Herself as Biracial."
50. Markle, "I'm More Than an 'Other.'"
51. Glanton, "Meghan Markle Saw Herself as Biracial."
52. Low, "Meghan Markle Dresses Down for Radio Station Visit." (Note that the article was later renamed.)
53. "Times Digital Archive," Gale North America.
54. Ford, "Racist Abuse at Stephen Lawrence Memorial."
55. Low, "Meghan Markle Backs MeToo Movement."
56. Weidhase, "Feminist Politics of Meghan Markle."

57. Kulz, "British Migrants in Berlin."
58. Clancy, *Running the Family Firm.*
59. Dowler and Bartos, "Comfort Feminism."

## Works Referenced

Adekoya, Remi. "Europe Needs to Talk About Race Too." *Foreign Policy,* June 12, 2020. https://foreignpolicy.com/2020/06/12/europe-needs-to-talk-about-race-too/.

Agility PR Solutions. "Top 10 U.K. Newspapers by Web Visitors." Last updated February 2025. https://www.agilitypr.com/resources/top-media-outlets/top-10-uk-newspapers-by-circulation/.

Ahmad, Waqar I. U., and Sardar, Ziauddin. *Muslims in Britain: Making Social and Political Space.* London: Routledge, 2012.

Austin, Sharon D. Wright. *The Caribbeanization of Black Politics: Race, Group Consciousness, and Political Participation in America.* Albany, State University of New York Press, 2018.

Awan, Imran, and Irene Zempi. "'You All Look the Same': Non-Muslim Men Who Suffer Islamophobic Hate Crime in the Post-Brexit Era." *European Journal of Criminology* 17, no. 5 (2020): 585–602. https://doi.org/10.1177/1477370818812735.

Bailey, Moya. *Misogynoir Transformed: Black Women's Digital Resistance.* New York: New York University Press, 2021.

*BBC News.* "Prince Harry and Meghan to step back as senior royals." January 8, 2020. https://www.bbc.com/news/uk-51040751.

Burnett, Jon. "Racial Violence and the Brexit State." *Race and Class* 58, no. 4 (2017): 85–97.

Busari, Stephanie. "Cloud of Colonialism Hangs Over Queen Elizabeth's Legacy in Africa." *CNN,* September 10, 2022. https://www.cnn.com/2022/09/10/africa/colonialism-africa-queen-elizabeth-intl/index.html.

Clancy, Laura. "'If You Move in the Same Circles as the Royals, Then You'll Get Stories About Them': Royal Correspondents, Cultural Intermediaries, and Class." *Cultural Sociology* 17, no. 3 (2022): 331–50. https://doi.org/10.1177/17499755241252192.

Clancy, Laura. *Running the Family Firm: How the Monarchy Manages Its Image and Our Money.* Manchester: Manchester University Press, 2021.

Conboy, Martin. *Tabloid Britain: Constructing a Community through Language.* London: Routledge, 2006.

Davies, Caroline. "Meghan Calls for Tabloid Industry Overhaul as Mail on Sunday Loses Appeal." *The Guardian,* December 2, 2021. https://

www.theguardian.com/uk-news/2021/dec/02/mail-on-sunday-loses-duchess-of-sussex-meghan-privacy-case-appeal.

Dorling, Danny, and Sally Tomlinson. *Rule Brittania: Brexit and the End of Empire London*: London: Biteback Publishing, 2019.

Dowler, Lorraine, and Ann E. Bartos. "Comfort Feminism and the Cruelty of a 'Post-Racial' Monarchy in Britain." *Gender, Place, and Culture: A Journal of Feminist Geography* 30, no. 4 (2021): 1–7. https://doi.org/10.1080/0966369X.2021.1997939.

Duncan, Emma, and Valentine Low. "Thoroughly Modern Meghan Can Be the Royals' Biggest Asset or Greatest Danger." *The Times*, May 19, 2018. https://www.thetimes.co.uk/article/thoroughly-modern-meghan-can-be-the-royals-Biggest-asset-or-greatest-danger-v8j5h6gw0.

Elkins, Caroline. *Legacy of Violence: A History of the British Empire*. New York: Alfred A. Knopf, 2022.

Favell, Adrian. "Crossing the Race Line: 'No Polish, No Blacks, No Dogs' in Brexit Britain? or, The Great British Brexit Swindle." In "Europe's Malaise: The Long View," edited by Francesco Duina and Frédéric Merand, special issue, *Research in Political Sociology* 27 (October 2020): 103–30. https://doi.org/10.1108/S0895-993520200000027012.

Ford, Richard. "Racist Abuse at Stephen Lawrence Memorial." *The Times*, April 23, 2018. https://www.thetimes.com/uk/crime/article/racist-abuse-at-stephen-lawrence-memorial-7t5rgtfn8.

Gale North America. "Times Digital Archive: 1785–2014 Digital Archive." Accessed January 30, 2026. https://www.gale.com/product-catalog/266619.

Garbus, Liz, and Erica Sashin, dirs. *Harry & Meghan*. Aired December 2022 on Netflix. https://www.netflix.com/watch/81478159.

Glanton, Dahleen. "Column: Meghan Markle Saw Herself as Biracial, but the Royals Saw Her as Black." *Chicago Tribune*, March 9, 2021. https://www.chicagotribune.com/columns/dahleen-glanton/ct-glanton-meghan-markle-race-royals-20210309-tggn36w3brcupb2ptqvcxsnara-story.html.

Goodwin, Matthew J., and Oliver Heath. "A Tale of Two Countries: Brexit and the 'Left Behind' Thesis." *LSE British Politics*, July 25, 2016. https://blogs.lse.ac.uk/politicsandpolicy/brexit-and-the-left-behind-thesis/.

Kulz, Christy. "British Migrants in Berlin: Negotiating Postcolonial Melancholia and Racialised Nationalism in the Wake of Brexit." *Ethnic and Racial Studies* 45, no. 7 (2022). 1326–46. https://doi.org/10.1080/01419870.2021.1924390.

Low, Valentine. "Meghan Markle Dresses Down for Radio Station Visit with Prince Harry." *The Times*, January 10, 2018. https://www.thetimes.com/uk/royal-family/article/meghan-markle-dresses-down-for-radio-station-reprezent-fm-visit-with-prince-harry-7b6flm7f6.

Low, Valentine. "Meghan Markle Backs MeToo Movement in Debut with Duchess of Cambridge." *The Times*, May 20, 2018. https://www.thetimes.com/uk/royal-family/article/meghan-backs-metoo-movement-in-debut-with-duchess-pxfkzl0l7.

Mahfouz, Iman M. "The Representation of Meghan Markle in Facebook Posts: A Discourse Historical Approach (DHA)." *International Journal of Language and Linguistics* 5, no. 3 (2018): 246–59. https://doi.org/10.30845/ijll.v5n3p24.

Markle, Meghan. "Meghan Markle: I'm More Than an 'Other.'" *Elle*, updated December 22, 2016. https://www.elle.com/uk/life-and-culture/news/a26855/more-than-an-other/.

Morgan, Kenneth. *Slavery and the British Empire: From Africa to America*. New York: Oxford University Press, 2007.

Patel, Tina G., and Laura Connelly. "'Post-Race' Racisms in the Narratives of 'Brexit' Voters." *The Sociological Review*, 67, no. 5 (2019): 968–84. https://doi.org/10.1177/0038026119831590.

Phillips, Melanie. "Meghan's 'Woke' *Vogue* Is Shallow and Divisive." *The Times*, July 29, 2019. https://www.thetimes.com/uk/royal-family/article/meghan-s-woke-vogue-is-shallow-and-divisive-0qsjj537n.

Pramaggiore, Maria, and Páraic Kerrigan. "Brand Royal: Meghan Markle, Feuding Families, and Disruptive Duchessing in Brexit era Britain." *Feminist Media Studies* 22, no. 8 (2022): 2037–57. https://doi.org/10.1080/14680777.2021.1928258.

Reddie, Anthony G. *Theologising Brexit: A Liberationist and Postcolonial Critique*. London: Routledge, 2019.

Rose, Hilary. "Meghan—oh How the Royal Family Need You." *The Times*, November 1, 2016. https://www.thetimes.com/uk/royal-family/article/oh-meghan-the-royal-family-needs-you-067w6jbx.

Schuller, Kyla. *The Trouble with White Women: A Counterhistory of Feminism*. New York: Bold Type Books, 2021.

Schwarz, Hunter. "'I'm Proud to Be a Woman and a Feminist': The Politics of Meghan Markle." *CNN*, May 19, 2018. https://www.cnn.com/2018/05/18/politics/politics-of-meghan-markle/index.html.

Sobolewska, Maria, and Robert Ford. "British Culture Wars? Brexit and the Future Politics of Immigration and Ethnic Diversity." *Political Quarterly* 90, no. S2 (2019): 142–54. https://doi.org/10.1111/1467-923X.12646.

Taylor, Alex. "Harry and Meghan: What's the Media's 'Invisible Contract' with British Royalty?" *BBC News*, March 11, 2021. https://www.bbc.com/news/entertainment-arts-56326807.

*The Times*. "Welcome to the Firm." May 21, 2018. https://www.thetimes.com/article/85520658-5d0f-11e8-881d-a1499f0c9519.

Venäläinen, Venla. "Meghan Markle in the British Tabloid Press: A Corpus-Based Critical Discourse Analysis." Master's thesis, Tampere University, 2022. https://trepo.tuni.fi/bitstream/handle/10024/228435/Nykanen Noora.pdf?sequence=3.

Virdee, Satnam, and Brendan McGeever. "Racism, Crisis, Brexit, Ethnic and Racial Studies." *Ethnic and Racial Studies* 41, no. 10 (2018). 1802–19. https://doi.org/10.1080/01419870.2017.1361544.

Weidhase, Nathalie. "The Feminist Politics of Meghan Markle: Brexit, Femininity, and the Nation in Crisis." *European Journal of Cultural Studies* 20, no. 3 (2022): 916–33. https://doi.org/10.1177/1367549420980010.

Woldemikael, Eve, and Olivia Woldemikael. "From Suits to Royals: The Politics of Meghan Markle's Racial Ambiguity." *Women's Studies International Forum* 85 (2021). https://doi.org/10.1016/j.wsif.2021.102439.

CHAPTER 4

# JOURNEY TO THE CENTER OF THE EMPIRE

## *Meghan Markle and the Threat to the British Royal Family*

MARISSA KESSENICH

On March 7, 2021, CBS aired a groundbreaking ninety-minute interview conducted by Oprah Winfrey with Prince Harry and Meghan, Duke and Duchess of Sussex.[1] After their "Megxit" from the royal family in early 2020, the coronavirus lockdown forced everyone into isolation and removed the couple from the public eye for an entire year. The interview allowed the world to hear their side of the story, which had become steeped in controversy and intrigue. For the first time, the couple, whose engagement in 2017 took the world by storm, were able to discuss their journey to freedom from the restraints of royal protocol.

Nearly two years later, the royal couple released a six-part Netflix series that offered an in-depth narrative account of the same story—this time conceived, produced, and edited by Archewell Productions, the creative arm of Meghan and Harry's nonprofit organization. Like the 2021 interview, the December 2022 documentary series created an uproar across the globe—both among those supporting the couple and those accusing them of lying, overindulgence, and self-aggrandizement. Consistent in both versions of the Sussexes' story, however, is Meghan's testimony, which speaks to an experience of neglect, apathy, and aggression that, though often only implied, resulted from racist sentiments within the institution of the monarchy. Oprah asks a crucial question toward the end of her interview, when the duchess reveals that her experience turned particularly sour after garnering excellent press on her first tour in Australia and the South Pacific in 2019: "Isn't that what you [the royal family] want?"[2] Wouldn't someone like Meghan Markle—a humble, charismatic, intelligent woman of color—be an asset to an institution that continues to preside over a Commonwealth populated by majority Black and Brown citizens?

I argue that Meghan's entry into the royal family created a crisis of power. Her embodied existence within the institution of the monarchy revealed its true function not as a uniting body for the Commonwealth but as an active preservation of white supremacy. Stuart Hall's conception of race as a sliding signifier and the figure of the "white" mulatta provide lenses through which we can understand the threat that the American duchess poses to the English imperial order—even (and especially) in a postcolonial context. By reading through Meghan's biographical experience and her relationship with an English prince, we can see more clearly these cultural and historical processes of empire and race. With these processes and players established, I analyze how the British press and the monarchy reacted to Meghan. I identify two of the push factors that caused "Megxit"—both the abuse by the British tabloids and the lack of protection from the royal family—and discuss how they exist within global, systemic patterns of anti-Black racial violence.

Meghan's story brings together a rupture that Hazel Carby identifies between African American studies and Black studies more generally. The African American experience is held as singular in the United States, as if incomparable within the diaspora. However, Carby argues that to hold Black American history as unrelated to international Black experience, ignores the common inheritances of coloniality.[3] To understand Meghan's background as a biracial African American woman is important, as I will demonstrate. However, her movement across the Atlantic connects that experience to a context of Britishness that, despite glorifying itself as a post-racial modern society, remains mired in the cultural and historical processes enacted centuries ago.

## Sliding Signifiers and the Spectacle of the "White" Mulatta

In his lecture "Race—the Sliding Signifier," Stuart Hall lays out the entanglements of race, history, language, and power. He addresses discussions of race within the field of cultural studies, emphasizing the slipperiness of identifying how and why race is so pervasive. Analyzing the work of W. E. B. Du Bois and Kwame Anthony Appiah, Hall traces a genealogy of Black intellectuals' struggle to understand race. While Du Bois recognized early on that race is not biological, he failed to disentangle his metaphors from mention of bloodlines and physical traces. Appiah sees race as a purely social construct, arguing that the concept should be abandoned entirely—despite the very real effects of phenotypical difference on the lived experience of people of color.

Recognizing, rebutting, and reconciling these arguments, Hall sees race functioning precisely as discourse, as language. He describes race as a sliding signifier that does not reference facts "but the systems of meaning that have come to be fixed within the classifications of culture." Those meanings are not inherently true but are derived from the hierarchical scaffolding of perceptible traits that became formalized within a climate of white supremacy. The "Euro-imperial adventure" used science to arrest racial meaning as guaranteed, permanent, and transhistorical by virtue of nature rather than human design. However, this rigidity masks the impossibility of the racial binary. Meaning is mobile and highly contextual in the formation of identity. Thus, miscegenation and mulatto-ness present a threat to racial epistemology by undermining the "inscription of racial difference on the skin."[4]

Hall's conception of race as discourse offers a lens through which to read Meghan Markle's experience as a biracial woman. In a piece for *Elle* magazine in 2015, Markle describes her upbringing and early professional career. She is the daughter of an African American woman and a white man and grew up in Los Angeles, California, in the 1980s and 1990s. Her experience speaks to a perverse fascination with light-skinned Black bodies. She begins her article with the Question—"What are you?"—and discusses how her very existence renders her incomprehensible and paradoxical to people's understanding of race. In her own words, Meghan describes this existence as embodying "a blurred line that is equal parts staggering and illuminating."[5] It is a topic she admits to feeling uncomfortable discussing because it invites so much needling—so much scrutiny.

Two anecdotes in particular provide biographical examples of the slipperiness of race. The first is a story Markle tells of encountering the arbitrarily defined categories of race. In her seventh-grade class, she was forced to fill out a census. The boxes listed a number of races and ethnicities—white, black, Hispanic, or Asian—and asked students to choose the (singular) box that applied to them. Markle describes the turmoil this engendered for her as an eleven-year-old, "my curly hair, freckled face, my pale skin, my mixed race," and her dismay at having to choose one part of her identity over the other. In the end, she left the box blank, "a question mark, an absolute incomplete—much like how I felt." The second incident surrounds Markle's career as an actress. Her industry experience was characterized by not being "black enough for the black roles . . . [nor] white enough for the white ones, leaving me somewhere in the middle as an ethnic chameleon who couldn't book a job."[6] Landing her big break on the television drama *Suits* ended this constant racial recoding, but still had interesting repercussions. When her character was revealed to be biracial, like Markle herself, fans of the show retaliated. "She's not black," said one tweet. "Ew, she's black? I used to think she was hot," said another.[7] These were not isolated reactions. There was a sense among audiences that they had been tricked, that the showrunners had lured them into sympathizing with, being attracted to, or relating to a Black woman in a white-passing body.

The ethnic ambiguity that Markle highlights in her autobiographical experience is a modern continuation of what P. Gabrielle Foreman details in her discussion of the "white" mulatta in the nineteenth century. In the antebellum South and in the years following emancipation, mulatta women were often accused of passing *for* white. However, this perceived whiteness was not necessarily an active deception on the part of the subject but an external observation and classification that preserved the racial binary. These women created an epistemological crisis for those with racial power.[8] This crisis invited intense scrutiny that aimed to recover and inscribe the racial difference that upheld established systems of meaning. In other words, this scrutiny allowed white people to solidify their "authentic" whiteness by identifying "fraudulent" whiteness.

Foreman directly addresses the influence of the daguerreotype in the nineteenth century as creating a public obsession with looking. The imaging and imagining of the mulatta figure created conversations about the perceptibility of Blackness that aimed to train white viewers to "recognize putatively authentic visual and racial codes" "in the penumbras, rather than epidermis, of the women on display."[9] Even in the twenty-first century, Markle's experience as a white-passing biracial woman is marked by evidence of extant white anxiety. Her light-skinned body earns her privileges associated with whiteness—playing a racially ambiguous character on a successful television series and openly dating and then marrying an English prince, as two examples. However, because she "passes *through*" whiteness, her continued identification with her biracial-ness recuperates her Blackness and makes her subject to the intense scrutiny of the white gaze.[10] Her visibility as a public figure exposes the mobility and meaninglessness of racial identification, but also demonstrates how race is constantly (and often violently) reinscribed in order to masquerade as a stable and fixed system.

This white anxiety only increased when Markle's relationship with Prince Harry went public in 2016. Harry is an integral member of the British royal family and, through this association, personifies a history of empire and power. As an embodiment of an ideal of Britishness that "harbors the deepest interconnections of class and race and gender," Harry represents a direct link between the present iteration of the monarchy and its history of invasion, exploitation, and enslavement. By marrying Meghan, Harry unknowingly brought "geographies of pain" and the "continuing aftermath of enslavement" to the surface of mainstream British culture and society.[11] The fallout from this was shocking.

## The Press, the Palace, and Echoes of Empire

> *Harry's Girl Is (Almost) Straight Outta Compton: Gang-Scarred Home of Her Mother Revealed—so Will He Be Dropping By For Tea?*
>
> —STYLES, "HARRY'S GIRL"

Meghan Markle's arrival in London was met with mixed reactions. While many praised Prince Harry's modern choice, the recognition of Markle as an unlikely partner was widespread. A biracial Black American actress, she seemed to many an unfit addition to the paragon of Britishness represented by the royal family. The publication of the above *Daily Mail* headline in response to the couple's new relationship captures this reaction. Most horrifying was the adamant refusal of the British press to recognize that the headline was, indeed, racist.[12] However, Meghan and Harry do not solely cite the abuse from the press for their stepping back from royal life. The lack of support given to Meghan by the palace, both publicly and privately, created a dangerous environment. My analysis of the press focuses on print publications (and their online extensions) precisely because of the compounding and deleterious effect of the royals' symbiotic relationship with influential British print media outlets. In order to fully understand the involvement of the press and the monarchy in Meghan and Harry's departure from the royal family, it is important to highlight the relationship among the monarchy, media culture, and power.

Not all the British press's racist treatment was as visible as the aforementioned *Daily Mail* headline. The stark contrast between coverage of Meghan and of her sister-in-law, Kate Middleton (Duchess of Cambridge at that time), was perhaps more insidious *because* of its implicit anti-Blackness. Media and cultural studies scholar Laura Clancy points out the unfortunate timing of Meghan's entry into British society. Her engagement to Prince Harry came eighteen months after the British public voted in favor of Brexit, and their tenure in the royal family paralleled the nation's withdrawal period from the European Union. Brexit was largely animated by a "postcolonial melancholia" that made Meghan's racial Otherness a target for scrutiny and criticism.[13] This Otherness was all the more visible in contrast to Kate's conservative, traditionally British image. In a piece by *The Sun*, published after Meghan and Harry announced their engagement in 2017, the line between the two women was drawn. "NOT A DUPLI-KATE," the headline ran, adding, "Seven reasons why Meghan Markle is nothing like Kate Middleton." The article goes on to point out differences of class, upbringing, and "sophistication." Kate is portrayed as having "aristocratic roots" and being "more of a public figure than a career girl." Her style is described as modest, classic, and stylish—befitting a future queen. Meghan, on the other hand, is always mentioned second, as if a runner-up in every category. The article portrays her as a "grafter" and struggling artist with a string of former suitors, a gaggle of Hollywood friends, and a penchant for "racy clothes."[14]

The article makes no explicit critiques or analyses of the two women's differences, but the implications are obvious. Of the six photos included in the article, only two are of the Duchess of Cambridge and both are taken at official royal engagements, thus underscoring the tabloid's description of her as "Classy Kate." In both photos, she has a neutral facial expression, maintaining an air of typical British calm and reserve. The other four photos—all of Meghan—provide visual evidence of the differences drawn up in the article. A photo of Meghan on the red carpet depicts her looking directly into the camera. Dressed in leather pants and made up with red lipstick, Markle's sultry look contrasts heavily with the shots of Kate in formal gowns and business-professional dress. The other three photos depict Meghan smiling widely, almost as if to mock her American gaiety and naïveté. Most notable, however, is that despite mentioning both Kate's and Meghan's families, the only family photo the article includes is one of Meghan and her mother. The careful decision to exclude an image of the Middletons emphasizes that the point here is not family as much as it is "bloodlines." The photo of Meghan and her mother makes a spectacle of the future duchess's biracialness and cements the article's message: Meghan does not belong.

The article in *The Sun* was only the beginning. Once the couple married, the British press became relentless in their attacks on the Duchess of Sussex, ranging from her consumption of avocados—"a fruit linked to water shortages, illegal deforestation and all round general environmental devastation," according to *Express*—to disrespecting the institution of the monarchy by guest editing the September 2019 issue of British *Vogue*.[15] The stories turn Meghan into a villain, portraying her variously as selfish, ignorant, irritating, and opportunistic. In a particularly crude article criticizing the duchess for cradling her pregnant stomach in public, a contributor pithily asks, "I do wonder what is to come once Meghan begins to breastfeed . . . will she milk it for all she's worth?"[16] The comment is followed by over a dozen other opinions, ranging from those given by psychologists and birthing experts to newspaper columnists. The scrutiny is endless and, while not all negative, points to an abnormal level of interest in Meghan's body. In their depiction of Meghan, these tabloids effectively deconstruct her humanity in a way that continuously breeds and invites further scrutiny and deleterious criticism.

This process echoes the photographic scrutiny described by Foreman, but also incorporates a phenomenon of disembodiment in the way the tabloids write about (and write over) Meghan's body. Hortense Spillers discusses how the Black female body is the site of mutilation, dismemberment, and exile. She analyzes how the concept of flesh precedes the body, and without a sense of ownership or an ability to protect one's own flesh, there can be no embodiment or selfhood. While Spillers speaks specifically about the historical flesh of enslaved women brought from Africa to the Americas, her article connects this experience to present generations of Black women who continue to feel the effects of the destruction of Black subjecthood "over and over again by the passions of bloodless and anonymous archaism, showing itself in endless disguise." What she describes is an "American grammar," but this phenomenon is not singular to Black American life.[17] The aggressive and callous treatment of Meghan by the British press is a manifestation of a pervasive, global sentiment of misogynoir that seeks to exercise control over Black women's bodies, behavior, and lives.[18]

Even worse than the sentiments expressed by the press, however, was the utter lack of retaliation from the palace. The royal family made no effort to correct or redress the abuse carried out by the tabloids, nor did they make any attempt to support the newest active member of the family. In the interview with Oprah, Prince Harry comments that the relationship between the press and the palace keeps the latter "scared . . . of the tabloids turning on them."[19] Their symbiotic—yet strained—relationship allows the palace to control certain stories but also empowers the press to take advantage of their guaranteed access to royal news. This cooperation between the two entities gives the distinct impression that one cannot survive without the other. Because the monarchy is largely symbolic, it requires people to constantly buy into its legitimacy to ensure its survival. Constant press coverage of the royal family lends the monarchy the credibility it requires, but the maintenance of such an outdated colonial remnant means that this coverage must uphold certain "traditional" values. Especially considering the conservative bent of many of the publications in the royal rota—including the *Daily Express, Daily Mail, Daily Mirror, Evening Standard, Telegraph, Times,* and *Sun*—sentiments of disdain for Meghan reflect a larger concern about the sustainability of the monarchy.[20] While Meghan represents the larger community of the Commonwealth, the existence of the royal family depends on a sense of exceptionalism and untouchability. The press made a point of solidifying Meghan as the metonymic "Other" in order to ensure the survival and stability of the imperial institution they serve (and that serves them).

How the institution itself reacted to Meghan reveals the threat she poses to their preeminence. In the interview with Oprah, Meghan recalls the promises made to her when she became a working royal: "I did anything they told me to do—of course I did, because it was also through the lens of 'We'll protect you.' . . . It was only once we were married and everything started to really worsen that I came to understand that not only was I not being protected but *they were willing to lie to protect other members of the family but they weren't willing to tell the truth to protect me and my husband*" (emphasis mine).[21]

"The Firm," a popular nickname for the operational arm of the royal family, not only allowed lies and rumors about her to circulate through the press but actively fed the papers false narratives. They forced her to stay out of the public eye for months—ostensibly to let the smoke clear from all the media attention, but also as a way to disillusion her of any sense of freedom or autonomy. During this time, Meghan and Harry also found out that their unborn son, the first member of color born into the royal family, would not be given a royal title or security. Pregnant, alone, and panicking for her family's safety in the midst of a media maelstrom, Meghan admits that she became a threat to herself. She describes going to the Firm and to human resources to request help and hospitalization—and being denied.[22]

It is this neglect for Meghan's mental health that ultimately led the Sussexes to leave the institution. In order to remove themselves from the media circus and raise their young son in peace, the couple were forced to abandon their roles as active members of the royal family. The palace, as a result of this, also stripped Harry, Meghan, and Archie of their security detail. In the Netflix documentary series, Harry describes his desperate (and ultimately unsuccessful) discussions with his father to maintain their security.[23] With the onset of the COVID-19 pandemic on the heels of this news, the couple struggled to put together a means of protecting themselves. Unique among the royal family, Harry and Meghan were the victims of intense online hate campaigns that amassed shocking support, particularly among those with affiliations to violent far-right ideologies.[24] In an emotional interview for the documentary, Meghan describes reading some of the things written by people online, threatening (among other things) to murder her—just for existing as a Black woman and having married into the royal family.[25] For the palace to pull the couple's security with barely any notice amid this level of threat, one unprecedented among other members of the family, put their lives in very real danger. The fact that Black entertainment mogul Tyler Perry, a loose acquaintance of the Sussexes, provided more reliable security than the palace, highlights just how violently negligent the Firm truly was.

The Firm's actions speak volumes about the priorities of the monarchy and whom they deem worthy of protection. These repeated instances of deliberate neglect of Meghan's mental and physical health are demonstrative of Black life in the wake of slavery and colonialism.[26] That the palace sacrificed the safety of the only Black woman in the family to protect the reputation and prestige of its white members is an act of violence characteristic of an institution built upon, fed by, and surviving on the global, all-encompassing climate of anti-Blackness. Even as the royal family sought to capitalize on the diversity Meghan brought to their ranks, the Firm could not control the symbolic overload that her presence created.[27] Meghan's visibility, rather than absolving the royal family's racism, emphasized it. The power of the British monarchy, buoyed for centuries by various designs of superiority, relies on the myth of white supremacy to survive—and the palace's actions paint Meghan as a threat. If Meghan, Archie, and Lilibet's exclusion from King Charles III's coronation in May 2023 confirms anything, it is that the monarchy cannot afford to welcome "outsiders" whose mere presence shatters the illusion.

## Conclusion

Public reaction to Harry and Meghan's version of their story was, as usual, split. However, among Black Britons, it was overwhelmingly unanimous. After the couple's interview with Oprah, viewers took to Twitter to express their support for the duchess, sharing their similar experiences. "The passive aggressive, denial tactics that Meghan talks about is something we've all experienced in this country, it's very traumatic," commented Twitter user @itsKayokayyy. While still empathizing with Meghan, many Black Britons also expressed their frustration that "it literally took a light-skinned biracial american woman for people to believe how sexist + racist this island is to us," wrote Twitter user @helloalegria.[28] Indeed, colorism afforded Meghan many privileges. But similar to her experience in Hollywood, she was not white enough to be safe from the overwhelming forces of anti-Blackness within the British royal family. The colonial attitudes demonstrated by the press and the monarchy are not isolated. They represent larger systems of power that continue to pervade British society. Entering the royal family as a biracial woman, Markle threatened the carefully drawn boundaries that maintain definitions of race, class, and "Britishness" that originated in the empire's colonial pursuits. One way or another, the institution was going to attempt to remove her to save itself.

However, the damage may already be done. It is becoming increasingly evident that the monarchy is unsalvageable. Despite the continued barrage of opinions against Harry and Meghan, the royal family has been forever changed by Meghan's brief time among their ranks. The death of Queen Elizabeth II and the coronation of King Charles III have reopened debate about the necessity of the monarchy, highlighting its antiquated values, exploitation of British taxpayers, and failure to reflect modern Britain. Amid these conversations, Meghan arises as an inevitable example of the monarchy's failure to go beyond superficial gestures of diversity to welcome, protect, and nurture a more modern vision of the institution's commitment to public service and representation. King Charles now rules over a Commonwealth that is falling apart at the seams, with at least six Caribbean nations seeking to extricate themselves from the Crown's influence. In 2021, Barbados officially removed the British monarch as its head of state. In 2022, during visits by the Duke and Duchess and Cambridge and the Duke and Duchess of Wessex, Jamaica, Belize, and Grenada demanded official apologies and reparations. While it is unlikely that Meghan's departure from the royal family directly influenced these events, her treatment at the hands of the institution undoubtedly calls into question the ability of the royal family to accommodate a new era of post-colonial reckoning. Only time will tell if (or, rather, how much longer) the institution can survive through myths alone.

## Notes

1. Jones and Linton. "Harry and Meghan Detail Royal Struggles." See the full interview transcript in Sun Reporter, "Mark My Words."
2. Jones and Linton. "Harry and Meghan Detail Royal Struggles."
3. Goffe, Tao Leigh. "Who Inherits?"
4. Hall, *The Fateful Triangle*, 45, 53, 62.
5. Markle, "I'm More Than an 'Other.'"

6. Markle, "I'm More Than an 'Other.'"
7. Cited in Markle, "I'm More Than an 'Other.'"
8. Foreman, "Who's Your Mama?"
9. Foreman, "Who's Your Mama?," 148.
10. Foreman, "Who's Your Mama?," 135 (emphasis in original).
11. Carby, *Imperial Intimacies*, 4.
12. Bland, "Society of Editors in Turmoil."
13. Clancy, *Running the Family Firm*, 22.
14. Roberts, "NOT A DUPLI-KATE."
15. Read, "Meghan Markle's Beloved Avocado Linked to Human Rights Abuse"; Vine, "My Memo to Meghan Markle."
16. Jones, "Why Can't Meghan Markle Keep Her Hands Off Her Bump?"
17. Spillers, "Mama's Baby, Papa's Maybe," 68.
18. Lynch, Holly (@HollyLynch5). 2019. "Women MPs from all political parties have put aside our differences to stand in solidarity with the Duchess of Sussex today and are sending her this open letter." *Twitter*. https://twitter.com/HollyLynch5/status/1189175248035483648.
19. Jones and Linton. "Harry and Meghan Detail Royal Struggles."
20. "Media," website the Duke and Duchess of Sussex, Sussex Royal, accessed December 19, 2025, https://sussexroyal.com/media/.
21. Jones and Linton. "Harry and Meghan Detail Royal Struggles."
22. Jones and Linton. "Harry and Meghan Detail Royal Struggles."
23. Garbus and Sashin, *Harry & Meghan*, episode 5.
24. Newman, "Exclusive: Meghan Markle Faced Credible Threats."
25. Garbus and Sashin, *Harry & Meghan*, episode 5.
26. Sharpe, *In the Wake: On Blackness and Being*.
27. Clancy, *Running the Family Firm*.
28. These tweets are no longer available at the time of publication but were accessed at time of writing.

## Works Referenced

Bland, Archie. "Society of Editors in Turmoil over Its Statement on Meghan." *The Guardian*, March 10, 2021. https://www.theguardian.com/media/2021/mar/09/society-of-editors-claim-uk-media-not-racist-laughable.

Carby, Hazel V. *Imperial Intimacies: A Tale of Two Islands*. London: Verso, 2019.

Clancy, Laura. *Running the Family Firm: How the Monarchy Manages Its Image and Our Money*. London: Manchester University Press, 2021.

Foreman, P. Gabrielle. "Who's Your Mama? 'White' Mulatta Genealogies, Early Photography, and Anti-Passing Narratives of Slavery and Freedom." In *Pictures and Progress: Early Photography and the Making of African American Identity*, edited by Maurice O. Wallace and Shawn Michelle Smith, 132–66. Durham, NC: Duke University Press, 2012.

Garbus, Liz, and Erica Sashin, dirs. *Harry & Meghan*. Aired December 2022 on Netflix. https://www.netflix.com/watch/81478159.

Goffe, Tao Leigh. "'Who Inherits?': A Conversation Between Tao Leigh Goffe and Hazel V. Carby." *Public Books*, February 3, 2020. https://www.publicbooks.org/who-inherits-a-conversation-between-tao-leigh-goffe-and-hazel-v-carby/.

Hall, Stuart. *The Fateful Triangle: Race, Ethnicity, Nation*. Cambridge: Harvard University Press, 2017.

Jones, Liz. "Why Can't Meghan Markle Keep Her Hands off Her Bump? Experts Tackle the Question That Has Got the Nation Talking: Is It Pride, Vanity, Acting—or a New Age Bonding Technique?" *Daily Mail*, January 26, 2019. https://www.dailymail.co.uk/news/article-6636233/Why-Meghan-Markle-hands-bump-Experts-tackle-question.html.

Jones, Zoe Christen, and Caroline Linton. "Harry and Meghan Detail Royal Struggles, from Discussions of Baby's Skin Tone to Suicidal Thoughts." *CBS News*, March 8, 2021. https://www.cbsnews.com/live-updates/oprah-winfrey-interviews-meghan-markle-prince-harry/.

Lynch, Holly (@HollyLynch5). 2019. "Women MPs from all political parties have put aside our differences to stand in solidarity with the Duchess of Sussex today and are sending her this open letter." *Twitter*. https://twitter.com/HollyLynch5/status/1189175248035483648.

Markle, Meghan. "Meghan Markle: I'm More Than an 'Other.'" *Elle*, updated December 22, 2016. https://www.elle.com/uk/life-and-culture/news/a26855/more-than-an-other/.

Newman, Cathy. "Exclusive: Meghan Markle Faced Credible Threats to Her life, Says Former Head of Counterterrorism." *Channel 4 News*, November 29, 2022. https://www.channel4.com/news/exclusive-meghan-markle-faced-credible-threats-to-her-life-says-former-head-of-counter-terrorism.

Read, Carly. "Meghan Markle's Beloved Avocado Linked to Human Rights Abuse and Drought, Millennial shame." *Express*, January 23, 2019. https://www.express.co.uk/news/world/1076626/meghan-markle-news-avocado-toast-vegan-instagram.

Roberts, Sophie. "NOT A DUPLI-KATE: Seven Reasons Why Meghan Markle Is Nothing Like Kate Middleton . . . from Relationship History to Fashion Sense." *The Sun*, November 27, 2017. https://www.thesun.co.uk/fabulous/5010683/meghan-markle-kate-middleton-differences/.

Sharpe, Christina. *In the Wake: On Blackness and Being*. Durham, NC: Duke University Press, 2016.

Spillers, Hortense. "Mama's Baby, Papa's Maybe: An American Grammar Book." *diacritics* 17, no. 2 (1987): 65–81. http://www.jstor.org/stable/464747?origin=JSTOR-pdf.

Styles, Ruth. "Harry's Girl Is (Almost) Straight Outta Compton: Gang-Scarred Home of Her Mother Revealed—so Will He Be Dropping By for Tea?" *Daily Mail*, November 2, 2016. https://www.dailymail.co.uk/news/article-3896180/Prince-Harry-s-girlfriend-actress-Meghan-Markles.html.

Sun Reporter. "Mark My Words: Meghan Markle Oprah Interview." *The Sun*, January 31, 2024. https://www.the-sun.com/news/2475583/meghan-markle-oprah-interview-full-transcript/.

Vine, Sarah. "My Memo to Meghan Markle Following Her Vogue Editorial—We Brits Prefer True Royalty to Fashion Royalty." *Daily Mail*, July 29, 2019. https://www.dailymail.co.uk/debate/article-7298911/SARAH-VINE-memo-Meghan-Markle-Brits-prefer-true-royalty-fashion-royalty.html.

## CHAPTER 5

# GASLIGHT, GATEKEEP, GIRLBOSS

## *The Postfeminist American Dreams of Meghan Markle and Kim Kardashian*

AMELIA RYAN

Millennial women are the first in history to be able to market themselves, their spouses, their families, and their lifestyles on social media; in doing so, they have harnessed the ability to control their own narratives and build their own brands. Hard work and individualism lie at the heart of this endeavor as they "lean in" to achieve professional and personal success, epitomizing the girlboss. Few embody this shift more than Meghan Markle and Kim Kardashian. The two women are only a year apart in age, both born in Los Angeles at the cusp between Generation X and millennial. Their life paths mark a trajectory of ascendance to overwhelming fame, and are characterized by multiple marriages and either relatively late or later than personally desired childbearing. The two women also share a unique status as members of families whose prominence and influence meet that of royal standards. Markle and Kardashian use their sexuality, their choice of controversial but prominent spouses, and their ethnic/racial ambiguity to build a desirable brand.

I begin this chapter by contextualizing these women's success through the ever-changing American dream and the role that celebrity plays in reinforcing its neoliberal values. Then I examine the increasing convergence of celebrity and royalty and how these two women personify this development, arguing that they both constitute a new kind of royalty: girlboss royalty. Following this contextualization, I analyze Markle's and Kardashian's use of their sexuality and racial ambiguity as tools to advance their professional careers, marrying high-profile, wealthy, and controversial men to achieve this status. Next I contrast Markle's embrace of feminism and Kardashian's rejection of it. Subsequently, I introduce postfeminism and tie it back to the neoliberal American dream. I contend that these two women represent progress, as their modernity includes divorce, interracial marriage, motherhood after establishing a career, bearing mixed-race children, and practicing working motherhood. I define postfeminism and interrogate whether Markle and Kardashian have provided a feasibly replicable blueprint to achieve a twenty-first-century dream of family, global wealth, and influence: a royal postfeminist American dream. However, I ultimately assert that these women espouse neoliberal postfeminist values that reinforce systems of inequality.

## The American Dream and Celebrity

In her book, *Celebrity Culture and the American Dream: Stardom and Social Mobility*, Karen Sternheimer outlines the ways in which celebrity has reinforced the American dream through its various iterations. The expression "American dream" became popular in the 1930s but has been deeply embedded in the nation since its founding. Sternheimer associates our freedom from European-style monarchy with freedom to achieve economic success without a title. She argues that the "practically endless amounts of land and opportunity for homesteaders" built the myth that individual success was rooted in determination and ingenuity. Thus, we cannot ignore the role that privilege plays in success and how it is often used to justify inequality. Sternheimer asserts that celebrity culture "seems to provide a continual reaffirmation that upward mobility is possible in America and reinforces the belief that inequality is the result of personal failure rather than systematic social conditions."[1] She identifies eight dreams told through celebrity, situating each in historical context. They include modest ambitions like entry to the middle class and the simple desire to live comfortably at the outset of the 1900s, and an idealized family life following World War II. The two most recent aspirations, she proposes, are extreme wealth after the economically and politically unstable decade of the 1970s, and accessible celebrity in the age of the internet and reality television, the latter coinciding with the Great Recession of 2008 and deep economic inequality.

Sternheimer acknowledges that some critical theorists view celebrity media as propaganda that brainwashes the public into accepting the current socioeconomic system. However, she argues that it is less of a top-down effort from the elite class of celebrity aimed at stifling dissent and more so derived from a collective desire for the American dream to be possible. I am inclined to agree with her analysis, as the former requires too much forethought to be practically implemented. Today, we cling ever so tightly to the idea that achieving celebrity and wealth is more accessible than ever through social media and reality television because of the immense wealth gap and stagnant wages that bar us from social mobility. We also thoroughly enjoy getting glimpses into deeply personal aspects of celebrities' and influencers' lives. The relatively low cost of this type of content production and its popularity have mutually reinforced each other and have rapidly transformed our consumption of celebrity culture. Now consumers of media expect to have access to intimate details about celebrities' lives even outside of the context of reality television or social media.

## The Convergence of Royalty and Celebrity

In an age when reality television stardom and billionaire-hood intersect with the presidency, the line between long-respected institutions and tawdry celebrity blurs. In recent history, celebrity and royalty have started to resemble each other, and in the process, have redefined their respective conceptions. In Sternheimer's reflections on celebrity, she adds that it serves other purposes in addition to reinforcing the American dream. For example, we as a society can bond over shared values when celebrities act in ways we deem inappropriate. Sternheimer compares these shared celebrity stories to what sociologists Daniel Dayan and Elihu Katz have written about how media events like royal weddings and state funerals create social integration through shared rituals, as "celebrity culture also provides a window into broader, macro-level social processes." This mirrors the larger social significance that famous families like the royal family possess in the way we identify with and emulate them.[2] There is some kind of fundamental sociological need for people to watch the famous proceed through various life stages. While the United States was founded in opposition to the convention of monarchy, the public's desire to witness public family life remained. With our own head of state changing every four to eight years, the Kardashians filled a niche that has rewarded them with astonishing fame and wealth. The Kardashian-Jenners comprise four out of the ten most followed people on Instagram, each with at least 290 million followers. Kim Kardashian is worth an estimated $1.7 billion. They are truly the American equivalent to the British royal family. Her own 2011 "fairy-tale wedding," which was coincidentally also her second and featured a big, white dress and veil, raked in 10.5 million views on *E!*[3] At the time, media outlets drew comparisons to the 2011 royal wedding. The family has also been labeled "America's royal family," even if only used as a snappy title or evoked in a thoughtful if brief contextualization/analysis of the family. Sternheimer argues that celebrity further exhibits ideals of the American dream in that it is disconnected from family lineage despite myriad celebrities who were greatly aided by the connections of their rich or famous family members. Public discourse has shifted in the years since Sternheimer's book was published, to include conversations about "nepotism babies." I contend that the Kardashians shattered the illusion that Sternheimer describes—that the American dream is accessible to all kinds of people—and constitute a new kind of royalty.

As mentioned, it is not just celebrity that has evolved to mirror royalty but royalty that has evolved to mirror celebrity. Royalty is associated with a famous family, far-reaching fame, and immense wealth. In their article "Brand Royal: Meghan Markle, Feuding Families, and Disruptive Duchessing in Brexit Era Britain," Maria Pramaggiore and Páraic Kerrigan state that "the contemporary understanding of families—famous, infamous, royal or obscure—is strongly informed by tabloid and reality television. . . . These anti-meritocratic dynasties, though far from royal, are often associated with lucrative international business empires. The family unit represented by reality TV both foregrounds and masks ideologies of class, gender, and race within a sentimentalizing rhetoric of bonded kinship."[4] In a way, royals, especially those who are ceremonial, are the original influencers: a notable and select few who live lavishly off the masses in exchange for a peek into their lives. The distinction between royalty and modern celebrity is diminished by coverage of royal lives that are "served up reality television style."[5] Prince Harry and Markle themselves have perpetuated this dynamic by profiting from sharing intimate details of their lives in the prince's memoir, *Spare*, and in their Netflix series. While they have done a lot to align with the influencer space in their commercial endeavors (rumored to be worth $135 million) following their departure from the royal family in 2020, they still cling to their royal titles. *The Cut* author Allison P. Davis reflects on the contradiction between influencing and royalty: "That specific type of very American ambition just isn't really compatible with being a princess. Though it is compatible with her current life, which seems to be the best of all worlds: a palace in a better climate, still culturally considered royalty while having freedom from the royal family, a level of celebrity that exceeds what she could have gotten through *Suits* or the Tig." In the end, as *Jacobin* writer Ryan Zickgraf puts it, "maybe she modernized the monarchy after all."[6]

Both Meghan Markle and Kim Kardashian now belong to an elite class of uber-wealthy, famous families. Interestingly, they share similar upbringings, as they were both born and raised in greater Los Angeles, had fathers who were in the entertainment industry, and attended all-girls Catholic high schools despite not being Catholic. They each established their careers and joined the upper class before they married the men who would become the fathers of their children. These weddings were extravagant affairs in which each woman walked down the aisle in custom Givenchy with cathedral veils over their faces. Today they are mothers who possess even more wealth. Markle and Kardashian even share social circles: Markle sent Kris Jenner jam from her new brand, American Riviera Orchard (recently renamed As Ever).

Next I explore the ways in which both women leveraged their sexuality, racial ambiguity, and choice of controversial spouse to attain girlboss royalty.

## Sexuality

Both Markle and Kardashian have used their sexuality as a tool to gain status and financial security. The most apparent example is Kardashian's sex tape with Ray J, released in 2007, which propelled her to fame and gave her name recognition. A much-discussed *Playboy* shoot and the premiere of a TV reality series, *Keeping Up with the Kardashians*, followed later that year. Interestingly, at the 2023 Met Gala, Kardashian seemingly paid homage to her 2007 *Playboy* photoshoot by wearing just shapewear and many strands of pearls, suggesting that she seeks not to hide her past but to celebrate it. This tribute was intentional and easily recognizable as her 2007 *Playboy* look, wearing only pearls, is immortalized in the legendary meme of Kris Jenner telling her daughter "You're doing amazing, sweetie" during the photo shoot.[7] It also served as an opportunity to indirectly advertise her own shapewear line, SKIMS. Kardashian brilliantly garnered attention for herself, and in doing so, reinforced her brand recognition.

Both Kim Kardashian and Meghan Markle starred as themselves in suggestive food video advertisements, for Carl's Jr. (2010) and *Men's Health* (2013), respectively. In the Carl's Jr. commercial, Kardashian seductively eats a salad in bed, dressed in a robe; later, she appears in a bathtub, where she is seen unclothed. The camera zooms in as she puts the salad in her mouth. When dressing drips off the salad, the camera pans to her cleavage. In her commercial, Meghan Markle is labeled "the ultimate guy's girl." She seductively takes down and shakes out her hair, gives the camera a sultry look while unbuttoning her shirt to reveal her bra, and bites her lip while flipping burgers. Similar to Kardashian's commercial, the camera makes several sweeps of her figure and features close-ups of her eating a burger and sucking her finger. These two commercials are expertly sculpted for the male gaze.

Markle held lower-status acting jobs while trying to earn a living early on in her career. In 2006, she was a *Deal or No Deal* "briefcase girl," in which her purpose was to look hot and open a briefcase if instructed. In an episode of her erstwhile podcast, *Archetypes*, she describes how she felt objectified and like a bimbo: "I would end up leaving with this pit in my stomach, knowing that I was so much more than what was being objectified on the stage." Ultimately, her discomfort led her to quit.[8] She also appeared very briefly on *90210* as a character who is caught performing oral sex on a main character in a car. It is her character's only appearance besides a brief reference to the event in the following episode. This role is at odds with Markle's values that led her to quit *Deal or No Deal* a couple of years before. In the podcast episode, Markle recounts that while working for *Deal or No Deal*, she was grateful to have a job with a regular paycheck and health insurance. While she ultimately decided that the financial stability was not worth the objectification, it is possible that she fell on harder times and felt that she had to take the *90210* role. Additionally, while she has not commented directly on her *Men's Health* advertisement, she describes herself as a "girl's girl" in the podcast episode, a characterization that directly contradicts *Men's Health*'s branding of her as "the ultimate guy's girl," further demonstrating that her early public identity was built around the profitability of the male gaze.

Unlike Markle, Kardashian embraces objectification. While promoting her book of selfies in 2015, she shared that she "think[s] that you have the power—women objectify themselves, too—to put out there what you want people to look at, what you want to portray about yourself."[9] Both women have evidently used their sexuality to earn a living and to raise their status in the entertainment industry, regardless of their feelings about objectification. This suggests that not only is objectification a helpful tool, but it is perhaps a necessary strategy for success in today's world or at least the early twenty-first century. This serves as a sharp contrast to a generation ago when Prince Harry's mother, Princess Diana, was chosen as Prince Charles's bride for her virginity, beauty, and nobility. Regardless of the reception and implications of their sexuality in the public eye, Kardashian's and Markle's sexualities do not simply exist for the public eye; they are also a key part of their private lives and marriages.

## Controversial Husbands

Both Markle's and Kardashian's most well-known marriages are to very prominent and wealthy men—Prince Harry and Kanye West, respectively. The two men are no strangers to controversy and both have made racist and antisemitic comments and/or participated in such actions. In 2005, Prince Harry dressed up as a Nazi at a costume party. In the couple's 2022 Netflix documentary series, he refers to this act as "one of the biggest mistakes of my life."[10] In his 2023 memoir, he takes a different tone. He blames his brother and sister-in-law for telling him to wear the outfit to their themed party, compares the humiliation he experienced to the humiliation his father felt when his "most intimate conversations were leaked" (Tampongate), and discusses how he felt shame and self-loathing. He recounts a conversation he had with the Chief Rabbi of Britain in which the rabbi taught him about the Holocaust. A year later, he filmed himself calling a comrade at his military academy racial and religious slurs ("Paki," "raghead"). In his memoir, he explains that he thought "Paki" was a term like "Aussie," adding that he wanted to issue his own apology in 2009 but his father advised him not to. He also shares that he "cared about not being a racist."[11] He does not reference the religious slur that he used. A more relevant controversy concerns his relationship with Chelsy Davy, circa 2005. While discussing the relationship with the Zimbabwean woman to the press, Prince Harry stated "She's not black or anything, you know."[12]

These are actions of a self-described ignorant and privileged young man. People are capable of personal growth; however, Prince Harry, who was thirty-eight when his memoir was published, does not take full accountability for his actions and frames the first two in terms of familial conflict and media backlash. Indirectly comparing his racist and antisemitic actions to his father wishing to be Camilla Parker Bowles's tampon is trivial. In his memoir, he treats his Nazi controversy similarly to when he was photographed naked while partying. In doing so, he dismisses the power of his actions, and, while he acknowledges that he was wrong, he does not focus on the harmful consequences to others or their larger societal implications. This is especially important as a public figure in a family that has long benefited from colonizing other nations. He fails to connect that his casual use of an anti-Muslim slur may have made it easier to dehumanize (by his own admission) the twenty-five Muslim men he claims to have later killed in war. His silence regarding his statement about Davy is disturbing, especially considering his marriage to Markle and the opportunities he has had to address it in his 407-page memoir, his and Markle's Netflix documentary series, and countless media interviews. He, instead, chose to spend pages talking about his frostbitten penis. Interestingly, Markle has never publicly addressed these three instances of prejudice.

In contrast, Kanye West's racist and antisemitic remarks are more recent, significantly more egregious, and more difficult to summarize. In 2018, five years after the birth of West and Kardashian's daughter, North, and four years after their wedding, West called slavery "a choice" while showing support for Donald Trump. He later apologized for "how [the comment] made people feel," for the "one-two punch effect of the MAGA hat into the slave comment," and how it let people down. Kardashian defended his comments publicly, but shared that she screamed, cried, and fought about them.[13] West's public antisemitism is immensely worse than Prince Harry's ever was. In 2022, over a year after Kardashian filed for divorce, he threatened the lives of Jewish people: "I'm a bit sleepy tonight but when I wake up I'm going death con 3 [*sic*] on JEWISH PEOPLE." He later declared that he "loves Nazis," and "likes Hitler." Kardashian condemned his antisemitic tirade in a Tweet: "Hate speech is never OK or excusable. . . . I stand together with the Jewish community and call on the terrible violence and hateful rhetoric towards them to come to an immediate end."[14] Kardashian exhibited a unified front with West while in the marriage despite his controversial stances. However, she finally contradicted and disavowed West's problematic beliefs after the marriage ended.

These two women have set an interesting example for other high-profile women in relationships with high-profile men. They largely have either remained silent or defensive regarding their husbands' comments while in the marriage. This leads us to interrogate the question of why these women are or were in relationships with men of questionable judgment or character. Is it to secure status? Without Prince Harry, Markle may have continued to live a comfortable life as an actress and a United Nations Women's advocate, but would not have access to the same remarkable fame, wealth, and influence that she has as the Duchess of Sussex. As for Kardashian, her relationship with West elevated her from reality TV star to member of a power couple. West reinvented Kardashian as a high-fashion icon and connected her to brands like Balenciaga, affiliations that brought her legitimacy and considerable wealth.[15] Is the goal to raise children with even more privilege to create or extend a dynasty of their own? Both Markle and Kardashian will leave a legacy of privilege and wealth to their children that very few people in history have known.

Next I dive into racial ambiguity and the role it has played in these women's romantic lives.

## Racial Ambiguity

Meghan Markle, a biracial woman, and Kim Kardashian, a woman of Armenian descent, both possess racial ambiguity. This is evident in the public's difficulty in categorizing their racial identities and the ways in which they intentionally align with a specific racial identity. In Prince Harry and Markle's Netflix documentary series, the couple and Markle's mother, Doria Ragland, reflect on the shift she experienced from being treated like a mixed-race woman to a Black woman. Markle explains, "It is very different to be a minority but not be treated as a minority right off the bat. Obviously, now people are very aware of my race because they made it such an issue when I went to the U.K., but before that, most people didn't treat me like a 'Black woman.'" Markle had not anticipated the racist backlash she faced once she was publicly linked to Prince Harry. Doria recalls warning her daughter: "I said to her . . . that this is about race and Meg said, 'Mommy, I don't want to hear that.' I said, 'You may not want to hear it but this is what's coming down the pike.'" Markle, who has much lighter skin than her mother, appeared to be stunned that she was now experiencing a racism similar to what her mother has experienced.

Nylah Burton elaborates on Markle's mixed-race privilege in an article for *Andscape*, a website that delivers "news and commentary that explores the intersections of race, sports, culture and more." She highlights that "while many light-skinned people have the *ability* to pass, passing as an *act* is intentional." Burton supports this claim by emphasizing that Markle distanced herself from her blackness by not being seen with curly hair after adolescence, joining a white sorority, and dating mostly white men: "effectively . . . living a white life."[16] Another writer, Elaine Musiwa, reflects on Markle's mixed-race identity and how Markle reminded of her of women in her own life:

> Markle looks like some of the mixed-race girls who I went to high school with in my suburban town. When the Internet was still new, I used a few of their pictures to catfish white boys so I could hear them say that they loved me, even if it was only digitally and not really me. Instinctually, I knew that white men had more dexterity with romance when it came to dating ambiguously looking black women rather than ones that couldn't be mistaken as anything else: dark skin, big nose, big lips, big eyes, big hair. Ambiguous blackness could be forgotten, at the very least easily forgiven, when introduced to white families, to white friends, to white neighbors.[17]

And that forgiveness is what Markle and Prince Harry anticipated from the British public and press upon announcing their engagement. After all, her racial ambiguity had been a strong-enough force for Prince Harry, a man who once scoffed at the idea of dating a Black woman, to propose that she join the royal family.

Whereas Meghan Markle's racial ambiguity acted as a shield to protect her from racism, Kim Kardashian has distanced herself from whiteness in an attempt to commodify exoticism and has lived a Black-adjacent life. Whiteness has a history of heavy regulation in the U.S. While Armenians were legally categorized as white in 1909 by the U.S. Supreme Court, lower courts called into question the legitimacy of this classification in 1923 after many fled to the U.S. as the result of the Armenian Genocide. Ultimately, a federal district court affirmed the initial decision. So, while technically white by this standard, Kardashian sits at the outskirts of whiteness. Kim Kardashian's racial identity has caused so much confusion that it was even the subject of an article in the *Houston Law Review*. In it, John Tehranian attempts to understand her race, tracing its historical, legal, and social constructions and analyzing the roles of racial fluidity and personal expression as a potential moderator of this understanding. In an article for *Vice*, Anya Zoledziowski, a woman of Armenian and Polish descent, explores Kardashian's influence on her own racial identity. She describes Kardashian's racial identity as "malleable and label-free, allowing her to shift from white to brown and back to white, effectively building a palatable brand of off-white that's easy to sell because *we* get to define *her* however we want."[18] Kardashian's racial and ethnic ambiguity make her both more popular and profitable. She is so widely celebrated for her curvaceous body and plump lips that American beauty standards have transformed from the worship of extreme thinness in the early aughts to an obsession with being "slim thick" in the 2010s. These features, often seen on Black women, were neither nationally acclaimed nor sought after until they were seen on a racially ambiguous woman. Now the Kardashians capitalize on this new standard in their commercial ventures with their makeup lines, SKKN (formerly KKW Beauty) and Kylie Cosmetics, and shapewear company, SKIMS.

Kardashian has been accused of "blackfishing" throughout her career as she alters her physical appearance with cosmetic procedures to accentuate her body and lip shape, regularly darkens her skin, and repeatedly sports braids often worn by Black women. Moreover, her proximity to Blackness is not limited to her physical appearance. She and most of her female family members have almost exclusively dated well-known Black or biracial men.[19] This pattern was obvious to her late father, Robert Kardashian, who she claims knew she "would probably end up with a Black guy."[20] Kim has been romantically linked to Damon Thomas, Ray J, Nick Cannon, Reggie Bush, Miles Austin, Kris Humphries, Kanye West, and Odell Beckham Jr.[21] Additionally, Kim, Khloe, and Kylie have all had children with Black men. On an episode of *Keeping Up with the Kardashians,* Kim almost characterizes Kanye West as a sperm donor, sharing, "When I got pregnant with North, I had no idea if Kanye and I would end up together and I was like, 'We can break up, but let me at least have some sperm so, like, I can have another one, so I can have siblings.'"[22] West outright referred to himself, Tristan Thompson, Travis Scott, and Scott Disick (the fathers of Khloe's, Kylie's, and Kourtney's children, the latter of whom is white) as sperm donors, showing he believed that he and other men were used, not as partners in creating a family, but as genetic material.[23] In 2022, after she and her sisters finished having children with Black men, the sisters started distancing themselves from Blackness. Kim started dating a white man, Pete Davidson, and she and Khloe both lost a considerable amount of weight and drastically reduced their signature curves. She has since been publicly linked to Odell Beckham Jr.

## Feminism

Kardashian and Markle have dueling opinions regarding their identification with feminism. Meghan Markle has long identified as a feminist. Her first public appearance with this identity was at age eleven, when she appeared in a *Nickelodeon News* segment. In it, she describes how she successfully advocated for their dish soap commercial to change its marketing to include all people as opposed to only women; she did this by writing a letter to

Procter & Gamble and a few influential women. She shared that she did not think it was right for kids to grow up thinking that "just Mom does everything." Markle served as a United Nations women's advocate for political participation and leadership before she met Prince Harry. In a speech given to the UN in 2015, she stated that she is proud to be a woman and a feminist. She has continued her advocacy for women both inside and outside her duties as a working royal. Additionally, her podcast, *Archetypes* (2022–23), is centered on "investigat[ing], dissect[ing], and subvert[ing] the labels that try to hold women back." Markle is also friends with the second-wave feminist Gloria Steinem, who gifted her a bracelet engraved with "We are linked not ranked." Steinem has publicly praised Markle as a "great human being" who is "smart and funny and devoted to social issues" and shared her motivation for the engraving as a reflection on race, gender, and class.[24] I interpret these gestures as a gentle push for Markle to consider class more thoughtfully in her personal interpretation of feminism, which sharply contrasts with how she continually evokes her ranking as the Duchess of Sussex.

Contrastingly, Kim Kardashian has long denied being a feminist. She elaborates on this identification in an essay she published on her website in 2020:

> For me, [a] feminist is someone who advocates for the civil and social rights and liberties of all people, regardless of their gender; anyone who believes that women should have the same choices and opportunities as men when it comes to education and employment, their bodies and their lifestyles. . . . Of course I want these things! I'm all about empowering and uplifting women. . . . Obviously, there are things about me that people might say make me a feminist: I work hard, I make my own money, I'm comfortable and confident in my own skin, and I encourage women to be open and honest about their sexuality, and to embrace their beauty and their bodies. . . . I don't need to be defined by those beliefs. . . . I feel that being grouped or labeled can create sep-

> aration between people who do (or don't) fall into certain categories, when they may actually share many of the same beliefs and goals.[25]

It is unclear why she rejects the label of feminist while she admittedly believes in its core tenets. She appears to not want to alienate those who do not identify as feminist. Perhaps it would hurt her carefully constructed brand, driving away social media followers and potential customers. Kardashian appears to have shifted away from this mentality as she took a stand in 2022 when *Roe v. Wade* was overturned. In an Instagram story, she posted, "In America, guns have more rights than women."[26] Supporting the bodily autonomy of women is a feminist act. While Kardashian denies labeling herself a feminist, her beliefs about female empowerment, financial independence, and bodily autonomy suggest otherwise.

## Breaking Barriers

Kardashian and Markle teach us that feminism is more complex than identity. Their lives serve as testaments to the complexity of womanhood and the desire "to have it all." Both women publicly shared their desire to be mothers before they started their families. Markle expressed her desire to start a family in press interviews in 2015 and 2016. She shared that "it's all about balance, and I have so much happiness in my career and am fortunate to travel the world and see so many amazing things—it will also be nice to be anchored to something grounded and in the same place. Raising a family will be a wonderful part of that."[27] Markle established herself as a professional actress before she started a family at thirty-seven. Her career ambitions did not conflict with her wish to have her own family. Kardashian recounted her dream of being a mother in a 2012 episode of *Keeping up with the*

*Kardashians*. While crying about her separation from Kris Humphries, she said, "At thirty years old, I thought I'd be married with kids and I'm not. I've failed at this."[28] Despite this setback, she gave birth to her daughter North at thirty-two years old. Markle and Kardashian represent a generational shift in the age at which women have kids. Both of their mothers gave birth to them in their midtwenties, while Markle and Kardashian had their first children in their thirties. Markle and Kardashian demonstrate that motherhood is not only attainable later in life compared to previous generations but desirable, as both women already had successful careers, financial stability, and well-established personal and public identities before they became mothers.

These two women also set the example for younger generations in terms of marriage in general. Markle and Kardashian were both previously married before they met the fathers of their children. Neither had children with their ex-husbands, demonstrating that marriage does not exist for the sole purpose of having children. They also show young women that marriages can end but their world does not. Women do not have to stay in relationships that no longer suit them or that harm them. In a more practical sense, these women show how marriage can help build wealth and gain influence. Markle, while financially successful in her own right, gained many millions more dollars in her marriage to Prince Harry and the two have built wealth together with their Netflix series and other ventures. Kardashian, also a millionaire before her marriage to West, is now a billionaire. These women are not solely beneficiaries of their husbands' wealth but members of a financial team. Markle and Kardashian teach young women that marriage does not have to last forever, can happen multiple times in your life, and can be a very lucrative financial arrangement.

Markle and Kardashian also break barriers as women who are/were in interracial marriages and as mothers of mixed-race children. While many young people may not see anything unusual about interracial marriage and mixed-race children, this has not always been the case. In 1967, just over a decade after Markle's and Kardashian's mothers were born, the Supreme Court ruled that interracial marriage must be legal across the country in its decision in the *Loving v. Virginia* case. Markle, a mixed-race woman, struggled with her identity growing up and felt that she was forced by both Black and white people to choose which category she fit into. Hopefully, Markle's and Kardashian's children will not have to struggle with their identities in the same manner, as the public is more familiar with the concept of being mixed race and it is a more common experience today. These two women normalize and further reduce the stigma of interracial relationships by simply living their own lives.

Meghan Markle and Kim Kardashian represent generational progress in the way women are perceived and the manner in which they shape their public perceptions. These millennial women have constructed brands for themselves that showcase "having it all." Both Markle and Kardashian took advantage of their sexuality and racial ambiguity to propel themselves forward professionally and to marry high-profile men. These high-profile marriages resulted in both personal and professional success as they were able to start the families they longed to have, benefit from an elevation in their fame and influence, and build extraordinary wealth. The price of these advantages involved aligning themselves with controversial men and institutions. However, they demonstrate that under very narrow circumstances, women can have both family lives and remarkable professional and financial success.

## Is "Royal Feminism" Postfeminist and Neoliberal?

I'd like to contextualize Markle's and Kardashian's girlboss journeys through the lenses of postfeminism and neoliberalism. The girlboss is derived from the same neoliberal ideas that Sheryl Sandberg lauded in her book *Lean In*. Former Nasty Gal CEO Sophia Amoruso coined the term "girlboss" in her 2014 memoir in an effort to empower women to thrive under capitalism.[29] The term did not enjoy popularity solely in the context of female executive leadership and was even co-opted by victims of multilevel marketing. Alex Abad-Santos characterizes the girlboss as "one of the cruelest tricks capitalism ever perpetrated" as, much like bell hooks argues in her critique of Sandberg's memoir, female leadership in corporate settings does not challenge the inextricably linked structures of systemic inequality under capitalism.[30] Much of Generation Z keenly understands the hypocrisy in this faux feminism, and as we do, we've made it into a meme. Thus, the mantra "Gaslight, Gatekeep, Girlboss" was born on social media in June 2021. My friends and I invoked it frequently in college and it still makes appearances on social media. The terms were already established staples of Generation Z's vernacular. "Gaslight" refers to lies fiercely defended in the face of blatant truth. "Gatekeep" is a verb used to describe preventing certain people from attaining a desired outcome and is invoked in conversations from fandom to discrimination. The mantra demonstrates an intersectional awareness that the promise of women's liberation through capitalistic achievement is a farce, as it completely ignores the discriminatory circumstances that prevent its universal adoption. Moreover, individual achievement within the bounds of capitalism cannot change a system that is rooted in patriarchy, racism, and classism. In Generation Z terms, girlbosses have tried to gaslight us into believing that a system that is inextricably linked to gatekeeping can empower us. Individuals can find success, but it is not accessible to all. This meme rejects the neoliberal prioritization of the individual and favors collective liberation.

Unbeknown to many of us, Generation Z's astute mockery mirrors postfeminist theory. Postfeminism simultaneously rejects feminism as no longer necessary and appropriates the themes of sexual liberation and empowerment. Marston, citing previous scholarship, presents a definition of postfeminism as "a capitalistic sensibility in which female empowerment is largely reduced to the pursuit of financial success and active participation in consumer culture, rigorous self-monitoring, and the physical embodiment of beauty standards in adherence to a normative model of white, western, middle-class heterofemininity."[31] Postfeminism is neoliberal because it relies on the individual to make a choice to work hard to build wealth, ultimately empowering the self. Here, women must pull themselves up by their (heeled) bootstraps, as they also have to perform femininity and be sexy. Under this theory, women are empowered because they are not objectified without agency: they choose sexualization, subjectification.

In "Selling Sunset . . . and My Postfeminist Sexual Capital: New Sexual Subjectivities in Reality TV," Silvia Díaz Fernández analyzes how two female real estate agents gain and use their sexual capital to acquire financial capital. She clarifies that it is not simply aesthetic sexiness or desirability they are cultivating; it is a state of being. She argues that not only do they employ subjectification as a tool to succeed but it is "fundamental" to their success. Díaz Fernández defines success as personal and professional, framing an agent's marriage as "landing . . . a multi-millionaire." Ultimately, Díaz Fernández finds limitations in this theory and stipulates that "sexual freedom to grow one's sexual capital is only available for a privileged few, and in the context of popular culture, these few tend to be heterosexual, wealthy, white and white-passing women who are idealised as the norm."[32] I, and French feminist Virginie Despentes, do and would find further limitations in sexual subjectivity, as (1) there is no real choice to self-sexualize if it is required to succeed, and (2) sexual subjectivity relies on performance for the male gaze and must meet its beauty standards, and is therefore not a genuine expression of sexuality.

Meghan Markle and Kim Kardashian are better understood within this framework. I am neither the first to contextualize these women in terms of postfeminism explicitly nor am I alone in comparing the two simultaneously, as scholar of postfeminism Kendra Marston does in her book chapter "Hating Meghan Markle: Drawing the Boundaries of British Whiteness Against Postfeminist Femininity":

> Her perceived failure . . . is framed as evidence of an alignment with a "lower class" of celebrity linked implicitly to blackness, with Markle often compared to Kim Kardashian, an iconic, albeit maligned, reality star notorious for achieving a stratospheric level of fame disconnected from accomplishment. The likening of Markle to Kardashian, a woman of colour considered by many as undeserving of fame, raises questions about the interrelationship between the public regulation of women of colour enacting postfeminism, the "authenticity" (or lack thereof) of different kinds of celebrity, and how this judgement of authenticity may relate to peculiarly white interests, investments and fantasies, such as the investment in the British monarchy.[33]

Marston's work was helpful in aiding this chapter's understanding of postfeminism in general and in relation to Meghan Markle specifically. I did not read this chapter before drawing comparisons between Markle and Kardashian. Class and race undoubtedly lie in some of these comparisons from "haters." However, there are legitimate criticisms of both women's postfeminism and legitimate comparisons between the two. They both possess excessive amounts of wealth that no one deserves or should be entitled to. Markle does come from a "lower class" of celebrity in which she was reality television adjacent. *Suits* does not have the same cultural cache as *Rear Window*. But to become a princess, you no longer need the status of Grace Kelly. Our world, informed by social media, reality television, and personal branding, values wealth above almost all else.

## Conclusion

Meghan Markle and Kim Kardashian are not conniving villains who are responsible for our economic system. They are symptomatic of our neoliberal postfeminist society. These girlbosses are not the gatekeepers, but it does feel like gaslighting when Kardashian tells women to "get your fucking ass up and work. It seems like nobody wants to work these days," or when Markle tells little girls, "You have the power within you to create a life greater than any fairy tale you've ever read. I don't mean that in terms of 'You could marry a prince one day.'"[34]

Much like with the historical American dream, the postfeminist American dream is something the overwhelming majority of us will not attain. The specific dangers in the royal postfeminist dreams of Meghan Markle and Kim Kardashian lie in their racially ambiguous backgrounds, fostering the illusion that it is not tied to whiteness, and their reliance on controversial partners to fulfill these dreams, potentially exchanging ideal companionship for status. The postfeminist American dream is deeply flawed in its conception of empowerment and reliance on systems of oppression like patriarchy, capitalism, and white supremacy. It perpetuates the myth that women can "have it all" and that a failure to "have it all" is a reflection on the individual, as opposed to the society.

### Notes

1. Sternheimer, *Celebrity Culture*, 10, 4.
2. Sternheimer, *Celebrity Culture*, 7.
3. *Forbes India*, "10 Most Followed Instagram Accounts"; Berg, "Kim Kardashian West Is Officially a Billionaire"; *TODAY*, "10.5M Watched Kim Kardashian's Wedding."
4. Pramaggiore and Kerrigan, "Brand Royal," 2041.
5. Pramaggiore and Kerrigan, "Brand Royal," 2052.
6. Davis, "Meghan of Montecito"; Zickgraf, "Meghan Markle Is Not the People's Princess."
7. Leighton, "Kim Kardashian's Met Gala Look."
8. Markle, "Breaking down 'the Bimbo.'"
9. Maloney, "Kim Kardashian."

10. Garbus and Sashin, *Harry & Meghan*, episode 3.
11. Prince Harry, *Spare*, 104, 161, 162; Dockterman, "Tampongate."
12. Summerskill, "Charles, Prince of the Prudes."
13. Arnowitz, "Kim Kardashian Tried (and Failed) to Explain"; Gonzalez, "Kanye West Apologizes"; Hassan, "Kim Kardashian Condemns Hate Speech"; *BBC News* "Kim Kardashian West 'Cried' over Kanye Slavery Comments."
14. Romano, "Kanye West's Antisemitic Spiral."; Hassan, "Kim Kardashian Condemns Hate Speech."
15. Logan, "Kim Kardashian Opened Up About Kanye's Fashion Influence."
16. Burton, "Meghan Markle Thought Being Biracial Could Protect Her."
17. Musiwa, "Problem with Calling Meghan Markle the 'First Black Princess.'"
18. Tehranian, "Is Kim Kardashian White?"; Zoledziowski, "Kim Kardashian Helped Me with My Own Racial Identity."
19. Lang, *"Keeping Up with the Kardashians Is Ending."*
20. Maloney, "Kim Kardashian."
21. Gurley, "Kim Kardashian's Dating History."
22. Corinthios, "Kim Kardashian Didn't Know If She and Kanye West Would Last."
23. Centeno, "Kanye West Says He's a 'Sperm Donor.'"
24. Richards, "Gloria Steinem on Her Friendship with Meghan Markle."
25. Quoted in Corinthios, "Kim Kardashian West on Why She Doesn't Call Herself a Feminist."
26. Quoted in Clark, "Kim Kardashian Condemns Supreme Court's Decision."
27. Petit, "Meghan Markle Once Said She Dreams of Being a 'Mom.'"
28. Woodward, "Kim Kardashian Wept About Feeling Like a 'Failure.'"
29. Amoruso, *#Girlboss.*
30. Abad-Santos, "Death of the Girlboss"; hooks, "Dig Deep."
31. Marston, "Hating Meghan Markle."
32. Díaz Fernández, "Selling Sunset," 70, 72.
33. Marston, "Hating Meghan Markle."
34. *Variety*, "Kim Kardashian's Business Advice"; Davis, "Meghan of Montecito"; Davis, "Meghan of Montecito."

## Works Referenced

Abad-Santos, Alex. "The Death of the Girlboss." *Vox*, June 7, 2021. https://www.vox.com/22466574/gaslight-gatekeep-girlboss-meaning.

Amoruso, Sophia. *#Girlboss*. New York: Portfolio, 2014.

Arnowitz, Leora. "Kim Kardashian Tried (and Failed) to Explain Why Kanye West Said Slavery Is a 'Choice.'" *USA Today*, December 6, 2018. https://www.usatoday.com/story/life/people/2018/12/06/kim-kardashian-kanye-west-never-said-slavery-choice/2226101002/.

*BBC News*. "Kim Kardashian West 'Cried' over Kanye Slavery Comments." June 6, 2018. https://www.bbc.com/news/entertainment-arts-44380715.

Berg, Madeline. "Kim Kardashian West Is Officially a Billionaire." *Forbes*, April 6, 2021. https://www.forbes.com/sites/maddieberg/2021/04/06/kim-kardashian-west-is-officially-a-billionaire/?sh=35c6d7921bba.

Burton, Nylah. "Meghan Markle Thought Being Biracial Could Protect Her from Racism. She Was Wrong." *Andscape*, December 16, 2022. https://andscape.com/features/meghan-markle-harry-race-netflix/.

Centeno, Tony M. "Kanye West Says He's a 'Sperm Donor' & Goes off on Kim Kardashian's Family." iHeart, September 2, 2022. https://www.iheart.com/content/2022-09-02-kanye-west-says-hes-a-sperm-donor-goes-off-on-kim-kardashians-family/.

Clark, Meredith. "Kim Kardashian Condemns Supreme Court's Decision to Overturn Roe v. Wade: 'In America, Guns Have More Rights Than Women.'" *The Independent*, June 24, 2022. https://www.independent.co.uk/life-style/kim-kardashian-roe-v-wade-abortion-b2109090.html.

Corinthios, Aurelie. "Kim Kardashian West on Why She Doesn't Call Herself a Feminist." *People*, December 2, 2020. https://people.com/tv/kim-kardashian-west-on-why-she-doesnt-call-herself-a-feminist/.

Davis, Allison P. "Meghan of Montecito." *The Cut*, August 29, 2022. https://www.thecut.com/article/meghan-markle-profile-interview.html.

Despentes, Virginie. "Porn Witches." In *King Kong Theory*, 83–104. Translated by Frank Wynne. New York: Macmillan, 2021.

Díaz Fernández, Silvia. "Selling Sunset . . . and My Postfeminist Sexual Capital: New Sexual Subjectivities in Reality TV." In *Working Women on Screen: Paid Labour and Fourth Wave Feminism*, edited by Ellie Tomsett, Nathalie Weidhase, and Poppy Wilde, 53–75. London: Palgrave Macmillan, 2024.

Dockterman, Eliana. "Tampongate: True Story behind the Crown's Phone Sex." *Time*, November 9, 2022. https://time.com/6226657/crown-charles-camilla-tampongate/.

*Forbes India*. "The 10 Most Followed Instagram Accounts in the World in 2023." *Forbes India*, updated April 28, 2025. https://www.forbesindia.com/article/explainers/most-followed-instagram-accounts-world/85649/1.

Garbus, Liz, and Erica Sashin, dirs. *Harry & Meghan*. Aired December 2022 on Netflix. https://www.netflix.com/watch/81478159.

Gonzalez, Sandra. "Kanye West Apologizes for How Slavery Comment 'Made People Feel.'" *CNN*, updated August 30, 2018. https://www.cnn.com/2018/08/29/entertainment/kanye-west-apology/index.html.

Gurley, Alex. "Kim Kardashian's Dating History: From Kanye West to Pete Davidson." *People*, updated April 30, 2024. https://people.com/tv/kim-kardashian-dating-history/.

Hassan, Jennifer. "Kim Kardashian Condemns Hate Speech after Kanye West's Antisemitism." *Washington Post*, updated October 25, 2022. https://www.washingtonpost.com/lifestyle/2022/10/25/kim-kardashian-kanye-ye-antisemitism/.

hooks, bell. "Dig Deep: Beyond Lean In." *Feminist Wire*, October 28, 2013. https://thefeministwire.com/2013/10/17973/.

Lang, Cady. "*Keeping Up with the Kardashians* Is Ending. But Their Exploitation of Black Women's Aesthetics Continues." *Time*, June 10, 2021. https://time.com/6072750/kardashians-blackfishing-appropriation/.

Leighton, Mara. "Kim Kardashian's Met Gala Look Is a Shapewear-ified Reference to the 'You're Doing Amazing, Sweetie' Meme." *Business Insider*, May 2, 2023. https://www.insider.com/kim-kardashian-met-gala-look-youre-doing-amazing-sweetie-meme-2023-5.

Logan, Elizabeth. "Kim Kardashian Opened Up About Kanye's Fashion Influence and How She's Moved On." *Glamour*, November 17, 2022. https://www.glamour.com/story/kim-kardashian-opened-up-about-kanyes-fashion-influence.

Maloney, Devon. 2015. "Kim Kardashian, Coy and Unprovocative, Delivers as Promised in Talk to Prestigious San Francisco Club." *Vanity Fair*, July 1, 2015. https://www.vanityfair.com/hollywood/2015/07/kim-kardashian-inforum-talk.

Markle, Meghan. "Breaking Down 'the Bimbo' with Paris Hilton and Iliza Shlesinger." *Archetypes*, October 18, 2022. Podcast audio. https://open.spotify.com/episode/6S3Y5mKB9nJAk6wvZdbVo8.

Marston, Kendra. "Hating Meghan Markle: Drawing the Boundaries of British Whiteness Against Postfeminist Femininity." In *Routledge Handbook of Critical Studies in Whiteness*, edited by Shona Hunter and Christi van der Westhuizen, chapter 8 (ebook). London: Routledge, 2021.

Musiwa, Elaine. "The Problem with Calling Meghan Markle the 'First Black Princess.'" *Vogue*, November 28, 2017.

Petit, Stephanie. 2022. "Meghan Markle's Trailblazing Feminism through the Years, in Honor of Women's History Month." *People*. https://people.com/royals/meghan-markle-trailblazing-feminism-through-the-years/.

Pramaggiore, Maria, and Páraic Kerrigan. "Brand Royal: Meghan Markle, Feuding Families, and Disruptive Duchessing in Brexit era Britain." *Fem-*

*inist Media Studies* 22, no. 8 (2022): 2037–57. https://doi.org/10.1080/14680777.2021.1928258.

Prince Harry. 2023. *Spare.* Random House of Canada.

Richards, Bailey. "Gloria Steinem on Her Friendship with Meghan Markle: 'She Is Different from the Picture of Her in the Media.'" *People,* November 22, 2022. https://www.yahoo.com/entertainment/gloria-steinem-her-friendship-meghan-191013625.html.

Romano, Aja. 2022. "Kanye West's Antisemitic Spiral, Explained." *Vox.* https://www.vox.com/culture/23400851/kanye-west-antisemitism-hitler-praise.

Sternheimer, Karen. 2014. *Celebrity Culture and the American Dream: Stardom and Social Mobility.* Routledge.

Summerskill, Ben. 2005. "Charles, Prince of the Prudes." *The Guardian.* https://www.theguardian.com/g2/story/0,3604,1383309,00.html.

Tehranian, John. 2020. "Is Kim Kardashian White? (And Why Does It Matter Anyway?): Racial Fluidity, Identity Mutability & the Future of Civil Rights Jurisprudence," *Houston Law Review,* 58.

*TODAY.* "10.5M Watched Kim Kardashian's Wedding." October 11, 2011. https://www.today.com/popculture/10-5m-watched-kim-kardashians-wedding-wbna44866092.

*Variety.* "Kim Kardashian's Business Advice: 'Get Your F**king Ass Up and Work.'" March 9, 2022. YouTube video, 6:52. https://www.youtube.com/watch?v=XX2izzshRmI.

Woodward, Ellie. "Kim Kardashian Wept About Feeling Like a 'Failure' and a 'Loser' as Her Marriage to Kanye West Ended After Admitting She'd Been Unhappy 'for Years.'" *BuzzFeed,* June 4, 2021. https://www.buzzfeed.com/article/elliewoodward/kim-kardashian-failure-loser-kanye-west-divorce-kuwtk.

Zickgraf, Ryan. 2022. "Meghan Markle Is Not the People's Princess." *Jacobin.* https://jacobin.com/2022/09/meghan-markle-royal-family-british-monarchy-girlboss-feminism-peoples-princess.

Zoledziowski, Anya. 2020. "Kim Kardashian Helped Me with My Own Racial Identity, Until She Didn't." *VICE.* https://www.vice.com/en/article/ep4nxw/kim-kardashian-helped-me-with-my-own-racial-identity-until-she-didnt.

CHAPTER 6

# MOTHER OF THE REALMS

## *Dueling Narratives of Womanhood in Queen Elizabeth II's Funeral*

SARAH OLUTOLA

## Introduction: Monsters and Heroines

In her book *Diana and Beyond* cultural studies scholar Raka Shome contemplates the death of Princess Diana, former Princess of Wales. Particularly, she notes how, at the time, national and transnational narratives consolidated within the media to tell the perfect story of heroes and villains, victimizers whom we should despise, and victims who deserve our outpouring of sympathy. Importantly, she poses the following potent questions: "What script of white femininity was being so successfully spun and mediated such that this highly British woman became a simultaneous signifier of a national popular and a global popular? What ideologies of white femininity did this script tap into and stabilize such that this woman soon became an idealized signifier of a modern woman of the millennium? Why would a similar idealization not have occurred of a nonwhite woman, an immigrant woman, or a non-Western woman?"[1]

Queen Elizabeth II's age may have barred her death from achieving the same emotional effect as the untimely demise of Princess Diana; the princess's beauty and youth had long transformed her into a global signifier of "light and life," as well as "hope and future for the nation at the very time that nation . . .

saw itself as being violated by Others." Nonetheless, the script of Queen Elizabeth II's death in 2022, as spun by Western media, very much mobilized the "spectacularization of white femininity" in such a way that heroes and villains, victims and monsters, once again emerged for the public to consume.[2]

In posing similar questions to Shome, in this chapter I concentrate specifically on the word "script" to detail how the discursive linking of white femininity to the light, life, hope, and future of England and the British Empire necessarily dragged nonwhite women—and specifically Black women—into the narrative as the victimizers, villains, monsters, and Others. Standing in the middle of this continuum from Princess Diana to Queen Elizabeth II is Meghan Markle, Duchess of Sussex through her marriage to Diana's youngest son, Prince Harry. Amid the televised national mourning of Queen Elizabeth II's death, the biracial Meghan Markle, along with other Black women, emerged as a threat in counterpoint to Queen Elizabeth II's symbolic "timeless Englishness." Their treatment in the wake of the queen's death explodes the fantasy of a changed, happily multicultural England, which some cultural scholars took the global grieving of Princess Diana in 1997 to represent.[3] I examine the media-constructed script of Queen Elizabeth II's death and its spectacularization of white femininity through the lens of storytelling and myth as a discursive language utilized in empire building.

Western myth has employed the "Dark Other" as a storytelling archetype since at least the Greek classical tradition. The figure of the "Dark Other" in fantastical tales manifests as "the monster," a being understood as terrifying solely because of its status as the counterpoint of the living being.[4] "Monstrosity is the accidental and conditional threat of incompleteness or distortion in the formation of the form," according to philosopher George Canguilhem.[5] More specifically, monstrosity is the error, the *difference* that confronts the "normal man," in the words of Guillaume Le Blanc.[6]

Looking at children's fantasy novels, scholar Elizabeth Ebony Thomas, borrowing from Jeffrey Jerome Cohen's *Monster Theory*, argues that monsters are "analogous to those who are positioned as different in the realm world."[7] In doing so, Thomas ultimately makes clear the logic of race that ties the "Dark Other" to the "monster." This matters beyond fairy tales, epics, and novels. If we, like Michel Foucault and George Canguilhem, think of storytelling as encompassing the telling of *history* and the knowledge making arising from tales of "truth,"[8] then we can consider how various kinds of monsters emerge in the tales we tell about ourselves. So as historical events unfold in the present, narrativized by media, public figures, and other powerful actors capable of storytelling on a global level, we must ask ourselves: Who are the protagonists and who are the monsters of this tale?

On Thursday, September 8, 2022, history did indeed unfold: Queen Elizabeth II, Britain's longest-reigning monarch, died at age ninety-six. As mainstream media outlets and social media alike breathlessly eulogized the queen, framing her as a kind of heroine—the moral (grand)mother of the Commonwealth realms—on many of those same platforms, Black women seemed to materialize as her counterpoint, her Dark Other. The British newspaper the *Daily Mail* expressed its disgust at Dr. Zoé Samudzi, a Zimbabwean American professor at the Rhode Island School of Design for writing, "As the first generation of my family not born in a British colony, I would dance on the graves of every member of the royal family if given the opportunity." The *Daily Mail* also targeted Dr. Ebony Elizabeth Thomas, of the University of Michigan, for calling the queen a colonizer.[9] Queen Elizabeth II's death drew celebrations and challenging discussions from many anti-imperialists unwilling to acquiesce to the whitewashing of her (and Britain's) colonial past. However, it was Black women who drew the most attention and were targeted the most for harassment by the British royal family's supporters.

Most baffling is the case of Dr. Uju Anya, a Nigerian linguistics researcher at Carnegie Mellon University, who was only one of the many public figures who took to Twitter to express her unapologetic abject lack of pity for the queen's passing. In a tweet inevitably deleted by Twitter, she wrote, "I heard the chief monarch of a thieving raping genocidal empire is finally dying. May her pain be excruciating." In another tweet removed by Twitter, the professor also wrote, "That wretched woman and her bloodthirsty throne have f***** generations of my ancestors on both sides of the family, and she supervised a government that sponsored the genocide my parents and siblings survived. May she die in agony." In a shocking twist, her tweet was met with backlash from none other than Jeff Bezos, executive chairman of Amazon and one of the richest men in the world, worth approximately $136 billion: "This is someone supposedly working to make the world better? I don't think so. Wow." Jeff Bezos's public admonition brought global attention to Dr. Anya's remarks. But in response to the ensuing harassment that Dr. Anya began to receive, her employer chose to reprimand, humiliate, and publicly disown her: "We do not condone the offensive and objectionable messages posted by Uju Anya today on her personal social media account," they wrote in an official statement on their Twitter account.[10]

As much as their statement went on to laud "free expression," the university's condemnation of their own professor made clear that certain voices in the public arena are respected while others must be silenced. Carnegie Mellon and Jeff Bezos helped to transform Dr. Anya into a monster in the whitewashed, celebrated tale of the British monarchy. And as many Black women writers and academics became targeted for their outspokenness during the queen's death and funeral, essayist and historian Panashe Chigumadzi zeroed in on the specific racialized and sexist demonization of Black women in particular: "In our analysis of Power and Empire's Violence we have to ask—why are the tweets of two Global South Black women academics more threatening to Empire and deserving of its violence than an entire Irish stadium of mostly men publicly declaring their delight in the

Queen's death?"[11] In this tweet, Chigumadzi is referring to a video that emerged on social media of Irish soccer fans chanting "Lizzy's in a box" just hours after the announcement of Queen Elizabeth II's death.[12] But as Thomas seems to anticipate in *The Dark Fantastic*, white men were never going to be the monsters of this tale, not when there were dark people readily available to serve as the "Dark Others":

> In the West, the mysterious unknowability of darkness in nature was extended to a corresponding fear of unknown and unknowable dark things, including imaginary monsters beyond the boundaries of the known world during medieval times and, in the modern period, conquered and enslaved people from its margins. 'Darky,' a colloquial term for people of African descent during the late eighteenth century, signals that in modern English, darkness has never been just a metaphor. Darkness is personified, embodied, and most assuredly racialized.[13]

This is the answer to Chigumadzi's question, the reason why Black women were singled out as the foremost enemies of the British Empire following Queen Elizabeth II's passing, despite the wide range of anti-imperialists celebrating her death. That they were outspoken and openly critical of empire is only *partly* the reason for their perceived pathology. Black women, simply by being racialized and gendered, simply by existing beyond the boundaries of Europe's "known world," were easily slotted into the story of Queen Elizabeth II's death as monsters. These Black women did not have to speak to be figured as "darkness personified." They simply had to be. No other example makes this fact more clear than that of Meghan Markle, Duchess of Sussex.

Indeed, Markle, the Duchess of Sussex through her marriage to Prince Harry, son of now-King Charles III and grandson of Queen Elizabeth II, became the single most targeted Black woman during the queen's funeral coverage. British media outlets followed her every move during the funeral, with some, like the *Daily Mail,* lamenting the friction in Prince Harry and Prince William's brotherly relationship and insinuating that Meghan was to blame. Tom Bower, a royal biographer and author of *Revenge: Meghan, Harry and the War Between the Windsors,* criticized Meghan Markle for shedding a tear during the queen's funeral, telling GB News that the duchess "was only crying for herself."[14] Much hatred from British royalists was also lobbed at Markle for holding Prince Harry's hand during the funeral, with one social media user writing, "They can't keep their hands to their sides for two seconds to mourn the Queen (as if Meghan would care to anyway). Though unsurprising as they never fail to disrespect the protocol and the Queen."[15]

As Dr. Shola Mos-Shogbamimu asserts, (white) Britain's relentless criticism of Meghan Markle is racist in nature: Markle is an African American woman who transgressed social norms by marrying a British white prince.[16] But when juxtaposing the bullying of Meghan Markle and the bullying of Black women in general during the queen's funeral, a deeper discussion emerges—one that understands Queen Elizabeth II's death as a story of two kinds of women: the heroine and the monster. This story includes violence and race, exposing especially women's bodies as a psychic terrain upon which the meaning of the British Empire can be built or torn down.

## Women and Empire: Meghan Markle and Blackness as Britain's "Monster"

Queen Elizabeth II, a monarch of the British Empire, directly profited from the spoils of colonial violence, which included the slave trade and brutal suppression of communities across the globe. She not only acted as a symbol of this terrible history; she also chose to be complicit in its continuing debilitating effects, remaining silent on the historical and ongoing tragedies wrought upon colonized peoples by the British Empire and flaunting the spoils of colonial conquest—most notably the crown jewels plundered from continents such as Africa. Dr. Uju Anya made clear the historical, political, and even personal background for her words against Queen Elizabeth II: "My experience of who she was, and the British government she supervised, is a very painful one," she said in an interview following her public shaming. Referring to the Nigerian Civil War (1967–70), she continued: "The harm shaped my entire life and continues to be my story and that of the people she harmed—that her government harmed, that her kingdom harmed, however you want to frame it. The genocide of the Biafra killed 3 million Igbo people and the British government wasn't just in political support of the people who perpetrated this massacre; they directly funded it. They gave it political cover and legitimacy."[17] This context did not save her from being framed as the monster in Queen Elizabeth II's narrative.

The bullying of Black women on behalf of the Queen of England acted as a strategy to suppress critical dialogue about Britain's history. Not only did this public bullying aim to whitewash the history of the British Empire; it also worked to protect the very meaning of the British Empire and its psychic boundaries of belonging. Many invest in the hegemonic ideological framing of England as a white nation and the royal family as its white bourgeois center that rules over colonized peoples. These colonized (Dark) Others may be figured as "children" of the British Empire but are understood implicitly to be only marginalized members who don't quite belong. My focus on women here is not by accident. The racial, gendered, and sexual hierarchies within the British Empire's categories of belonging depend on Britain's sociopolitical management of bodies, and Britain's biopolitical regulation has, since the colonial era, revealed white anxieties and obsessions over women.

As theorists such as Ruth Feldstein, Patricia Hill Collins, and Ann Stoler have noted, women have long been seen as crucial to empire building.[18] Women are considered physical and ideological reproducers of the next generation of a nation's citizens. Historically, this has made women of key importance to state power and regulation. In *Race and the Education of Desire*, Ann Stoler specifically discusses Britain's discursive framing of women in the nineteenth century, an important era during which Britain consolidated itself as an imperial power through its colonies. Women, through their production of children, were crucial to civil society not in that they were expected to participate in the public sphere. Quite the contrary: Their importance stemmed from their sexual relationship with men, which would "insure that marriage, sexual morality, and family provided the natural foundations of civil life." Motherhood, then, was a kind of "national service."[19] But it was also heavily racialized. To reproduce the foundations of civil life, white women's sexual activity was to be monitored and controlled in such a way that it would reproduce whiteness as the national norm as well as social notions of whiteness as possessing inherent racial superiority.

It's ironic, then, that Meghan Markle has become symbolic terrain upon which discourses of British nationalism, sexuality, and racial thinking converge. Meghan Markle is an African American woman. Specifically, she is half-Black, with a Black mother and a white father. Her facial features are ambiguously "ethnic" and in many cases, she does not unambiguously present as "Black" like Dr. Uju Anya, Dr. Elizabeth Ebony Thomas, Dr. Zoé Samudzi, and other Black women who were bullied following Queen Elizabeth II's passing. Her framing as a Black woman comes from racial and sexual management strategies of the colonial era devised to protect the definition of whiteness.

Specifically in America, from where Markle hails, laws were crafted to control the legal definition of children born of white male slave masters and their Black female slaves. According to these laws, the free or slave status would be dependent on the condition of the mother, meaning that if the mother was a Black slave, the child would be as well.[20] These laws were created to protect the inheritance of white male slave owners, ensuring that any child a slave owner begot through raping his enslaved women could not legally own his land and property (as the child was legally considered property based on the condition of the mother). Thus, generational wealth and power would remain in the possession of white bourgeois men, which had the larger significance of maintaining America as a white patriarchal nation. The unofficial but colloquially understood one-drop rule served the same purpose. In America, it was socially understood that as long as a person had one drop of Black blood, he or she was Black.[21] This protected the perceived exceptionalness of whiteness, maintaining the integrity of the construction of white racial purity.

The British public's perception of Meghan Markle as a Black woman is itself based on commonly accepted colonial-era discourses about who is *truly* white that were perpetuated in both America and Britain through the insidious race knowledge produced through and as a consequence of the British slave trade. According to Ann Stoler, these discourses "hinged on the state's moral authority to defend the social body against degeneration and abnormality."[22] Here, it was not the slave master's raping of his enslaved women that constituted deviant morality, but the supposed sexual danger and "moral terror" that Black people posed to white Europeans and their white descendants. This story of the slave trade cast the Black body as the monstrous Dark Other. It cast the Black body, impure with only one "drop" of Black blood, as the threat to white nations. White women, conversely, acted as the heroines of this story. As Stoler writes, "Bourgeois women in colony and metropole were cast as the custodians of morality, of their vulnerable men, and of national character."[23] The word "vulnerable" matters here, displaying the contradictions tied up in white anxieties about nation and empire. The common perception during the colonial era was that white men were vulnerable to the advances of women of color. Common still was the fear that white men could "go native" in colonized lands by engaging in sexual acts with Indigenous women, and thus destroy the moral fabric of their European nation and the meaning of whiteness itself.[24] Such fears are echoed in criticisms of Prince Harry. When Times Radio, a British digital outlet partly owned by *The Times* and *The Sunday Times*, interviewed royalists camping outside Buckingham Palace awaiting King Charles III's coronation on May 6, 2023, many framed Harry as a traitor who betrayed his family through his marriage to and continued defense of his wife. "Her name's 'Meghan Marble,'" one white British man told the interviewer, perhaps deliberately getting Markle's name wrong. "But I call her Miss Marple. Because she's caused so much trouble. Harry isn't the same as what he used to be. You know, he's . . . he's completely changed . . . he's degraded himself . . . It's not the Harry that we used to know. And why? Because of her. She's changed him."[25] His words make clear the commonly held belief that Meghan Markle, through her marital union and sexual relationship with Prince Harry, degraded the purity of a vulnerable white man, a white prince, most unforgivingly. Most tellingly, the royalist's complaints emphasize the continued power of Europe's racial thinking of the colonial era.

Indeed, since the colonial era, Black women's bodies have been overburdened with meaning as a consequence of European anxieties over the racial, social, and moral boundaries of whiteness. Black feminist scholars including Ange-Marie Hancock and bell hooks have researched and parsed white narratives of Black women's supposed deviancy: the sexually irresponsible Jezebel who pursues sex over rearing her own children, or the sexless mammy who cares for the slave master's child instead of her own.[26] Black women have long been narrativized as the ideological opposite of the moral white middle-class woman who reproduces the white nation; Black women, thus, exist in this narrative as dangers lurking on the edge of empire. Though Black women have always been crucial to empire's survival through the labor they provide and especially, in the context of slavery, their ability to produce more laborers, their existence also signaled to the white imagination a constant threat to the body politic, in particular because of how their bodies and sexual capabilities destabilized categories of racial membership.

We can see what Homi Bhabha describes as "the deep fear of the Black figured in the psychic trembling of Western sexuality"[27] very clearly in a published attack on Meghan Markle by Jeremy Clarkson, a British columnist for the newspaper *The Sun*. In December 2022, Clarkson's column was all about his hatred of Markle in response to her and Prince Harry's 2022 Netflix docuseries that criticized the British media and the royal family for their attacks on Markle. Clarkson writes that while he feels sorry for Prince Harry, he hates Meghan Markle, but the specific words he uses to describe his hatred for her reveal contemporary manifestations of the "power of fantasy, imagined terror, and perceived assaults on the European self that made up the anxious and ambivalent world in which European colonials lived."[28] In this now-deleted article, Clarkson tells his audience, "I hate her. Not like I hate Nicola Sturgeon or Rose West. I hate her on a cellular level. . . . At night, I'm unable to sleep as I lie there, grinding my teeth and dreaming of the day when she is made to parade naked through the streets of every town in Britain while the crowds chant, 'Shame!' and throw lumps of excrement at her."[29]

It's not by accident that he compares Meghan Markle to Nicola Sturgeon, formerly the first minister of Scotland and leader of the Scottish National Party, and Rose West, a serial killer who helped her husband rape, torture, and murder at least twelve young women in the 1970s and 1980s. These are women who transgressed the moral order of bourgeois white patriarchy in different ways, one by holding political power in public space and another by breaking the legal and moral laws against killing. But the transgressions of both women also reveal themselves as part of a fantasy of sexual violence against women. Rose West's serial murder was sexual in nature, but Clarkson still does not hate her as much as he hates Meghan Markle. His description of this hatred is also sexual in nature. He admits that he lies awake fantasizing about the sexual humiliation, sexual debasement, and sexual brutalization of a Black woman. He aligns the implicit sexual violence he wishes to see done to her with the sexual violence of Rose West and names Sturgeon as the "kind of woman" who he perhaps implicitly sees as deserving of violence because of her unwillingness to uphold the white woman's moral and domestic service to empire. There's a reason why many scholars, like Octavio Mannoni, Albert Memmi, and Ashis Nandy, have drawn on Freudian psychoanalysis to discuss European male desire in the colonies.[30] White male fear and anger toward Black women bring sexual desire into the terrain of power and violence. Clarkson's expression of hatred against Meghan Markle, born out of her transgressing racial boundaries and threatening the meaning of the British empire, reveals the interrelatedness of sexual obsession, race making, and empire building. As Stoler writes, "What is striking about the sexual stories that European colonials and their metropolitan observers told about their own desires and thus about what distinguished themselves is how boldly they turned on defining and affirming the bourgeois order in specific ways." We can look to Victorian-era discourses of childhood—Europe's obsession with educating its white children on the dangers of the "habitual licentiousness" of the colonies.[31] The notion that white children needed to be protected from native sexuality only brings back into the discussion the figure of the white bourgeois mother, the heroine who reproduces and upholds the nation. Such was the precise framing of Queen Elizabeth II after her passing.

## Conclusion: White Heroines and Compulsory Affection

Throughout the queen's funeral, she was eulogized as a mother, not only of the nation but also of the commonwealth. White womanhood as an ideological invention has emerged as a site of critical discussion among scholars.[32] If a normal white woman's motherhood was considered a service to the nation, then how much more so was that of Queen Elizabeth II? The far-reaching global political significance of her framing as a moral white woman and global mother needs to be contextualized. Raka Shome insists that white femininity is a *transnational* phenomenon, one that must be "related to histories of Western colonialism, foreign policy initiatives, war, Western militarism, and financial policies of organizations such as the World Bank and IMF, all which have had a role to play in decimating local family structures in so many underprivileged worlds that today result in abandoned children, or children plagued by poverty whom the white woman then rescues and brings into her familial folds."[33]

In her analysis of Princess Diana, Shome mentions the proliferation and circulation of media representations of her body as producing a figure that shored up affect worldwide. In the 1980s and 1990s, images of the late princess's humanitarian work circulated in a similar way to UNICEF ads in the 1950s, symbolizing the altruism of the Global North, and with it, the economic, political, and cultural superiority of the Western world. Her death was a global phenomenon as images of her demise and recollections of her story were circulated and consumed worldwide. As Shome writes, "No other mass spectacle of our times provides such overwhelming evidence of how the production of Anglo nations is visualized through white femininity."[34] It's not by accident, then, that many Western media outlets compared Queen Elizabeth II's death to Princess Diana's, clambering to narrativize her as a kind of relatable "People's Princess" in life (despite this being Princess Diana's moniker), reporting on every detail of the royal family in the wake of her passing.[35]

White femininity, womanhood, and motherhood were crucial to the public mourning of Queen Elizabeth II, a whitewashing of her history that required a villain—specifically the villainous Black female as the Dark Other. Queen Elizabeth II is not the only British monarch to receive this posthumous treatment. The last British female monarch, Queen Victoria, was often depicted as a kind of matriarchal figure and was specifically thought of as the mother of the "British imperial family," which, of course, extended beyond Britain to the colonies. Seen as concerned in a pious, motherly way for all her subjects, Queen Victoria's white femininity was mobilized to normalize Britain's colonial domination; as Victoria Smith argues in her doctoral dissertation "Constructing Victoria," "the image of a maternal Victoria allowed for the representation of the empire not as a project of domination or conquest but of familial love and domestic duty."[36]

The same conservative white patriarchal politics that placed what postcolonial scholar Daniel Coleman calls a "muscular Christian" manliness at the center of Victorian England's representation as an empire whose global domination was a moral mission also promoted as its twin bourgeois white femininity, complete with the ideals of piety, kindness, discipline, and family.[37] Jeff Bezos attacked Dr. Uju Anya for criticizing the queen because he could not imagine that critiquing such a symbol could be in the service of making the "world a better place"; Queen Elizabeth II, as a white global mother, already served as a humanitarian symbol of bettering the world simply by existing. Likewise, Meghan Markle's existence as part of the British royal family threatens the ideological integrity of the white family and exposes the constructed nature of the white nation, thus threatening white power. If white femininity normalizes "the white man's burden" and the logic of domination, then so too does violence against Black women as a consequence of racial purity discourses.

## Notes

1. Shome, *Diana and Beyond*, 1–2.
2. Shome, *Diana and Beyond*, 62, 2.

3. Nava, "Diana and Race: Romance and the Reconfiguration of Race"; Brown, *Imagining the New Britain.*
4. Thomas, *Dark Fantastic.*
5. Canguilhem, *Monstrosity and the Monster,* PAGE NUMBER.
6. Le Blanc, *Les maladies.*
7. Thomas, *Dark Fantastic,* 20.
8. Delaporte, "Foucault, Canguilhem et les monstres."
9. Alexander and Oliveira, "Have They No Shame?"
10. All quoted in Dutton, "Carnegie Mellon Refuses to Condone Uju Anya."
11. Panashe Chigumadzi, (@PanasheChig), Twitter, September 10, 2022, https://twitter.com/PanasheChig/status/1568580412477145088.
12. Farberov, "Irish Soccer Fans Celebrate Queen's Death."
13. Thomas, *Dark Fantastic,* 20.
14. Nsubaga, "Royal Biographer Slammed."
15. Tarah Heuss (@HeussTarah), Twitter, September 14, 2022, https://x.com/HeussTarah/status/1570062437113794560.
16. Naomi, "Dr. Shola on Racial Inequality."
17. Quoted in Bansinath, "I Won't Cry."
18. Feldstein, *Motherhood in Black and White*; Collins, *Black Feminist Thought,* Stoler, *Race and the Education of Desire.*
19. Stoler, *Race and the Education of Desire,* 131–32.
20. Courtney, *Hollywood Fantasies of Miscegenation.*
21. Nama, *Black Space.*
22. Stoler, *Race and the Education of Desire,* 134.
23. Stoler, *Race and the Education of Desire,* 134, 135.
24. Stoler, *Race and the Education of Desire,* 182.
25. *Times Radio,* "Harry's a Traitor."
26. Hancock, *Politics of Disgust*; hooks, *Black Looks.*
27. Quoted in Stoler, *Race and the Education of Desire,* 169–70.
28. Stoler, *Race and the Education of Desire,* 169.
29. Quoted in Rosney, "Jeremy Clarkson and Meghan Markle."
30. Stoler, *Race and the Education of Desire,* 170.
31. Stoler, *Race and the Education of Desire,* 178.
32. See Frankenberg, *White Women, Race Matters*; Feldstein, *Motherhood in Black and White.*
33. Shome, "Global Motherhood," 389.
34. Shome, "Global Motherhood," 324.
35. *MSNBC,* "Queen Elizabeth II Could 'Relate to People.'"
36. Smith, "Constructing Victoria," PAGE NUMBER.
37. Coleman, *White Civility*: PAGE NUMBER.

## Works Referenced

Alexander, Harriet, and Alex Oliveira. "Have They No Shame? Woke Liberals Writing for *The New York Times, New York Magazine* and *The Atlantic* Waste No Time Attacking the 'Colonizer' Queen Mere Hours After Her Death Aged 96—and Hours After Twitter Took Down Vile Post Mocking Monarch." *Daily Mail,* September 8, 2022. https://www.dailymail.co.uk/news/article-11195181/Woke-liberals-waste-no-time-attacking-colonizer-Queen-mere-hours-death.html.

Anderson, Natasha, and Stephen M. Lepore. 2022. "Royal Expert Slams 'Inappropriate and Opportunistic' Comments by American Professors Who Said They Had 'Nothing but Disdain' for the Queen's Death and Claimed Her Reign Was 'Violent.'" *Daily Mail,* September 10, 2022. https://www.dailymail.co.uk/news/article-11199409/Royal-expert-slams-inappropriate-opportunistic-comments-Majestys-death.html.

Bansinath, Bindu. "I Won't Cry Over the Death of a Violent Oppressor." *The Cut.* September 9, 2022. https://www.thecut.com/2022/09/uju-anya-on-her-tweet-about-queen-elizabeth-ii.html.

Brown, Yasmin. *Imagining the New Britain.* London: Routledge, 200.

Canguilhem, Georges. "Monstrosity and the Monstrous." Translated by Therese Jaeger. *Diogenes* 10, no. 40 (1962): 27–40. https://doi.org/10.1177/039219216201004002.

Coleman, Daniel. *White Civility: The Literary Project of English Canada.* Toronto: University of Toronto Press, 2006.

Collins, Patricia Hill. *Black Feminist Thought: Knowledge, Consciousness and the Politics of Empowerment.* New York: Routledge, 2000.

Courtney, Susan. *Hollywood Fantasies of Miscegenation: Spectacular Narratives of Gender and Race, 1903–1967.* Princeton, NJ: Princeton University Press, 2005.

Delaporte, François. "Foucault, Canguilhem et les monstres." In *Canguilhem: Histoire des Sciences et Politique du Vivant,* 91–112. Paris: Presses Universitaires de France, 2007.

Dutton, Jack. "Carnegie Mellon Refuses to Condone Uju Anya Over Queen's Death Remarks." *Newsweek,* September 9, 2022. https://www.newsweek.com/carnegie-mellon-refuse-condone-uju-anya-over-queens-death-remarks-1741404.

Farberov, Snejana. "Irish Soccer Fans Celebrate Queen's Death, Chant 'Lizzy's in a Box' at Game." *New York Post.* September 9, 2022. https://nypost.com/2022/09/09/irish-soccer-fans-celebrate-queens-death-chant-lizzys-in-a-box/.

Feldstein, Ruth. *Motherhood in Black and White: Race and Sex in American Liberalism: 1930–1965.* Ithaca, NY Cornell University Press, 2000.

Frankenberg, Ruth. *White Women, Race Matters*. Minneapolis: University of Minnesota Press, 1993.

Hancock, Ange-Marie. *The Politics of Disgust: The Public Identity of the Welfare Queen*. New York: New York University Press, 2004.

hooks, bell. *Black Looks: Race and Representation*. Boston: South End Press, 1992.

Le Blanc, Guillaume. *Les maladies de l'homme normal*. Paris: Vrin, 2007.

*MSNBC*. "Queen Elizabeth II Could 'Relate to People at a Very Human Level' Says Fmr. Press Sec." September 12, 2022. YouTube video, 4:53. https://www.youtube.com/watch?app=desktop&v=OwxWwoVq7fY.

Nama, Adilifu. *Black Space: Imagining Race in Science Fiction Film*. Austin: University of Texas Press, 2008.

Naomi. "Dr. Shola on Racial Inequality, Meghan Markle, and Sarah Everard: No Filter with Naomi." March 23, 2021. YouTube video, 46:28. https://www.youtube.com/watch?v=3USH_-0OaEM.

Nava, Mica. "Diana and Race: Romance and the Reconfiguration of Race." *Mourning Diana: Nation, Culture and the Performance of Grief*, edited by Adrian Kear and Deborah Lynn Steinberg, 108–19. London: Routledge, 1999.

Nsubaga, Jimmy. "Royal Biographer Slammed After Claiming Meghan Markle 'Was Only Crying for Herself' at Queen's Funeral.'" *Yahoo News UK*, September 30, 2022. https://ca.style.yahoo.com/tom-bower-queen-prince-harry-meghan-markle-184829116.html.

Oppenheim, Maya. "Meghan Markle Critics in Denial About Their Misogyny and Racism, Prominent Activist Warns." *The Independent*. March 9, 2023. https://www.independent.co.uk/life-style/women/meghan-markle-trolling-misogyny-racism-b2297293.html.

Rosney, Daniel. "Jeremy Clarkson and Meghan Markle: The Sun Column Gets 6000 Official Complaints." *BBC News*, December 19, 2022. https://www.bbc.com/news/entertainment-arts-64025074.

Shome, Raka. *Diana and Beyond: White Femininity, National Identity, and Contemporary Media Culture*. Champaign: University of Illinois Press, 2014.

Shome, Raka. "'Global Motherhood': The Transnational Intimacies of White Femininity." *Critical Studies in Media Communication* 28, no. 5 (2011): 388–406. https://doi.org/10.1080/15295036.2011.589861.

Smith, Victoria Ruth. "Constructing Victoria: The Representation of Queen Victoria in England, India, and Canada, 1897–1914." PhD diss., Rutgers University, 1998.

Stoler, Ann. *Race and the Education of Desire: Foucault's History of Sexuality and the Colonial Order of Things*. Durham, NC: Duke University Press, 1995.

Thomas, Ebony Elizabeth. *The Dark Fantastic: Race and the Imagination from Harry Potter to The Hunger Games*. New York: New York University Press, 2019.

*Times Radio*. "'Harry's a Traitor. You Can't Betray Your Own People, Your Family': Royal Fans on Harry & Meghan." May 4, 2023. YouTube video, 8:25. https://www.youtube.com/watch?v=k_zbSdBQC2I.

CHAPTER 7

# WHEN THE MONARCHY DOESN'T "PAPER OVER THE CRACKS"

## *Placing the Marriage of the Duke and Duchess of Sussex in the Context of Great Britain's Racialized Politics*

STEPHANIE L. WILLIAMS

The coronation of King Charles III and Queen Camilla was an extraordinary presentation of multiculturalism that influenced the way in which the world views the racial landscape of Great Britain. The program participants, choirs, and musicians represented multiple faiths, ethnicities, and races from many countries of the Commonwealth. They sang songs that defined their cultures. Men and women read the liturgy of the Church of England and made the declarations of sovereign power. The coronation procession was led by the Commonwealth's troops, composed mainly of people of color.

During the most sacred part of the ceremony, the king was shielded by the anointing screens. The screen facing the audience carried the names of the countries of the Commonwealth, which are predominantly comprised of nonwhite citizens, as the king received the sacraments of the holy oil. The first prime minister of color and a Hindu, Rishi Sunak, read a Bible verse. The Ascension Choir, comprised of eight members of the all-Black Kingdom Choir that also performed at the Sussexes' wedding in

2018, made history by singing the first gospel music performed at a coronation.

It is also notable that four Black women had prominent roles in the ceremony. Three of the women carried significant symbols of British power into the coronation. The bishop of Dover, the Right Reverend Rose Hudson-Wilkin, presented the queen consort's rod. Baroness Floella Benjamin, a Trinidadian British member of the House of Lords and Dame of the British Empire, carried the Sovereign's Sceptre with Dove, symbolizing the sovereign's spiritual role. Dame Elizabeth Anionwu, also a Dame of the British Empire, is of mixed Irish and Nigerian heritage and carried the Orb, the symbol of the world under Christ. Baroness Valerie Amos, the fourth woman, presented King Charles III to the people.[1] The baroness holds the highest honor of British chivalry as the first nonroyal Black person to have the title Knight or Lady of the Garter. This title was bestowed to her by Queen Elizabeth II in 2022. Haile Selassie (1892–1975) was a Knight of the Garter as the emperor of Ethiopia.[2] It is important to note that all the women earned their titles for their exceptional professional service to the nation.

The coronation program needed to be inclusive. The Commonwealth over which the king reigns is overwhelmingly nonwhite. Of the fifty-six member nations, only six countries (the United Kingdom, Canada, Cyprus, Malta, Australia, and New Zealand) are majority white.[3] Yet, the inclusiveness of the coronation program may give the appearance and assumption that the royal family can promote multiculturalism more easily and authentically than the leaders of the political class and British establishment. The British public and supporters can see on the royal family's social media pages that Black and minority ethnic (BME) people have been engaged for several decades in many of the over three thousand charities and patronages in the country and around the Commonwealth that receive their support. In addition, three of the most prominent of these patronages, the Prince's Trust (now the King's Trust), the Prince of Wales's Charitable Fund (now the King Charles III Charitable Fund), and the Duke of Edinburgh's Award patronages, have provided inclusive opportunities for children, teens, and young adults to promote personal growth and prepare them to be community leaders, and have supported higher education and the workforce.[4] Many BME British and Commonwealth citizens have been recognized for their extraordinary service in their profession, the arts, and sports, and for acts of heroism. Yet the diversity celebrated in the public is limited by the institutions of the royal household and the British establishments of nobility, politics, and the press.

The rightful multicultural display during national celebrations cannot paper over the nation's legacy of empire nor the contemporary racial indignities and inequities that promote and perpetuate institutional and systemic racism within the country. Great Britain's brutal history of empire, slavery, and race and class subjugation continues to influence who is accepted as an authentic member of British society. The coronation demonstrated the difficulty that the royal family has yet to overcome. Even with the splendor and demonstrations of multiculturalism, the monarchy still could not "paper over the cracks"—namely, that the king's biracial African American daughter-in-law, the Duchess of Sussex, was absent. Buckingham Palace said that the Duchess of Sussex would remain in the United States to celebrate Prince Archie's fourth birthday.[5] Surely, parents and grandparents would not want any child to miss their birthday celebration and would find a way to celebrate a historic occasion and a beloved grandchild's birthday. However, the fact that the one multicultural family member did not attend the ceremony demonstrates why their efforts to promote multiculturalism fall short. It is one major sign that the royal family is unable to confront the racial vitriol that forms the basis of the rejection of the Sussex marriage. It must also be stated that the British establishments have been extraordinarily harsh to other members of the royal family, such as King Edward VIII (1930s) and Princess Margaret (1950s), by denying them the right to marry the spouse of their choice.[6] Prince Charles paid a high price for the intrusion of the institutions when he was denied the right to marry Camilla Parker Bowles in the early 1970s, only to enter into a tragic marriage with Diana Spencer in 1981. After his divorce in 1996, he fought for his right to marry Parker Bowles and to have her be accepted among the establishment and the public.[7] By using his personal experiences as well as his roles as monarch, head of the Commonwealth, and Supreme Governor of the Church of England, he could use his influence to broaden the acceptance of his daughter-in-law. However, to do so, the royal family has to face the harsh reality that their power and wealth are deeply entwined with British institutions that insist that the House of Windsor remain all white.

The rejection of Markle by the institutions of the monarchy and significant segments of British society must be considered in the context of the nation's history of slavery, colonialism, and the treatment of Black immigrants. The privilege of being a member of the royal family does not preclude the public from imposing the same racist attitudes and barriers that have prevented other BME populations from receiving equal treatment within British society.

This chapter is organized into three parts. Part I discusses the historical challenges of Black people to be accepted within British society. This includes the government's role in reinforcing imperialistic values. Part II discusses the treatment of Markle as a private citizen and a member of the royal family, and Part III discusses how the royal family faces the demands by nonwhite citizens of the Commonwealth to be respected and their subsequent calls for independence.

## Part I: Can You Be Authentically British if You Are Not White in Contemporary Britain?

### Britishness: An Exclusive White Identity

A discussion of the hardships that BME populations face in British society must include a discussion of how the concept of

"Britishness" is used to establish which individuals can be considered authentically a member of the nationality. Britishness is a creed that is in many ways comparable to the belief in "American exceptionalism." To hold American citizenship means you hold a place in a global caste system that places you above citizens of all other countries around the world. However, within that caste system, nonwhite Americans are not entitled to equal rights of citizenship regardless of their station in life.[8] A report by the Runnymede Trust's Commission on the Future of Multi-Ethnic Britain explains how Britishness places limits on BME individuals, how a person may build a life on the values of what it means to be a "good and respectful" British person and still not be accepted by society: "Britishness, as so much as Englishness, has systematic largely unspoken, racial connotations. Whiteness nowhere features as an explicit condition of being British, but it is widely understood that Englishness, and therefore by extension, Britishness is racially coded."[9] This aspect of racial coding helps us to understand the anger and resentment regarding the dialogue surrounding who can be considered "authentically" British.

## Britishness and the Legacy of the Windrush Generation

It is critical to understand how the legacy of the British Empire continues to shape contemporary racialized politics, specifically, who belongs in the country and who can be considered British. At a 2022 event to celebrate the work of British charities, one of Queen Elizabeth II's former ladies-in-waiting, Lady Susan Hussey, repeatedly asked Ms. Ngozi Fulani, "Where are you from?" Fulani stated that she was born in the U.K. and is a British citizen. That answer did not satisfy Hussey until Fulani revealed that her parents were immigrants. At that point, Hussey incorrectly concluded that she was a Jamaican national.[10] Although Hussey's comments caused a global scandal, they were a reflection of conflicts between the values of Britishness and the inability to explain why Black Britons are assumed as one of the most recent immigrant communities.

A review of the 2021 census helps to put the percentage of Black people who reside in the U.K. into perspective and demonstrates the limitations of their political representation. The total population of England and Wales was 59.6 million. Eighty-two percent of the population was comprised of white ethnic groups; 2.4 million identified as either Black African or Caribbean descent, and 1.7 million were of mixed race. Black people comprised .42 percent of the population in Northern Ireland. In Scotland, approximately 30,000 people were identified as "African" and nearly 7,000 people identified as "Caribbean or Black."[11] The relatively small number of Black British citizens living in the U.K. is due to the fact the British government prevented Black people, Indians, and Pakistanis from residing in Great Britain until their services were needed to rebuild the country after World War II. In 1948, a passenger ship named the *Empire Windrush* would begin an era of immigration of thousands of West Indians to England.

In efforts to narrate the immigrant story during national celebrations, such as the 2012 Summer Olympics in London, the Windrush migration has been portrayed as a story of pride and national exceptionalism. However, these immigrants and other BME populations faced constant difficulties to integrate fully into British society. In addition, the government imposed regulations to prevent BME individuals from gaining the benefits of citizenship rights that were provided to white immigrants. And in subsequent decades, the Caribbean immigrants of this era, often named the Windrush generation, were subjected to immigration policies to keep these communities small.[12]

In future decades, the Windrush immigrants would be negatively impacted by a broader political anti-immigration campaign. During her tenure as home secretary (2010–19), Theresa May (who then served as prime minister from 2016 to 2019), oversaw the destruction of thousands of landing cards of immigrants who came to the U.K. from 1948 to 1971, which for many, served as the only proof that they had entered the country legally. These actions were part of May's effort to create a hostile environment, such as the loss of benefits and the denial of medical treatments, for immigrants who entered the country illegally. It was revealed in 2017, the year of Prince Harry and Meghan Markle's engagement, that the destruction of records meant that elderly immigrants and those who migrated as children no longer had documentation to prove when they entered the country. Many were unjustly detained, lost their jobs, and even deported. The Windrush immigrants who were deported by the British court system encountered extensive difficulties in establishing their identities, opening bank accounts, and securing homes back in their countries of origin.[13] The legacy of the past continues to influence contemporary current attitudes.

## The Royal Household as a Reflection of British Society

When everyday citizens have difficulty integrating into a highly structured society, one must assume that integrating into the most elite level of society is even harder. The history of institutional racism is central to the palace and the family's inability to see that the way they managed the Sussex marriage in 2018 is reflective of the way that the institution of the royal family has been allowed to remain all white. Recent reporting on how the royal household has actively sought to prevent people of color from having significant employment opportunities should concern and disappoint the British public. A 2021 report from *The Guardian* revealed that as late as 1968, nonwhite immigrants or foreigners were not permitted to work in clerical positions for the royal family. They were instead relegated to domestic service. Additionally, Buckingham Palace claimed that it did not record the race or ethnicity of its employees through the 1980s.[14] The first Black senior member of the royal household was not onboarded until 1998, when Prince Charles hired Colleen Harris to serve in his press office.[15] Other research indicated that Queen Elizabeth II had been exempted from following the anti-discrimination laws related to race and gender discrimination and equal pay. And processes were put in place so that discrimination charges from employees at Buckingham Palace would be sent to the home secretary's office instead of the courts. The exemption remains in place today.[16] Richard Stokes, Britain's first Black royal guardsman of the royal residences of Buckingham Palace, Windsor Castle, and Clarence House, revealed the racial harassment that he was subjected to as both a trainee and a member of the Grenadier Guards from 1986 to 1990. His promotion to the Grenadier Guards was a national story of pride in 1988. However, his personal story is one of shame. Stokes writes in his account, "On day one of my training, I was greeted with putrid racial slurs, interrogations, death threats and regular visitors to my barrack room who'd stare, shout abuse and snigger at the black spectacle in front of them. The racist behavior never stopped. I was subjected to ostracisation, cigarettes stubbed out in my food, bananas thrown at me and hate mail, including a bullet with my name etched on it. The first six months of my deployment were a living hell. But despite this, I persevered."[17]

Stokes resigned from his post. He stated that he was not prepared to endure more years of racism to advance through the ranks. One would hope that many improvements to the quality of life and working conditions for BME staff members have been made in the three decades since Stokes resigned from his post. However, it still appears that the royal household continues to lag in its efforts to promote diversity. In the 2023–24 Sovereign Grant Report, the monarchy failed to meet its own imposed quota to diversify its workforce. Buckingham Palace stated that they need to do more to improve their recruitment efforts and to be fair and transparent, as well as ensure that their culture is inclusive.[18]

Before the discussion begins examining the backlash to the Sussex marriage, one has to ask two critical questions. First, does the royal family believe that it is necessary to sacrifice their multicultural family members to keep the support of the conservative establishment so that the monarchy continues? And second, are they so unwilling to make it possible for people of color to be accepted within their inner circles? This question also pertains to whom they choose as their spouses instead of continuing the perception that they tacitly agree that the highest levels of the monarchy should remain all white.

## Meghan, the Unwanted Duchess

Meghan Markle, the Duchess of Sussex, Countess of Dumbarton, Baroness Kilkeel, officially joined the royal family on May 19, 2018. When she married Prince Harry, it would have been unfathomable to imagine that she would not later attend the king's coronation. However, in the intervening years, the racial harassment and bullying, combined with the lack of institutional and moral support from the royal family, made life so untenable that the Sussex family would be forced to live outside the U.K. It was evident that despite the social changes that have diversified the British culture, an interracial family and a biracial senior member of the royal family would not be welcomed by the British social and political establishment.

Black Americans often lament that no matter how hard they work and sacrifice for the good of the country, white Americans will never see them as legitimate and authentic Americans. There is an understanding that their achievements, human dignity, or right to exist do not matter to people who believe that their racial "inferiority" prohibits them from receiving what racist people and systems of power receive: what they view as their blessing or legitimacy to occupy elite social and political spaces.

It is hard for African Americans of all classes to live in the U.S. because the racial conditions of this country are so hostile. Power and privilege do not provide individual Black people with protection from white hostility. The U.S. witnessed these attitudes in action during the Obama presidency. Tea Partiers and other Republican elected officials regularly used signs at rallies depicting Obama as a savage African witch doctor. John Sununu, former Republican governor of New Hampshire, publicly stated that he wished that Obama "would learn how to be an American."[19] It must not be forgotten that Donald Trump built his political base of support by spreading conspiracy theories that Obama was born in Kenya, not the U.S., and propagating the lie that his birth certificate was fraudulent.[20]

From the beginning of Prince Harry and Markle's courtship, the British press and social establishment disapproved of the interracial couple as part of the royal family. There were numerous comments that British author Afua Hirsch calls "classic British racism—only half said, and half implied, a kind of polite prejudice that is only pernicious for its subtlety." Hirsch, also a biracial Briton, discusses how Markle was described as "(almost) straight out of Compton, a 'gang-scarred' neighborhood." Her "inappropriateness" to associate with Prince Harry was further elucidated by comments about her mother's dreadlocks and nose stud.[21] It is difficult to understand how Hirsch calls this type of racism subtle. The racial code words for Black crime, poverty, and an unacceptable standard for beauty are overtly racist. These are clear statements that people like Markle and her Black mother do not belong within British high society. The press was sending warning shots to Prince Harry that he would no longer be accepted by the press if he married a woman of color.

## Sanctioned Bullying by British Elites

It is really important to understand that the abuse and degradation that Markle continues to receive on social media have come from individuals with the highest connections in media, government, and, ultimately, the royal family, which is sending her clear and consistent messages that she does not have a right to be a part of the monarchy. It is as if Prince Harry should have asked the British elites, and not the monarch, as is the tradition, for permission to marry Markle. Hirsch explains that the anti-Markle commentary is not just demonstrating racial hostility; it is an open statement to the monarchy and the public that the royal family must remain white.[22] Ducey and Feagin have a similar assessment, noting that the racial frames used by the press as jokes are "veiled" or coded language to hide the overt racism of British society.[23] It is not unexpected that anonymous citizens would use social media to promote racial tropes that equate Markle and her children to apes and use banana emojis when they post comments about her. However, one would not expect the use of racial tropes from prominent members of the press. Danny Baker, an award-winning radio host for BBC, considered a premier British institution, sent out a derogatory tweet that read "Royal baby leaves hospital."[24] Baker was fired for this post, but would later claim ignorance for his "mistake" of calling the first mixed-race great-grandson of Queen Elizabeth II an ape when he made no effort to reference the eight previous great-grandchildren born before Prince Archie.

The royal family is aware of the racial symbolism of apes and bananas and has protested the use of this trope. As president of the Football Association, Prince William has condemned fans who frequently hurl bananas at Black footballers during games.[25] Yet it is unclear whether Buckingham Palace requested that the BBC issue a public apology. Nor was there a public statement from the palace indicating that the media outlet had done so. Columns and social media posts have continued to stoke public resentment toward Markle and to reiterate that she does not belong in British society. Sarah Vine, a controversial columnist from the *Daily Mail*, wrote a 2019 commentary considered particularly hostile to Markle.[26] At the time it was published, Vine was married to the highly prominent "Brexiter," conservative member of Parliament Michael Gove and a member of Prime Minister Boris Johnson's cabinet, who campaigned on the view that the U.K. should leave the European Union to stop nonwhite immigration. Gove and Vine had close personal relationships with former prime ministers David Cameron and Theresa May.[27] Much of Vine's column focuses on Markle's work as a guest editor for British *Vogue*. The column is a litany of attacks claiming that Markle had a poor understanding of her place as a member of the royal family. Vine also makes the point that the British "people don't have your 'woke' antennae" and suggests that Markle has no legitimate right to complain of personal pain because her belonging to the royal family is a privileged position. To be clear, while Markle's social status through her marriage to Prince Harry is privileged, Buckingham Palace has not released any statement to defend her dignity and clearly state that she should be treated with respect.

The palace's failure to defend Markle's dignity and her position as a member of the royal family became most evident when Jeremy Clarkson wrote that Markle should be subjected to brutal, inhumane treatment. In December 2022, Queen Camilla hosted a holiday luncheon that included British celebrity Jeremy Clarkson as one of her guests.[28] His invitation to the party begs one to question the integrity of Buckingham Palace. Clarkson's known use of racial slurs would, under most circumstances, exclude him from receiving any invitation from institutions that value multiculturalism, much less Buckingham Palace. In 2014, the BBC sanctioned him for using the word "nigger" in three recorded takes. There was public backlash and demands that he resign or be dismissed by the BBC. However, at the time, Clarkson was the host of *Top Gear*, the most-watched show in the world in 2013, and he was able to remain employed.[29] Two days after the holiday event at the palace, Clarkson published a column in *The Sun* in which he states, "I hate her. Not like I hate [former first minister of Scotland] Nicola Sturgeon or [convicted serial killer] Rose West. . . . At night, I'm unable to sleep as I lie there, grinding my teeth and dreaming of the day when she is made to parade through the streets in every town in Britain while the crowd chants, 'Shame!' and throw lumps of excrement at her."

Clarkson also states that he hated her "on a cellular level" and claims the "everyone his age felt the same way."[30] Although the "excrement" quote became the focus of the media's attention, the column is a diatribe of misogynistic comments directed at both the Duke and Duchess. He named the duke "Harold Markle" and used vulgar, violent, and graphic references to sexualize the duchess and insinuate that the duke and the royal family have been damaged because of her greed and need for attention.

Clarkson's remarks caused fury across the nation. A multi-party letter, headed by Conservative member of Parliament Caroline Nokes, was signed by sixty-five members of the Women and Equalities Select Committee of the British Parliament and was sent to the editor of *The Sun*. The letter expressed that the members "are horrified" by the contents of the column. They asserted that they "condemned in the strongest of terms the violent misogynistic language against Markle." The letter also expressed their level of concern about recent violent threats that required the attention of the Metropolitan Police and stated that the language used by Clarkson only worsened the situation.[31] (It is important to note that the former head of counterterrorism in England, also the country's most senior law enforcement officer, Neil Basu, verified in an interview that there were genuine threats against the duchess from the far right. Those threats were investigated and prosecuted.[32]) Additionally, the signers expressed their deep concern for British society:

> We are deeply concerned about the role modeling being promoted to young men and boys, that they can verbally attack women without consequence or that it is OK to use violent language to address a woman that you might disagree with. You will no doubt know how violence against women has surged across Britain in recent years. We must do better. Enough is enough. We cannot allow this type of behaviour to go unchecked. We welcome The Sun's retraction of the article, we now demand action is taken against Mr. Clarkson and an unreserved apology is issued to Ms.

> Markle immediately. We further demand definitive action is taken to ensure that no article like this is published again.[33]

*The Sun* removed the column from its website. Clarkson issued the following public statement: "Oh dear. I've rather put my foot in it. In a column I wrote about Meghan, I made a clumsy reference to a scene in *Game of Thrones* and this has gone down badly with a great many people." He also sent a note of apology to Prince Harry on Christmas Day, 2022. However, he did not make a direct apology to Markle.[34] The royal family failed to issue a letter of condemnation to support the duchess. They should have been deeply concerned with the letter's statement about domestic violence. Queen Camilla's webpage discusses her long history and deep commitment to working with national and international organizations to advocate for victims of rape and sexual violence since 2013. A review of her work and speeches demonstrates that she is authentically connected to the problem of violence against women.[35] For example, in a February 2022 interview, she announced that her work in this area would continue when her husband ascended to the throne. And her reasoning and sincerity for her considering the fight against violence against women as her life's work echoed the same values that the members of Parliament outlined. She stated: "I think children at school have got to be taught self-respect. We have got to go back to the beginning and just build up this idea that you have to have respect for human beings, it's lack of respect. It's treating women like chattels and people thinking they can get away with it."[36]

Queen Camilla received justifiably harsh criticism on social media because she attended another holiday party in which Clarkson, along with Piers Morgan, who also has a history of making degrading comments about the Sussexes, was in attendance. One social media commenter questioned if she still advocated against misogyny, as well as whether Clarkson would continue to receive invitations from the royal family. Buckingham Palace did not release any comments related to Clarkson's statements. However, Kensington Palace has released statements in the past when the tabloids have made claims that Catherine, Princess of Wales, was too thin, wore hair extensions, or used Botox.[37] The decisions made by the royal family to not address the racially abusive and degrading actions of the press do have detrimental consequences to both their immediate family members and British society as a whole. These decisions also send a clear message that there are limits to their advocacy for promoting multiculturalism, precluding nonwhite citizens and immigrants from consideration as full and true British subjects. It is difficult to see that any compassion can exist in a family that lauds the value of multiculturalism but does not recognize that such racial degradation can potentially lead to physical harm from racists and take an unbearable mental toll on human beings who are referred to as animals. It is fair to ask if the royal family has authentic respect for people of color within their family and worldwide.

## Part II: The Royal Family and the Legacy of Colonialism

It is increasingly clear that members of the Commonwealth believe that Great Britain and the royal family should be held accountable for their historical actions. The increasing anger from BME communities within the nation and around the world comes from the view that the family would rather hold on to the perception that the Commonwealth is an organization based on mutual respect and interests. This is especially the case since the U.K. has refused to address difficult matters that perpetuate colonialist interests over truth and the right to be treated as an equal nation. The disconnect between the royal household, the general British public, and those nations whose history was negatively impacted by the British Empire comes from the nations who want history to be rectified. Kimberly Ducey and Joe Feagin discuss how British culture in films and literature reimagines the history of colonialism by portraying Queen Victoria as the "savior" to the savaged lands of the empire when she was brutally racist. While citizens lost their lives as they fought to reject the British confiscation of their lands, their wealth was stolen as well. This allowed the British to fund the Industrial Revolution. However, the history of the empire is depicted deceptively, portraying those who carried out the brutality as businessmen and merchants instead of slave owners. Such an approach is an attempt to make the national history more palatable.[38]

Yet the former colonies have not forgotten this history and remain determined to rectify it with both the British government and Buckingham Palace. This is evident in many current issues related to requests to return Crown Jewels in Africa and India, painful reminders of the atrocities that occurred during colonialism. Buckingham Palace is unwilling to return the jewels and artifacts but will make small gestures that do not go far in addressing the return request. For instance, the palace announced that Queen Camilla would not wear the 105.6-carat Koh-i-noor diamond that was presented to Queen Victoria but was stolen from an Indian prince in the 1840s.[39]

There is a similar request to return the body of an Ethiopian royal prince to that nation's government. Prince Alemayehu and his mother, Empress Tiruwork Wube, were taken into custody after his father, Emperor Tewodros II, committed suicide shortly after losing a battle to the British military in 1868.[40] The British proceeded to steal thousands of Ethiopian cultural, religious, and royal artifacts. The prince became an orphan when the empress died on their voyage to the U.K. Queen Victoria decided to have him raised in the royal household, and Prince Alemayhu was never permitted to return to Ethiopia. When he died at the age of eighteen, Queen Victoria arranged for his burial in Windsor Castle. The Ethiopian royal family has made several efforts to have his remains returned to his native land. However, Buckingham Palace has refused to do so because they said that they do not want to disturb the graves of other family members. Instead, the Ethiopian royal family has received a lock of his hair from the descendants of Captain Charles Sawyer Speedy, who raised the prince when he arrived in England.[41] The Ethiopian royal family vows to continue to press the British royal family and the British government for the return of his remains, as well as the repatriation of priceless artifacts looted from the country during the 1868 British expeditions to Magdala.

## The Commonwealth: Reparations, Truth and Reconciliation, and the Impact of the Royal Family

Coronation participants needed to reflect the diversity of the U.K. and the Commonwealth. Today, Great Britain is no longer an empire. However, as the empire began to fall away, it established the Commonwealth in 1949 to maintain economic and political links with its former colonies. The organization is currently comprised of countries in Africa (21), Asia (8), the Caribbean and the Americas (13), Europe (3), and the Pacific (11). The Commonwealth has a population of 2.7 billion people.[42] Queen Elizabeth II often discussed the organization as a permanent alliance that benefits the member nations. In her final message to the Commonwealth in 2022, she stated the following: "Our family of nations continues to be a point of connection, cooperation, and friendship. It is a place to come together to pursue common goals and the common good, providing everyone with the opportunity to serve and benefit. . . . I hope that we can deepen our resolve to support one another and endeavor to ensure the Commonwealth remains an influential force for good in our world for many generations to come."[43]

While the queen's messages to the Commonwealth expressed a sense of unity, citizens of these nations found it difficult to reconcile the need to have the British monarchy as the constitutional head of state and the cruelty and unrecoverable losses of resources. The queen, King Charles, and Prince William have all made statements to denounce the past atrocities of slavery.

Critics argue that these statements are not enough. What these citizens want, and what people of color around the world are demanding and expecting, is to be treated as equals and with respect.[44] This means BME British citizens with heritages from former British colonies must be respected as citizens, and the Commonwealth countries may demand that Great Britain and the crown own up to past atrocities and current structures and patterns of racist behavior that continue to prevent social integration in British society, including the monarchy. It is in the family's and institution's interests to demonstrate inclusivity beyond tours of the Commonwealth and the work of the royal patronages.

## Caribbean Protests Against the Royal Family

The increasing unfavorability of the royal family is growing among Commonwealth countries' constituents. Senior members of the family appeared to be significantly out of touch during their 2022 tours of the Caribbean to commemorate the queen's platinum jubilee. During their visit to Jamaica, the Duke and Duchess of Cambridge re-created images of a visit Queen Elizabeth II and Prince Phillip took to the island in the 1950s to reinforce British imperialism on behalf of the government.[45] Since the reign of King George V, members of the royal family have taken tours around the empire, now the Commonwealth, to reaffirm their position and reconnect the people with Great Britain by utilizing the glamour of the crown.[46] Read more bluntly, the British need to keep the Commonwealth countries connected to the U.K. so that these countries will not press for independence. The queen's message during her first tour in 1954 was to enforce the message that loyalty to the Commonwealth was also loyalty to her. And further, that the Commonwealth was a family of nations.[47]

The queen's children and grandchildren were not prepared to see that the deference given to her was not going to be given to them. It was as if they were unaware of the hardships of the Jamaican people under British colonial rule, as well as contemporary calls for accountability for slavery and the Windrush scandal. Protesters accused the royal family and the British economy of benefiting from the exploitation of slavery and made demands that reparations be paid to the nation. Jamaica's prime minister also informed them that the country is planning to go forward to end its formal ties with the crown and become a republic.[48]

As insensitive as it was to re-create an imperialist royal visit, the Cambridges' racist undertones didn't end there. The couple went on a walkabout in which young Jamaican children were placed behind a chain link fence. Photos of the white couple reaching between the openings of the fence to greet young, harmless Black children enraged the Jamaican public. The Cambridges—parents of young children, who also greet and advocate for children in their patronages—did not have the wherewithal to meet the children without the fence.[49]

Prince Edward, Earl of Wessex, and Sophie, Countess of Wessex, faced similar criticism and scrutiny in their 2022 plan to celebrate the queen's platinum jubilee. The couple were confronted by Gaston Browne, prime minister of Antigua and Barbuda, on the issues of slavery and reparation. Knowing that the Wessexes could not answer political questions, Browne asked Prince Edward if he and his wife would use their influence to advocate for the payment of slavery reparations to the people of the former British colonies. In addition, the prime minister stated that the world should understand the history of atrocities that took place under British rule. Prince Edward did not acknowledge the questions asked, but thanked Prime Minister Brown for his welcome. The couple appeared to be taken off guard by the question and looked very uncomfortable in photos taken during the event. It is not appropriate for them to answer political questions.[50] However, it is a fair criticism that there should have been a statement available for the earl to give the public a sense that the family appreciates the difficult history that has linked them to the history of imperial oppression.

## The Relevance of Reparations

The royal family should not have been surprised by the importance of reparations to the Caribbean. In recent years, the British government has rejected efforts to engage in conversations to address financial and social inequalities that were created due to their colonialist policies. During a 2015 visit to Jamaica, former prime minister David Cameron made a statement to the Jamaican Parliament that the current British government should be held responsible for past mistakes. Cameron argued, "I acknowledge that these wounds run very deep indeed, but I do hope that as friends who have gone through so much together since those darkest times, we can move on from this hateful legacy."[51]

Cameron's office reiterated that the government would not address issues that were centuries old. Instead, the prime minister announced that the government would invest $38 million from its foreign aid budget for the construction of prisons in Jamaica so that Jamaican-born citizens in British jails could be repatriated to serve out their sentences in their country of birth. It is important to note that Cameron had a distant relative who did receive reparations from the British slave trade. James Duff was a nineteenth-century member of Parliament and an army officer who received approximately £4,101—equivalent to £3 million, or $4.2 million today—in compensation for releasing 202 slaves on his sugar plantation at the end of the British slavery era.[52]

The British government and the royal family will continue to face calls for reparations from countries throughout the Commonwealth. The matter of reparations in the Caribbean that benefited Cameron's distant relatives is linked directly to policies and practices that extracted resources from those countries to create multigenerational wealth for British elites well into the twenty-first century. In 1834, the Slavery Abolition Act allocated £20 million to compensate slave owners who had businesses in

Jamaica, Barbados, Grenada, Trinidad and Tobago, and British Guyana for "property losses," which included enslaved people. Research estimates that 80 percent of the compensation went to the owners of British plantations residing in Great Britain. This wealth was central to financing British infrastructure that established railways, banks, and cultural institutions. The removal of this wealth from the people and places that produced it contributed to underdevelopment and multigenerational poverty. Formerly enslaved people never received compensation, and many Caribbean citizens still do not have access to the legal titles of the land on which they live today.[53]

The agenda for the 2022 visit, developed by the British government, and by extension the royal family, was that it was not in their interest to move on from the imperialist policies of their former colonies in the West Indies, Asia, and Africa. There was endless speculation during the king's tenure as Prince of Wales about how he would modernize the royal family. Although he has been recently crowned, the focus on the future should be placed equally on both the king and the Prince and Princess of Wales. It was shocking that two individuals in their early forties focused not on contemporary philanthropic work and conversations about their patronages but instead on re-creating a colonialist tour that took place nearly seventy years earlier when racial oppression was so harsh. As the future leader of the royal family, Prince William will be constrained by the government regarding what he can do and say as he travels abroad, but there is no excuse that he can use, such as he was unprepared by his staff, to understand that people of color will always defend their right to be free and demand that crimes against their people be recognized. His performance in 2022 shows that the relationship between the royal family and the people of the Commonwealth is likely to worsen over time unless they are better prepared and advised by courtiers who understand the concerns and legacies of the BME population.

## Conclusion: The Lost Opportunity

What should we conclude about Markle's experience as a senior member of the royal family? Was her and Prince Harry's marriage an example of "delusional post-racial progress?" Shantel Buggs argues that it was such a failure and that Markle was placed in an impossible situation. Her addition could not erase the racism and atrocities of the past. Nor could it show that nonwhite immigrants and native-born Britons are welcome to become equal citizens.[54] Instead, it revealed, if not proved, that the royal family is a symbol of white identity and the majority of British people want to keep the monarchy a white institution.[55] It is also very disappointing that as father, father-in-law, and grandfather, King Charles has failed to be more vocal about the harassment that has burdened the Sussexes, especially because of enormous personal difficulties that other members have faced in the press previously. In the aftermath of the Jeremy Clarkson controversy, British Black women were asking if the royal family had a "moral compass" when they questioned the family's treatment of Markle. There is a deep disappointment that she was constantly scapegoated as "an angry Black woman" when she was clearly the target of racial harassment. These women understand the mental toll that racism takes on an individual. And yet Markle was not allowed to receive any psychological treatment for her hardships.[56] The white majority of the British public may never give her the respect she deserves as a human being.

King Charles could choose to lead by example and do more to declare his love for the Sussexes, as he did during his first address to the nation as king.[57] As the head of the royal family, the Church of England, and the Commonwealth, he can be bold and vocally celebrate the diversity of his family as a bridge to the increasing diversity of the U.K. and the Commonwealth. The king cannot change the past racist treatment that the Sussexes have endured, nor that the empire has perpetrated. However, he can show the nation that above all else, he loves the duke and duchess as a son and daughter-in-law, and that he cherishes Prince Archie and Princess Lilibet in the same way that he cherishes Prince George, Princess Charlotte, and Prince Louis.

Family is family after all.

## Notes

1. "Coronation Day," official website of the British royal family, Royal Household, May 6, 2023, https://www.royal.uk/coronation-guide.
2. "The Order of the Garter," official website of the British royal family, Royal Household, accessed December 19, 2025, https://www.royal.uk/the-order-of-the-garter.
3. "Facts," the Commonwealth, Commonwealth Secretariat, accessed December 19, 2025, https://thecommonwealth.org/about/facts.
4. "Charities and Patronages," official website of the British royal family, Royal Household, accessed December 19, 2025, https://www.royal.uk/charities-and-patronages-1.
5. Westfall, "Prince Harry, but Not Meghan, Will Attend."
6. Gregory, "Princess Margaret Dies at 71."
7. Lyall, "How Time Softened the Judgement of Camilla."
8. See Rucker, *Obama's Political Saga*. 13ff.
9. Quoted in Travis, "British Tag Is 'Coded Racism.'"
10. Landler, "Former Palace Aide Makes Face-to-Face Apology."
11. "Facts," the Commonwealth, Commonwealth Secretariat, accessed December 19, 2025, https://thecommonwealth.org/about/facts.
12. Paul, "From Subjects to Immigrants"; Olusoga, *Black and British*.
13. *Economist*, "National Shame."
14. Pegg and Evans, "Buckingham Palace Banned Ethnic Minorities."
15. Harris, "Colleen Harris, the First Black Member of the Royal Household."
16. Pegg and Evans, "Buckingham Palace Banned Ethnic Minorities."
17. Stokes, "When I Guarded the Royal Palaces."
18. Crown, *Sovereign Grant and Sovereign Grant Reserve*.
19. MacAskill, "Romney Supporter John Sununu 'Sorry.'"
20. Dyson, *The Black Presidency*, PAGE NUMBER.
21. Hirsch, *Brit(ish)*, PAGE NUMBER.
22. Hirsch, *Brit(ish)*.
23. Ducey and Feagin, *Revealing Britain's Systemic Racism*.
24. Reproduced by Simon Lancaster (@bespokespeeches), Twitter, May 9, 2019, https://twitter.com/bespokespeeches/status/1126408674119958529?ref_src=twsrc%5Etfw%7Ctwcamp%5Etweetembed%7Ctwterm

%5E1126408674119958529%7Ctwgr%5E0b00457d185df0dd7be5ff39c11d890a1ab4dd00%7Ctwcon%5Es1_&ref_url=https%3A%2F%2Fwww.newsweek.com%2Froyal-baby-archie-harrison-danny-baker-bbc-meghan-markle-prince-harry-1420702.

25. Ducey and Feagin, *Revealing Britain's Systemic Racism.*
26. Vine, "My Memo to Meghan Markle."
27. MacLellan, "Godfather of Brexit Who Gave Theresa May a Lifeline."
28. See Booth, "Outrage in Britain"; Vanderhoof, "Jeremy Clarkson Has Apologized to Everyone but Meghan Markle."
29. Goldsmith, "BBC Rebukes 'Top Gear' Presenter Clarkson."
30. Quoted in Rosney, "Jeremy Clarkson and Meghan Markle."
31. Nokes, Caroline (@carolinenokes). "Letter to Vivian Newton from the Women and Equalities Select Committee." *Twitter*, 20 December 2022, @carolinenokes.
32. Russell, "Duchess of Sussex."
33. Nokes, Caroline (@carolinenokes). "Letter to Vivian Newton from the Women and Equalities Select Committee." *Twitter*, 20 December 2022, @carolinenokes.
34. Quoted in Vanderhoof, "Jeremy Clarkson Has Apologized to Everyone but Meghan Markle."
35. This commitment is also highlighted on the royal family website ("The Queen's Work on Violence Against Women," official website of the British royal family, Royal Household, accessed December 19, 2025, https://www.royal.uk/queen-consorts-work-violence-against-women).
36. *BBC News*, "Duchess of Cornwall Says Queen Consort Title Will Help."
37. Tufekci, "Prince Harry Is Right."
38. Ducey and Feagin, *Revealing Britain's Systemic Racism.*
39. Duncan, "Calls to Return Star of Africa Diamond"; Landler, "Jewels in Camilla's Crown."
40. Tamirat and Macaulay, "Ethiopia's Prince Alemayehu."
41. Tamuari, "Ethiopian Prince Alemayehu's Lock of Hair Returned."
42. "Facts," the Commonwealth, Commonwealth Secretariat, accessed December 19, 2025, https://thecommonwealth.org/about/facts.
43. Commonwealth, "2022 Commonwealth Day Message."
44. Dahir, Chutel, and Peltier, "In Africa, the Queen's Death Renews a Debate"; Goodbridge-Boyce and Llana, "Why Do We Have a Queen?"
45. Das, "Weeks After William and Kate's Controversial Caribbean Tour."
46. Sapire, "African Loyalism and Its Discontents."
47. Feingold, "Marketing the Modern Empire."

48. Das, "Weeks After William and Kate's Controversial Caribbean Tour."
49. Hall and Gentleman, "Perfect Storm."
50. Das, "Weeks After William and Kate's Controversial Caribbean Tour."
51. Kebede, "Legacy of Caribbean Slavery."
52. Bilefsky, "David Cameron Grapples with Issue of Slavery Reparations."
53. Rauhut, "Reassessing the Compensation Payments of the British Slave Owners."
54. Buggs, "Post-script—When Post-Racialism Fails."
55. Andrews, "Post-racial Princess."
56. Mohdin, "Where Is the Moral Compass?"
57. *Sky News*, "King Charles III's First Address."

## Works Referenced

Andrews, Kehinde. "The Post-racial Princess: Delusions of Racial Progress and Intersectional Failures." *Women's Studies International Forum* 84 (2021). http://doi.org/10.1016/j.wsif.2020.102432.

*BBC News*. "Duchess of Cornwall Says Queen Consort Title Will Help Her Causes." February 23, 2022. https://www.bbc.com/news/uk-60482173.

Bilefsky, Dan. "David Cameron Grapples with Issue of Slavery Reparations in Jamaica." *New York Times*, October 1, 2015. https://www.nytimes.com/2015/10/01/world/americas/david-cameron-grapples-with-issue-of-slavery-reparations-in-jamaica.html.

Booth, William. "Outrage in Britain after Tabloid Columnist Imagined Meghan Naked and Ashamed." *Washington Post*, December 12, 2022. https://www.washingtonpost.com/world/2022/12/20/uk-harry-meghan-jeremy-clarkson/.

*The Economist*. "The 'National Shame' of Britain's Treatment of Windrush Migrants." April 18, 2018. https://www.economist.com/britain/2018/04/18/the-national-shame-of-britains-treatment-of-windrush-migrants.

Commonwealth. "2022 Commonwealth Day Message by Her Majesty." March 14, 2022. https://thecommonwealth.org/news/2022-commonwealth-day-message-her-majesty-queen#.

Crawford-Smith, James. "Jeremy Clarkson Breaks Silence on Meghan Markle Column: 'Horrified.'" *Newsweek*, December 19, 2022. https://www.newsweek.com/jeremy-clarkson-breaks-silence-meghan-markle-comment-1768151.

Crawford-Smith, James. "Royals Fail to Meet Diversity Quota in Year of Palace Race Storm." *Newsweek*, June 29, 2023. https://www.newsweek.com/royals-fail-meet-diversity-quota-year-palace-race-storm-monarchy-1809798.

The Crown. *The Sovereign Grant and Sovereign Grant Reserve: Annual Report and Accounts 2023–2024*. London: The Crown, 2024. https://www.royal.uk/sites/default/files/documents/2024-07/Sovereign%20Grant%20Report%202023-24.pdf.

Dahir, Abdi Latif, Lynsey Chutel, and Elian Peltier. "In Africa, the Queen's Death Renews a Debate About the Legacy of the British Empire." *New York Times*, September 9, 2022. https://www.nytimes.com/2022/09/09/world/africa/Queen-africa-british-empire.html.

Das, Shanti. 2022. "Weeks After William and Kate's Controversial Caribbean Tour, More Nations Signal Plans to Ditch the Monarchy." *The Guardian*, May 1, 2022. https://www.theguardian.com/uk-news/2022/may/01/royals-republicanism-and-reparations-wessexes-feel-the-heat-on-antigua-visit.

Ducey, Kimberly, and Joe R. Feagin. *Revealing Britain's Systemic Racism: The Case of Meghan Markle and the Royal Family*. London: Routledge, 2021.

Duncan, Gillian. "Calls to Return Star of Africa Diamond in the UK Crown Jewels." *National News*, May 4, 2023. https://www.thenationalnews.com/world/2023/05/04/calls-to-return-star-of-africa-diamond-in-uk-crown-jewels/.

Dyson, Michael E. *The Black Presidency: Barack Obama and the Politics of Race in America*. Boston: First Mariner Books, 2017.

Feingold, Ruth P. "Marketing the Modern Empire: Elizabeth II and the 1953–1954 World Tour." *Antipodes* 23, no. 2 (2009): 147–54. https://www.jstor.org/stable/i40091500.

Goldsmith, Belinda. "BBC Rebukes 'Top Gear' Presenter Clarkson over Racist Language." Reuters, May 2, 2014. https://www.reuters.com/article/uk-britain-bbc-clarkson/bbc-rebukes-top-gear-presenter-clarkson-over-racist-language-idUKKBN0DI0XL20140502.

Goodbridge-Boyce, Anmar, and Sara Miller Llana. "Why Do We Have a Queen? Complex Reactions in the Commonwealth." *Christian Science Monitor*, September 13, 2022. https://www.csmonitor.com/World/Americas/2022/0913/Why-do-we-have-a-queen-Complex-reactions-in-the-Commonwealth.

Gregory, Joseph R. "Princess Margaret Dies at 71." *New York Times*, February 10, 2022. https://www.nytimes.com/2002/02/10/obituaries/princess-margaret-dies-at-71.html.

Hall, Rachel, and Amelia Gentleman. "'Perfect Storm': Royals Misjudged Caribbean Tour, Say Critics." *The Guardian*, March 25, 2022. https://www.theguardian.com/uk-news/2022/mar/25/william-and-kate-caribbean-tour-slavery-reparations-royals.

Harris, Colleen. "Colleen Harris, the First Black Member of the Royal Household, Recalls Her Years Working with King Charles III." *Vogue*, April 27, 2023. https://www.vogue.com/article/colleen-harris-king-charles-first-person.

Hirsch, Afua. *Brit(ish): On Race, Identity and Belonging*. London: Vintage Books, 2018.

Kebede, Rebekah. "Legacy of Caribbean Slavery Still Stings Despite British PM Saying 'Move On.'" Reuters, October 1, 2015. https://www.reuters.com/article/us-jamaica-reparations-idCAKCN0RV5UP20151001.

Landler, Mark. "Former Palace Aide Makes Face-to-Face Apology to Guest over Remarks." *New York Times*, December 16, 2022. https://www.nytimes.com/2022/12/16/world/europe/uk-royal-racism.html.

Landler, Mark. "Jewels in Camilla's Crown Will Not Include Famed Diamond Claimed by India." *New York Times*, February 14, 2023. https://www.nytimes.com/2023/02/14/world/europe/camilla-crown-koh-i-noor-diamond.html.

Lyall, Sarah. "How Time Softened the Judgement of Camilla and Fury over Diana's Death." *New York Times*, September 13, 2022. https://www.nytimes.com/2022/09/13/world/europe/princess-diana-camilla-queen-elizabeth.html.

MacAskill, Ewan. "Romney Supporter John Sununu 'Sorry' for Calling Obama Un-American." *The Guardian*, July 17, 2012. https://www.theguardian.com/world/2012/jul/18/john-sununu-apology-obama-unamerican.

MacLellan, Kylie. "The Godfather of Brexit Who Gave Theresa May a Lifeline—Michael Gove." Reuters, November 21, 2018. https://www.reuters.com/article/uk-britain-eu-gove-idUKKCN1NQ1T9.

Mohdin, Aamna. "'Where Is the Moral Compass?': Black Women on the Monarchy's Treatment of Meghan." *The Guardian*, December 15, 2022. https://www.theguardian.com/uk-news/2022/dec/15/black-women-feel-failed-by-royal-familys-treatment-of-meghan-markle.

Nokes, Caroline (@carolinenokes). 2022. "Letter to Vivian Newton from the Women and Equalities Select Committee." *Twitter* @carolinenokes.

Olusoga, David. *Black and British: A Forgotten History*. London: Pan Books, 2017.

Paul, Kathleen. "From Subjects to Immigrants: Black Britons and National Identity, 1948–62." In *The Right to Belong: Citizenship and National Identity in Britain, 1930–1960*, edited by Richard Weight and Abigail Beach, 223–48. London: I. B. Tauris, 1998.

Pegg, David, and Rob Evans. "Buckingham Palace Banned Ethnic Minorities from Office Roles, Papers Reveal." *The Guardian*, June 2, 2021.

www.buckingham-palace-banned-ethnic-minorities-from-office-roles-papers-reveal.

Rauhut, Claudia. "Reassessing the Compensation Payments of the British Slave Owners in Current Caribbean Claims to Reparations." *Sociologus* 70, no. 2 (2020): 123–41. https://DOI:10.3790/soc.70.2.123.

Rosney, Daniel. "Jeremy Clarkson and Meghan Markle: The Sun Column Gets 6000 Official Complaints." *BBC News*, December 19, 2022. https://www.bbc.com/news/entertainment-arts-64025074.

Rucker, Mary. 2013. *Obama's Political Saga: From Battling History, Racialized Rhetoric, and GOP Obstruction to Re-election*. Lanham, MD: Lexington Books, 2013.

Russell, Rachel. "Duchess of Sussex: Meghan Faced Very Real Threats, Says Met Chief." *BBC News*, November 30, 2022. https://www.bbc.com/news/uk-63804711.

Sapire, Hilary. "African Loyalism and Its Discontents: The Royal Tour of South Africa, 1947." *Historical Journal* 54, no. 1 (2011): 215–40. https://www.jstor.org/stable/i23017238.

*Sky News*. "King Charles III's First Address to the Nation: The Full Transcript." September 9, 2022. https://news.sky.com/story/king-charles-iiis-first-address-to-the-nation-the-full-transcript-12693814.

Stokes, Richard. "When I Guarded the Royal Palaces I Never Realised There'd Been a Ban on Black Staff." *The Guardian*, June 5, 2021. https://www.theguardian.com/commentisfree/2021/jun/05/i-guarded-royal-palaces-ban-on-black-staff-britains-first-black-guardsman.

Tamirat, Jibat, and Cecilia Macaulay. "Ethiopia's Prince Alemayehu: Buckingham Palace Rejects Calls to Return Royal's Body." *BBC News*, May 22, 2023. https://www.bbc.com/news/world-africa-65588663.

Tamuari, Hanna. "Ethiopian Prince Alemayehu's Lock of Hair Returned After 140 Years in the UK." *BBC News*, September 22, 2023. https://www.bbc.com/news/world-africa-66887597.

Travis, Alan. "British Tag Is 'Coded Racism.'" *The Guardian*, October 11, 2000. https://www.theguardian.com/uk/2000/oct/11/britishidentity.race3.

Tufekci, Zeynep. "Prince Harry Is Right, It's Not Just a Matter of Royal Gossip." *New York Times*, January 25, 2023. https://www.nytimes.com/2023/01/25/opinion/harry-meghan-tabloids.html.

Vanderhoof, Erin. "Jeremy Clarkson Has Apologized to Everyone but Meghan Markle for His *Sun* Column." *Vanity Fair*, January 18, 2023. https://www.vanityfair.com/style/2023/01/jeremy-clarkson-meghan-markle-sun-column.

Vine, Sarah. "My Memo to Meghan Markle Following Her Vogue Editorial—We Brits Prefer True Royalty to Fashion Royalty." *Daily Mail*, July 29, 2019. https://www.dailymail.co.uk/debate/article-7298911/SARAH-VINE-memo-Meghan-Markle-Brits-prefer-true-royalty-fashion-royalty.html.

Westfall, Sammy. "Prince Harry, But Not Meghan, Will Attend King Charles III's Coronation." *Washington Post*, April 12, 2023. https://www.washingtonpost.com/world/2023/04/12/harry-meghan-coronation-attend/.

## CHAPTER 8

# MEGHAN MARKLE'S MOTHERHOOD AND THE BOUNDARIES OF RACIAL MIXTURE AND ANTI-BLACKNESS

JASMINE MITCHELL

Meghan Markle's sexualized racial difference and mixed Blackness, as well as the birth of her children, threatens the imagined racial purity of Britain. The United Kingdom, largely in collective denial of its atrocious historical role in the slave trade, colonization, and imperialism, nonetheless perpetuates racial hierarchies. In the U.K., the erasure of Blackness from history, the present, and the future is paramount to a central British identity. Likewise, U.S. boundaries of race focus largely on demarcations of Blackness and the maintenance of white purity from colonial origins. By examining the British press's framing of Markle's racial identity, familial relationships, and motherhood, this chapter argues that Markle's presentation tapped into mulatta archetype tropes of temptresses who manipulate white men for social mobility and are also unfit mothers. Coupled with the way in which Meghan talks about herself, markers of resistance to white-dominated heteropatriarchal narratives persist yet are ultimately not radical counternarratives to anti-Blackness. While the marriage of Meghan Markle and Prince Harry incited symbolic hope in the union for a new Britain and imagined racial reordering, her motherhood resharpened racial boundary formations.

The association of whiteness with the British royal family, combined with the association of white motherhood as proper motherhood, makes Meghan Markle's motherhood out of place.

Not only is Meghan out of place in the hierarchy, but her future children would also be considered out of place due to their racial lineage. Markle's lack of fit within the British royal family is central to the cultural historical formations of British national identity. More broadly, the surveillance of Meghan Markle's body and motherhood is part of the racial and gendered surveillance of Black women's bodies. In the United States, the regulation of Black mothers and Black women's bodies, from enslavement to contemporary child protective services, welfare, and education, forms part of a system of institutionalized injustice.[1] With Markle as representative of the iconic British royal family and mother to future heirs, her sheer presence is a threat to the idea of Britain as a white nation.[2]

## Multiracialism and British Royal Lineage

Markle's light skin and ambiguous features signify her as symbolic of a new multiracial Britain. The ways in which Markle continued to identify as mixed determined a sense of allegiance to racial parameters outside the symbol and practice of whiteness within the British royal family. While Markle did not explicitly assert a Black identity, she nonetheless asserted a biracial identity: "My dad is Caucasian and my mom is African American. I'm half black and half white."[3] She dismissed the "other" label within U.S. racial landscapes and categories and has instead embraced "pride in being a strong, confident mixed-race woman."[4] Yet her ensuing treatment by the royal family—particularly the comments made about her children—politicized her racial experience and negated the professed ideal of color blindness. Markle initially perpetuated these color-blind logics surrounding her marriage to Prince Harry. With Markle's light skin and other phenotypical features, she was also in a unique privileged position to proclaim that race doesn't matter. By 2021, she did not show an allegiance to a white sentient identity. This refusal to fully assimilate into whiteness, coupled with the impossibility of full belonging in the British royal family, made racial ambiguity unrealizable.

For Markle, her light skin, straight hair, facial features, and biracial identity allow access to relative privilege in approximation of whiteness. Yet this approximation of whiteness does not grant full white privilege. On the contrary, Markle's "half Black" identity has also rendered her subject to anti-Blackness. Research into how families identify U.S. Black multiracial children suggests that family racial identification strongly correlates with how children will eventually self-identify.[5] While Harry's whiteness is not questioned but assumed, Meghan's "half Black" status nonetheless places her within British and global racial hierarchies that devalue Blackness. Meghan's African American heritage—coupled with the ways in which Blackness is viewed as foreign or as outsider—reinforces her interloper treatment by the British press. The colonial routes of Black enslavement and the imperial routes of Black migration stemming from the British Empire serve to both connect and distance Markle from British ideas of the nation and commonwealth.

Markle's claim of a mixed identity and her American citizenship are seemingly incompatible with ways of being a member of the royal family. As the British royal family deemphasizes race and ignores colonial and imperial histories in the very construction of race, Markle's visibility and knowledge of her Black descent become markers of difference that supersede British royal family claims of acceptance. In public discussions of Markle's African American mother, Doria Ragland, topics inevitably circle back to whether Markle's children could then possibly be perceived as Black. With U.S. histories of the one-drop rule, Markle's children are not globally understood as wholly white and British.

Markle's sexual attractiveness, her racial background, and her class status have all been highlighted to reinforce women of African descent as alluring, dangerous, and threatening, in contrast to the white femininity represented by Kate Middleton. News media representations hold Markle to a substantially higher standard than Middleton, with media commentary disapprovingly and harshly comparing Markle to her sister-in-law.[6] Through mechanisms of comparison, news sources such as the *Daily Mail* project Middleton's motherhood as an embodiment of traditional British femininity due, in part, to her supposed normal family structure, whereas Markle's motherhood was positioned as an inferior "other" due to her untraditional family dynamics. She is thus a threat to national identity in a post-Brexit context.[7]

In a highly publicized March 2021 televised interview with Oprah, Markle contrasts the use of "Waity Katie" as a nickname for Kate Middleton, who waited for William to marry her, as rude but not racist and not in the same vein as Markle herself had been treated.[8] The use of "Waity Katie" presented Middleton in a passive feminine role in which marriage becomes the pinnacle of her fulfillment. While initially deriding, the comments of "Waity Katie" became a way to contrast Middleton with racialized depictions of Markle as aggressive, improper, and lust inducing. In the *Daily Mail* article "No Tears or Tantrums Here, 'Waity Katie' Middleton Has Become the Royals' Crown Jewel After a Torrid Week for Prince Harry and Meghan Markle," Amanda Platell utilizes Middleton's white motherhood as a foil to a presentation of Markle as threatening white heteronormative patriarchal values. Platell highlights Middleton as a "smiling mother of three" who is "just a woman happy with her lot and who understands how to behave as a royal." And, she adds, "Kate was undoubtedly helped by the fact she came from a stable, loving family background—so different from Meghan, who didn't even have her own father and half-siblings at her wedding."[9] In the divide separating Middleton's prim maternal persona and Markle as an inauthentic gold-digging sexual influence, the article (1) spectacularizes Markle's difference through an emphasis on tropes of Black femininity and (2) presents her in alterity to the British identity.

Furthermore, the contrasting of Markle as the flashy, sexy woman against the honorable Middleton presents a narrative of the proper heroine and mother of the nation versus the seductive but ultimately unfit villain. The media depiction of Markle's motherhood and the future of the royal family through her lineage occurs within the context of a reconsideration of British identity through Brexit and a reexamination of the role of British royalty. As Maria Pramaggiore and Páraic Kerrigan argue, Markle was labeled as a "disruptive duchess" who was further imbued with angry Black woman tropes.[10] The later presentations of Markle and Middleton as enemies—the feuding duchesses narrative—pit Markle's Black femininity in constant tension with the upright white motherhood represented by Middleton. Black mothers are assumed to be unfit to meet traditional expectations of white motherhood.[11] Therefore, the early setup for Markle's integration into the royal family was one of a predicted racialized and gendered failure.

"Megxit," shorthand for the departure of Harry and Meghan from the British royal family in 2020, takes together the notion of Brexit and Meghan's retreat as a return to an imperial white patriarchal nostalgia. While Meghan's marriage into the royal family allowed for the optics of a post-racial fantasy, the hypervisibility of Markle and the role of the monarchy in signifying national unity also embodied a threat to the ideologies of Brexit.[12] With the xenophobic, racialized, and sexist media coverage of Markle prior to the Sussexes' move to the U.S., the Megxit hysteria also acted as a way to purge undesirable elements and restore a sense of white patriarchy symbolized by the monarchy. The threat of Meghan as a royal mother, with the prospect of contemporary Black lineage in the royal family through her son, Archie, was thereby mitigated.

## Sexualization of Meghan Markle as Temptress

The sexualization of Markle speaks to the transatlantic histories of enslavement, sexual exploitation, and racial mixing that continue to trouble the U.K. and former colonies. Markle is regarded as an exotic sexual artifact. As women of African descent have been understood a priori as sexualized, there was no justification required for headlines that emphasized Markle's sex appeal or "risqué" photos. The exposure of Markle's erotic body belongs to the transnational sensations of mixed Black female narratives. The British fascination with mixed Blackness emerges from British travel writers who were drawn to the antebellum Louisiana practice of plaçage, sexual unions between light-skinned free women of African descent and wealthy white men. The explosion of tragic mulatta narratives emerged after the British publication of Harriet Beecher Stowe's *Uncle Tom's Cabin* in 1852, as well as the London staging of the play *The Octoroon* in 1861.[13] The exclusion of women of African descent from the echelons of acceptance into white society also stems from these tragic mulatta narratives. As idealized white femininity also relies on motherhood, Markle's mixed-race identity is at odds with British royal mothers, the exemplar of idealized white femininity.

The British media projected suspicion and blamed Markle, suggesting that her Black feminine sexual power would be the downfall of the royal family. The media headlines around Prince Harry's attraction to Markle are bound to a historical imaginary of interracial desire, of inherent Black feminine sexual allure that cultivates white male lust. Markle is depicted as using Harry's lust as a white masculine weakness to her advantage. Headlines such as "Prince Harry Spent Two Years 'Lusting' Over Meghan Markle's Sexy *Suits* Character" include still images of Markle dressed in red lingerie, serving to introduce her as a symbol of desire.[14] Other headlines such as "Meghan Markle GYRATES with Suits Co-star in Outrageously Sexy Scene—Watch Out Harry!" warn of the potential danger and allure of Markle's sexuality.[15] After Markle's return to the U.S., similar headlines like "Prince William 'Wanted to Make Sure Harry Wasn't Blindsided by Lust' with Meghan" evoke Markle as a threatening corrupting influence.[16] The same article mentions that a royal family member referred to Markle as "Harry's showgirl," making explicit a linkage of Markle to sexualized performers. The hazy associations of showgirls as nightclub and burlesque performers also invoke sexual connotations. In particular, Markle's light-skinned body aligns with the advertising emblematic of early twentieth-century Black showgirl performers. The naming of Meghan as a showgirl calls into question her virtue and morality while also projecting her image as tawdry, rather than glamorous and respected. Markle had achieved economic independence and financial freedom through her work on *Suits*, but her bodily autonomy came under constant public scrutiny, especially around pregnancy and childbirth, once she was linked to Prince Harry.

The discourse of Prince Harry's marriage to Meghan Markle and the later expansion of the family through the birth of their two children paints him as a victim of Markle's manipulation and allure. This colonialist discourse follows the emphasis on white men's subjection to temptation that is rooted in ideas of racial and sexual difference, over which they can exercise no control. Presented as beautiful, modest, dutiful, and honorable, Middleton exemplifies idealized white womanhood and the heroic mother of the future nation, juxtaposed against Markle, her antagonist. The framing of Markle as an exotic beautiful temptress follows the legacies of the transnational circulation of mulatta in the cultural imagination. The discourse of seduction actually blamed enslaved Black women for their own sexual exploitation and depicted white male perpetrators as victims of Black women's sexual charms.[17] The hemispheric trajectory of the mulatta figure during enslavement and immediately after emancipation reflected the racial and sexual anxieties that justified Black subordination and white patriarchal control. For example, in the Brazilian literary canon—from *A escrava Isaura* (1875) to *O cortiço* (1890)—the seductive and dangerous mulatta is the downfall of white men and the imagined white nation. As a corrupting influence on white men, the Brazilian mulatta can be enjoyed as an object for sexual pleasure for white men but is not marriageable.

The positioning of Markle as sexy and irresistible posits a seduction based upon both racial and sexual difference. As a cunning, predatory mulatta, Markle is presented as being the one controlling the relationship and attempting to gain control over the royal family. While Markle functions in the British press as a sexual temptress, her ascension to British royalty through marriage and motherhood evokes fears of the dangers of devious mulatta women rising to power, with the prince as the white victim of Markle's self-serving designs.

## Racial and Class Lineage as Out of Place

The accusations that Markle is unfit for royal motherhood are primarily due to her racial and class lineage. The *Daily Mail* article "Harry's Girl Is (Almost) Straight Outta Compton: Gang-Scarred Home of Her Mother Revealed—so Will He Be Dropping By for Tea?" by Ruth Styles evokes the "hood genre" film and its gratuitous images of Black deviance, violence, gangs, and drugs in South Los Angeles.[18] The media tropes associating Black women with criminality, crime, and poverty is a strategy to discipline Black women's bodies through the vilification of single Black mothers in U.S. cities.[19] In this tabloid article, the question regarding stopping by for tea implies Markle's lineage and potential motherhood threaten practices of British civility, and by extension, traditional white British wealth and privilege. As Kehinde Andrews suggests, the article deems Markle as foreign to the privileged lifestyle of the monarchy due to her race and nationality. Without explicitly naming race, the use of a symbol like tea and the imagined landscape of Compton signal Markle as a racialized other who does not belong in the space of the British royalty or within the contours of British national identity. Markle's entrance to the British royal family and the emphasis on her Black mother implies a potential cultural and racial decline.[20]

Markle's whiteness, by way of her familial ties, is also presented as improper—her white family members are depicted as tawdry, tacky, and unfit for the British royal family. This presentation is invoked to differentiate a respectable upper-class British whiteness. Thomas Markle staged and sold paparazzi photos of himself getting measured for a wedding suit and reading a book about Britain, photos that were published in the *Daily Mail* right before Meghan Markle's wedding to Prince Harry. Meghan Markle's half brother, Thomas Markle Jr., submitted a letter to the prince pleading for him not to marry her. Despite not seeing each other for years, Samantha Markle, Meghan's half sister, has repeatedly criticized her sister in the press and published a book, *The Diary of Princess Pushy's Sister*.[21]

Press coverage such as "Burgered Off: Meghan Markle's Uninvited Family Celebrate Royal Wedding in Burger King with Paper Crowns" juxtaposed the "lavish" royal ceremony against her "unclassy" white relatives celebrating Markle's wedding at a fast-food restaurant. *The Sun* article emphasizes that while the royal family enjoyed "Scottish langoustines wrapped in smoked salmon, quail eggs, and lemon verbena, Meghan's relatives had a menu of Burger King's Double Bacon Breakfast Sourdough King and Hash Browns," underscoring the contrast between upper-class whiteness and working-class whiteness that lacks domesticity.[22] On the other hand, Doria Ragland, Markle's African American mother, performed respectability at the wedding while her physical Blackness facilitated the appearance of a post-racial royal family. The reframing of Doria Ragland as a symbol of poise and grace offered an image of a modern cosmopolitan nation while replicating conventional expectations of white femininity. Yet Markle's Blackness could not be integrated into the white supremacist underpinning of the nation and of the monarchy.[23]

## Surveilling Pregnancy

The coverage of Markle's baby shower in 2019 emphasizes her opulence and lack of taste. With press commentary describing "Meghan's lavish extravagance this week and the fact her baby shower looked so 'celebrity' rather than 'royal,'"[24] the press framed Markle as not understanding the difference between celebrity, which someone from any racial background can achieve, and royalty, which is rooted in whiteness. Markle's upward mobility converges with anxiety about possibly tainting the racial and class identities associated with British royalty. Headlines such as "Meghan Markle's 'Trashy' Baby Shower for Archie 'Horrified' Royal Aides" and "Palace Aides 'Rolled Their Eyes' When Meghan Had a 'Trashy and Common' $500,000 Baby Shower in New York When Pregnant with Archie" fueled these anxieties and moral judgements based upon class, racial, and gendered shaming.[25]

The focus on Markle's guests—in particular Serena Williams, Gayle King, and Amal Clooney, all independently successful women with careers, who do not identify with Anglo whiteness—also points to an anxiety surrounding white patriarchies and ideas of baby showers as a spectacle of domesticity. The characterization of Markle as staging the shower for paparazzi and as being common and trashy serve to separate ideas of white royalty from Markle's vision of upwardly mobile, successful, feminist women of color in celebration with one another. Markle later comments on the negative press of her baby shower in *Harry & Meghan*, the couple's Netflix docuseries, "These independent, strong, successful women choose to use their own money, and it's not taxpayer money, to throw a party for their friend from a place of love." While Markle certainly also feeds into capitalist consumerism, she calls attention to the way in which the focus on taxpayer money draws upon notions of good British citizenship to form a critique. The presence of confident, prominent, wealthy, and influential women of color and women outside British aristocracy represents a threat to white patriarchies based upon colonial orderings. As weddings and baby showers are all traditions and rituals marked as paths to womanhood, Markle's disruption of these rituals with a focus on her own Black maternity and community counters a spectacle of white upper-class femininity.

The surveillance of Markle's pregnant body is a means to control Black women's bodies. The antagonistic probing of Markle's cradling of her belly illustrates the antagonism toward Black women's bodies, even as the mother of future royalty. This common gesture was consistently speculated as a performance and described as "attention grabbing." In response to a January 26, 2019, *Daily Mail* article, "Why Can't Meghan Markle Keep Her Hands Off Her Bump? Experts Tackle the Question That Has Got the Nation Talking: Is It Pride, Vanity, Acting—Or a New Age Bonding Technique?," one reader commented, "Personally, I find the cradling a bit like those signs in the back of cars: Baby on Board. Virtue signaling, as though the rest of us barren harridans deserve to burn alive in our cars."[26] The abusive "mom shaming" comments on social media further entrenched the ways in which white patriarchal ideologies are enmeshed in not only the algorithms but also the ways in which digital users interact with each other.[27]

Both Markle's and Middleton's maternalism—with their impeccable appearance, slim bodies before and after pregnancy, and stylish clothing—all reflect an upper-class femininity. Yet Markle alone was consistently critiqued during her pregnancy, essentially excluded from attaining the ideal white royal femininity and motherhood. Instead, her body was relegated to the tropes of manipulative mixed Black women and the Black welfare queen who utilizes or fakes her pregnancy to obtain state funds.[28] Internet conspiracy plots that she had been faking her pregnancy and that her children do not even exist further associate Markle's motherhood as performative.[29]

Furthermore, Markle's pregnancy operates within a social matrix in which Black women's bodies have been regarded historically as stifling the nation, as lacking maternal feelings, or as not having rights to their own children. Black women's reproduction is controlled through racist histories, policies, and practices that have been circulating since enslavement.[30] While Markle is in a privileged position due to her status as Duchess of Sussex, she nonetheless is still situated within a highly racialized context, spanning high-income Western nations and the Global South, in which Black birthing parents receive disparate and inferior medical care.[31] In the U.K., the Black maternal mortality rate is five times higher than that of white women.[32] In the U.S., the Black maternal mortality rate is four times higher than those of white women. When comparing for education levels, U.S. Black women with a college degree die of pregnancy-related causes at 5.6 times the rate of white women with a college degree and 1.6 times the rate of white women with less than a high school education.[33]

Additionally, Markle and Prince Harry chose to maintain privacy for Archie's place of birth and did not pose for photos immediately after his birth. Throughout Markle's pregnancy, the British royal family and the general public expected her to follow in the footsteps of other royal mothers—her mother in-law, Princess Diana, and sister-in-law, Kate Middleton. Instead, she and Prince Harry left the hospital in private and only later did they disclose the hospital's location when the birth certificate for their son, Archie, was made public. As a Black woman, Markle made a radical demand to her rights to privacy and dignity. Markle's decision to use her status to maintain privacy, assert her agency, and protect her family was a disruption of deeply rooted racialized and gendered systems. Headlines from *OK! Magazine UK* included "Prince William 'Unimpressed' over Meghan's 'Prima Donna' Efforts to Hide Archie's Birth."[34] Markle's efforts to maintain privacy are embedded in a culture in which Black women are not permitted to assert their own agency, and thus threaten patriarchal systems of assumed protocols for the sake of duty. The expectations around the royal birth rely on ideas of power in which women's bodies help maintain a system of dominance.

## Bloodlines

From Markle's introduction to the British press onward, the notion of bloodlines and genes has been a way to control anxieties around race, especially racial ideologies in the U.S. and in the U.K. Originating from European ideas of noble and royal blood, European elites have long critiqued racial mixing and tried to subordinate "mixed bloods" within the colonial orders. The idea of noble blood charts royal inheritance and structures the ordering of hierarchy through blood from the past to the future. Meghan's status as an outsider to the aristocracy, to Britain, and to bounded parameters of whiteness elicits anxieties about racial mixing. As the British monarchy is "one of the premier symbols of whiteness," Markle subverts the linkages among royalty, race, and nation.[35]

From the outset of Prince Harry and Markle's relationship, the press demonstrated an obsession with bloodlines, genes, and ancestry. A 2016 *Daily Mail* column comments on their relationship: "Genetically, she [Meghan Markle] is blessed. If there is [an] issue from her alleged union with Prince Harry, the Windsors will thicken their watery, thin blue blood and Spencer pale skin and ginger hair with some rich and exotic DNA. Miss Markle's mother is a dreadlocked African-American lady from the wrong side of the tracks who lives in LA, and even the sourest spinster has to admit that the 35-year-old actress is extremely easy on the eye."[36] The allusion to their future child representing an ideal mixture—not diluting the visual appearance of whiteness but still enhancing the royal bloodline—still operates within the discourse of white supremacy. The discussion of the infusion of Markle's blood is similar to the ideas of "hybrid vigor" operating in Brazil, which proposes that the fusion of races creates a stronger new people and new nation. In the early twentieth century, Brazilian elites reconsidered the role of racial mixing from previous discourses of hybrid degeneracy and scientific racism. Gilberto Freyre, an influential anthropologist, argued that multiracials strengthened Brazil—he described Brazilians as a blend of European, African, and Indigenous peoples in his seminal 1963 work, *Sobrados e mucambos* (*The Mansions and the Shanties*).[37] While countering theories of racial mixing as a downfall to the nation, the espousal of hybrid vigor emphasized whitening and a dilution of Blackness.

The *Daily Mail* comments that focus on Markle's "diverse ancestry" or "exotic DNA"[38] position her race and her activism as both an asset and a threat to the British monarchy. To manage the anxieties surrounding racial purity and bloodlines, Markle's Blackness is diffused through an emphasis on the "exotic" to mark her as foreign. The exotic marker also positions Markle's mixed Black body within transnational constructions of race that reinforce national, colonial, and imperial fictions about white superiority and the romantic exotification of mixed Black women as sexual objects. Markle's light skin and other phenotypical features are assets, as physical whiteness neutralizes the fear of Blackness. At the same time, her ancestry presents a way for the royal family to present itself as modern and multicultural. Instead of a contamination of the family bloodline, Markle's blood is seen as actually enhancing whiteness. The idea of whiteness as overcoming Blackness is reminiscent of Latin American ideologies of whitening. In Brazil, *branqueamento* (whitening) has historically been a key tool for modernizing the nation. Mixed Black women, viewed as reproductive vessels, have been central in this national project.[39] Imbued with the next symbol of U.K., royal women's bodies are fetishized due to their function as reproducing the physical and metaphorical manifestation of the nation.[40] The fetishization of royal women's bodies and the British press framework of bloodlines and race is an evolutionist view of boosting the monarchy with connotations of Darwinist and eugenicist thought that resembles the rhetoric of early twentieth-century Latin American intellectuals.

By expanding tropes of the mulatta desire for upward mobility and whiteness, the British press has maintained white power structures, reinforcing a demarcation of bloodlines and racial lines. The *Daily Mail* headline "Now That's Upwardly Mobile! How in 150 Years, Meghan Markle's Family Went from Cotton Slaves to Royalty Via Freedom in the U.S. Civil War . . . While

Her Dad's Ancestors Included a Maid at Windsor Castle," recalls transatlantic mulatta tropes and whitening narratives.[41] This article features a family tree with Markle photographed in a short dress and positioned as a sex object whose own family history of racial mixing is eroticized. The first line of the article reads, "While Queen Victoria sat on the throne, Empress to a quarter of the world's population, a woman named Mattie Turnipseed gave birth to a 'mulatto'—the ugly, official term to describe those of mixed race—baby girl in a corner of America's Deep South." This story line explicitly sets up a contrast between Prince Harry's lineage and Markle's family history, which already includes racial mixture. Although the article condemns slavery and Jim Crow, it nonetheless does not focus on the British monarchy's role within these histories and sets up the contrast to maintain racial hierarchies. The article's dive into Markle's maternal and paternal lines, as well as the frequent mentions of the prince's royal bloodline, reflect an anxiety about racial mixing, racial boundaries, and notions of purity.

The framing of her father, Thomas Markle, suggests that his whiteness—while containing the possibility of an "impressive aristocratic line"—is nonetheless of inferior status due to his "not great wealth." The article also mentions that Meghan Markle and Prince Harry are to be wed at Windsor Castle; in a historical footnote, the article claims that Markle's great-great-great-grandmother, who came from Ireland, is "thought to have worked at the Castle as a teenager, probably in the kitchens or as a housemaid." The emphasis on the Irish maid as indicative of low social status downplays whiteness as a form of capital. As former colonial subjects, Irish migrants hold an insider and outsider status and have been racialized as other.[42] While the dive into Markle's family tree appears to give the potential for a multicultural Britain with greater social and class mobility, the framing reinforces rather than upends ideologies of white capitalist patriarchy. British anxieties about Black and Irish alterity are revealed through the possibility of alternate bloodlines to the royal family muddling national and racial identification. Furthermore, the specter of incestuous relations is implied: "Genealogists went further in their analysis to establish that Harry and Meghan are actually distant cousins."[43] Thus, Markle's relationship with Prince Harry causes anxiety both because she threatens to "contaminate" bloodlines as the descendant of enslaved Africans in the U.S. and because she is a blood relation to Prince Harry.[44] The upward mobility narrative follows transnational mulatta tropes of a desire for social mobility through sexual relationships with powerful white wealthy men.

## Phenotype

Color, as signifier of whiteness, became a primary concern regarding the future of the royal family. Markle's racial ambiguity, and the potential nonwhiteness of her children, still presented a threat to the tie between whiteness and royalty. During the 2021 internationally broadcast interview with Oprah Winfrey, Meghan and Harry discuss their 2020 departure from the British royal family. Pregnant with her second child, Meghan reveals that an unnamed royal family member inquired about her first child, Archie, and "how dark his skin might be when he is born." The speculation surrounding Meghan's pregnancy showcased anxieties of a white future threatened by Black women's bodies and the birth of mixed children. While narratives of whitening and the eventual dilution of Blackness is prominent throughout the Americas, the latent fear of Blackness remains. The presence of Markle's Black ancestry and the presence of Doria Ragland as the child's Black grandmother cannot remain wholly hidden. These fears of a genetic outlier to whitening, a recessive gene, phrases such as "Black behind the ears" or *torno atrás* (go back) in the Americas, from the U.S. to Brazil to the Dominican Republic, all reveal an anxiety of Black features showing up as a reminder of a Black past.[45] As skin color is not easily changed, the focus on Archie's color reveals existing racial hierarchies and the ways in which darker skin threatens a tie between whiteness and royalty. The dehumanization of people of African descent is apparent in how a British journalist tweeted photos of a well-dressed man and woman holding the hands of a chimpanzee in a suit as an allusion to newborn Archie.[46] The birth of Archie, the child of an interracial union, is imagined as animalistic and thus unnatural and antithetical to the idea of a white Britain, represented by the whiteness of the British royal family.

Since the birth of Archie and their daughter, Lilibet, the emphasis the British press places on the children's physical likeness to their father has further reinforced a desire for whiteness. By focusing on red hair and the prince's genes, the press also reifies the idea of race as ascribed to the physical bodies of Lilibet and Archie. The strong attachment to the idea of genes and redheaded lines acts as a kind of metonym for whiteness. Headlines included *The Mirror*'s "Prince Harry Thought 'the Ginger Gene Wouldn't Stand Up' in Kids with Meghan Markle" (O'Toole 2023) or "Four Generations of Ginger—how Lilibet Inherited the Royal Family's Iconic Look" (Bevan 2022).[47] Mixed Black individuals, such as Meghan, Archie, and Lilibet, challenge phenotypical and color codes of racial hierarchies and classification. Numerous photographs of Archie's and Lilibet's red hair serve as a kind of visual evidence to undermine the color coding of racial identity and as a reinforcement of Harry and his children's whiteness. The racial mixing, represented by Meghan and Harry's union, is thus neutralized with an emphasis on Archie's and Lilibet's red hair. Yet as Markle's children are often signified as white, she becomes the mother of an imagined white lineage that allows the nation to further whiten rather than maintain racial hybridity for the future.

While the British press has refrained from explicitly using the term "race" in these articles, the discussion of hair color and the likeness of the children to their father, such as the emphasis on Lilibet as "the spit of Harry," is a way to maintain a narrative of whitening.[48] This coding of racial desires happens through the highlighting of Harry's genes and generations of red hair in the family. Here, red hair becomes a marker of white masculine authority, while the presence of Markle allows for a kind of desirable mixed whiteness. Fascination with this particular feature speaks to a kind of exoticism and familiarity that mixed-race individuals are often subject to, revealed in statements like "When it came to Archie, many couldn't believe his beautiful locks and likened them to those of his dad, Harry" or the headline "Royal Fans Amazed by Archie's Hair in New Snap—and Notice Familiar Feature in Lilibet."[49] The desire for continuance of white privilege, as embodied by the royal family, is what allows for one generation to the next to utilize racial and class privilege. Prior to Archie's birth, an emphasis on visual racial logics showcased a concern with the blending of visual markers.

For example, Prince Harry's stepmother, Camilla, then-Duchess of Cornwall, supposedly asked Prince Harry if his unborn mixed-race child would have a "ginger Afro" when he grows up.[50] These questions, along with a lack of emphasis on Ragland's features, juxtapose an identifiable Blackness and a vision of racially ambiguous bodies that stand in for whiteness, Blackness, and racial mixture. Instead of a reflection on the inclusion of various representations of Blackness across color, complexions, hair color, and hair textures, Blackness here goes largely unrecognized. The preference for whiteness remains despite the disruptive presence of Markle, whose body then acts as a conduit of whitening through racial mixture.

## Navigating Family and Individual Racial Identity

Markle and Prince Harry's own navigation of racial identity refutes a reliance on whiteness. Although Markle has also invoked the significance of bloodlines, saying, "Harry and Archie have royal blood and no one can take that away,"[51] the issue of royal inheritance and titles does not disavow Blackness. While Meghan admits in her *Archetypes* podcast (2022–23) that it was only after dating Harry and moving to the U.K. that she "started to understand what it was like to be treated like a Black woman. Because up until then, I had been treated like a mixed woman. And things really shifted," she appears to separate mixed and Black identities rather than center how mixed and Black identities can coexist.[52] Furthermore, her comment implies that mixed-race women will not experience racism. Mixed-race identity becomes a source of individual personal choice rather than part of Black movements and struggles of social and political inequalities.[53] By seeing herself treated as Black, Meghan's Blackness also becomes legible to herself. In a 2020 speech to her alma mater, Northwestern University, Meghan explicitly addresses Black Lives Matter and recounts her experiences growing up during the 1992 L.A. riots.[54] The recognition of this Black identity as part of experiences of racism while also recognizing her Black lineage has implications for the way in which her children will also be racialized. The link between royalty and unexamined whiteness cannot operate alongside Markle's Black womanhood and her voicing her experiences with racism as a mother and the concerns over her children.

In the Netflix documentary *Harry & Meghan*, Doria Ragland reveals that she did not focus on helping Meghan forge a Black identity while growing up. She also admits that she regrets the decision and wishes she "could go back in time to have a real conversation about how the world sees you." While white parents frequently utilize color-blind perspectives or teach little about racism, Black families often center these issues in their parenting.[55] In interracial Black-white families, Black parents often take on the responsibility of racial socialization.[56]

Ragland's regret highlights an understanding of not adequately preparing Meghan for the racism she might encounter. It also shows that while Black mothers are pivotal in their children's formation of racial identity, discussions of race and enmeshment with Black communities are also essential to identity formation. Thomas Markle asserts that he argued with a doctor over his daughter's birth certificate and insisted the doctor write "mixed" rather than "Black" to identify her.[57] Indeed, the initial framing of Markle and Prince Harry's interracial romance, as well as Markle's racial identity, appeared individualistic rather than within a framing of multiracial and Black transatlantic histories and communities.

## Conclusion

Meghan Markle's motherhood shifts the discourse of white racial identity and royalty. While Markle was not socialized as Black in her upbringing, she does express a consciousness of how race impacts her family's life. In the U.S., research has shown that multiracial parents often actively cultivate racial identities in their multiracial children, whereas in the U.K., multiracial parents focus on cultivating a national identity.[58] Now that their titles of prince and princess have been conferred following Queen Elizabeth II's death, Archie and Lilibet are firmly entrenched in the royal family through their official titles. Although distanced from a white royal identity, the royal title confers a sense of national belonging. As royalty cannot be accessed except by bloodline, Archie's and Lilibet's royal titles also heighten how citizenship, belonging, and racial identity are implicated in their inclusion in the royal family.

Meanwhile, Markle and Prince Harry explicitly speak about their children as mixed race. When conversing with Alexis Ohanian, founder of Reddit and husband of Serena Williams, Markle reflected, "I know we have shared experiences of being in interracial marriages and raising small children who are of mixed race and how that plays into [our mission]."[59] Markle's comment creates a sense of multiracial community as well as highlights different experiences in terms of acceptance, belonging, and privilege.

In *Harry & Meghan*, Prince Harry asserts, "My son, my daughter, my children are mixed race, and I'm really proud of that."[60] He demonstrates how some white fathers of multiracial children develop a form of what France Winddance Twine names "racial literacy," which facilitates "a form of consciousness that enables them to perceive routine and subtle forms of everyday racism that were not previously visible to them."[61] Harry's awakening that "the world that we know has been created by white people for white people" reflects an acknowledgment of racial trauma and racial injustice as well as a renegotiation with white Britain; speaking on unconscious bias in 2020, he admitted, "I had no idea it existed. And then, sad as it is to say, it took me many, many years to realize it, especially then living a day or a week in my wife's shoes."[62] While Harry stops short of identifying anti-Blackness, he also refutes a color-blind narrative or a narrative of racial progress. Harry's legitimizing of a mixed-race identity counters the deep-rooted fear of reproducing darker-skinned children and tainting white purity and royalty.

Meghan Markle's podcast, the Oprah interview, and the documentary series all offer a discursive space for Markle to attempt to retain agency over her presentational self and to craft her own narratives. Following their departure from the royal family, Prince Harry and Markle founded Archewell Productions. Through collaborations with Netflix and Spotify, Archewell offered a platform for the couple to cultivate their own branded public personas while maintaining control over narratives about them, countering the British media's othering narratives premised on racial colonial ideologies. Markle's marketing of her celebrity persona also allows her to appear relatable through her focus on family life and motherhood. Markle's media productions and her interviews in the public sphere imagine domestic and family life as sites of racism and injustice, yet they do not go far enough to imagine the home as a site of collective social action. While Markle might represent a high degree of symbolic power, her actual power is limited.[63]

Markle's strategies for engaging media on her own terms—such as public writing, interviews, branding, docuseries, and podcasts—all offer up Black motherhood as a means to enact agency. Her focus on her right to control her own imagery and the imagery of her children runs counter to the ways in which the British media and royal family have attempted to control narratives and imagery of her Black sexuality, pregnancy, and motherhood. For example, in a 2022 interview, Markle commented about the practice of giving photos to the royal rota, the British press pool that covers the royal family: "Why would I give the very people that are calling my children the N-word a photo of my child before I can share it with the people that love my child? You tell me how that makes sense and then I'll play that game."[64] Markle positions the conflict as a struggle over control of her personhood and that of her children. Instead, her strategies for amplifying her own idea of motherhood and domestic life occur largely through Archewell Productions and media interviews. Markle's attempts to secure autonomy for herself and children resist colonial ideas of racialized ownership of Black women and children. Markle's framing of motherhood stops short of collective revolutionary Black mothering, but offers a reshaping of Black motherhood as a site of joy, power, and agency.

## Notes

1. Roberts, *Killing the Black Body.*
2. Gilroy, *There Ain't No Black in the Union Jack*; Jackson, "Imperial Suspect."
3. Markle, "I'm More Than an 'Other.'"
4. Markle, "I'm More Than an 'Other.'"
5. Roth, "End of the One-Drop Rule?"
6. McGill, "Question of Contrast."
7. McGill, "Question of Contrast."
8. Sun Reporter, "Mark My Words."
9. Platell, "No Tears or Tantrums Here."
10. Pramaggiore and Kerrigan, "Brand Royal," 1.
11. Handyside, "It's All About the Poise."
12. Weidhase, "Feminist Politics of Meghan Markle."

13. Manganelli, "Tragic Mulatta Plays the Tragic Muse."
14. Hope, "SUITS ME, SIR."
15. Miller, "Meghan Markle GYRATES with *Suits* Co-star."
16. Petter, "'Snob' Prince William 'Wanted to Make Sure Harry Wasn't Blindsided.'"
17. Hartman, "Seduction and the Ruses of Power."
18. Styles, "Harry's Girl Is (Almost) Straight Outta Compton"; Wiggins, "Race and Place at the City Limits."
19. Pimpare, *Ghettos, Tramps, and Welfare Queens.*
20. Andrews, "Post-racial Princess."
21. Waterson, "All the World's a Stage"; Tirschel, "Meghan Markle's Brother Writes Apology Letter"; Nardino, "Meghan Markle's Half-Sister Details Their Childhood."
22. Cox, "Burgered Off."
23. Handyside, "It's All About the Poise."
24. Bazaraa, "Meghan Markle NYC Spending."
25. Green, "Meghan Markle's 'Trashy' Baby Shower"; Johnston, "Palace Aides 'Rolled Their Eyes.'"
26. Jones, "Why Can't Meghan Markle Keep Her Hands Off Her Bump?"
27. Orgad and Baldwin, "How Any Woman Does What They Do"; Ward, "Making Black Motherhood (In)Visible."
28. Masters, Lindhorst, and Meyers, "Jezebel at the Welfare Office."
29. Gilbert, "Meghan Markle Fake Pregnancy Conspiracies."
30. Roberts, *Killing the Black Body.*
31. Davis, *Reproductive Injustice.*
32. Knight et al., *Saving Lives.*
33. Petersen et al., "Racial/ethnic Disparities in Pregnancy-Related Deaths."
34. Thompson, "Prince William 'Unimpressed' over Meghan's 'Prima Donna' Efforts."
35. Andrews, "Post-racial Princess."
36. Johnson, "Sorry Harry."
37. Freyre, *Mansions and the Shanties.*
38. Johnson, "Sorry Harry."
39. Schwarcz, *O Espetáculo das Raças.*
40. Shome, *Diana and Beyond.*
41. Wilson, "Now That's Upwardly Mobile!"
42. Walter, *Outsiders Inside.*
43. Wilson, "Now That's Upwardly Mobile!"
44. Woldemikael and Woldemikael, "From Suits to Royals."

45. Candelario, *Black Behind the Ears*; Duvall and Nerad, "Suddenly and Shockingly Black."
46. Hirsch, Afua. "Black Britons Know."
47. O'Toole, "Prince Harry Thought 'the Ginger Gene Wouldn't Stand Up'"; Bevan, "Four Generations of Ginger."
48. Rodger, "Holly Willoughby Reacts."
49. Newton, "Royal Fans Amazed by Archie's Hair."
50. Brown, "Palace Insiders Blast Nonsense Claims."
51. Vonow, "It's All for Archie."
52. Markle, "Duality of Diva."
53. Hernández, *Multiracials and Civil Rights.*
54. Zeigler, "Meghan Markle Addresses Black Lives Matter Protests."
55. Simon, "Role of Race and Ethnicity in Parental Ethnic-Racial Socialization."
56. Rockquemore and Brunsma, "Socially Embedded Identities."
57. O'Connell, "Thomas Markle Says He Blocked Doctor from Identifying Meghan as Black."
58. Sims and Njaka, *Mixed-race in the US and UK*; Song, *Multiracial.*
59. Ritschel, "Meghan Markle Discusses Being in an Interracial Relationship."
60. Garbus and Sashin, *Harry & Meghan*, episode 2.
61. Twine, *White Side of Black Britain*, 92.
62. Neal, "Prince Harry Talks About Anti-Racism."
63. Andrews, "Post-racial Princess"; Buggs, "Post-script—When Post-Racialism Fails."
64. Davis, "Meghan of Montecito."

## Works Referenced

Andrews, Kehinde. "The Post-racial Princess: Delusions of Racial Progress and Intersectional Failures." *Women's Studies International Forum* 84 (2021). http://doi.org/10.1016/j.wsif.2020.102432.

Bazaraa, Danya. "Meghan Markle NYC Spending Will Make Prince William 'Angry.'" *The Mirror*, February 22, 2019. https://www.mirror.co.uk/news/uk-news/meghan-markles-nyc-spending-make-14038764.

Bevan, Nathan. "Four Generations of Ginger—How Lilibet Inherited the Royal Family's Iconic Look." *Daily Star*, June 7, 2022. https://www.dailystar.co.uk/news/four-generations-ginger-how-lilibet-27168397.

Brown, Thomas. "Palace Insiders Blast Nonsense Claims that Camilla Joked How Harry and Meghan's Baby Would Have a Ginger Afro." *Daily Mail*, July 21, 2022. https://www.dailymail.co.uk/news/article-11036943/Camilla-asked-Meghan-Harrys-son-Ginger-Afro.html.

Buggs, Shantel Gabrieal. 2021. "Post-script—When Post-racialism Fails: Meghan Markle and the Limits of Symbolism." *Women's Studies International Forum* 84 (2021). https://www.sciencedirect.com/science/article/abs/pii/S0277539521000376.

Candelario, Ginetta E. B. *Black Behind the Ears: Dominican Racial Identity from Museums to Beauty Shops.* Durham, NC: Duke University Press, 2007.

Cox, Jamie. "Burgered Off: Meghan Markle's Uninvited Family Celebrate Royal Wedding in Burger King with Paper Crowns." *The Sun,* May 20, 2018. https://www.thesun.co.uk/news/6333254/meghan-markle-family-burger-king-royal-wedding/.

Davis, Allison P. "Meghan of Montecito." *The Cut,* August 29, 2022. https://www.thecut.com/article/meghan-markle-profile-interview.html.

Davis, Dána-Ain. *Reproductive Injustice: Racism, Pregnancy, and Premature Birth.* New York: New York University Press, 2019.

Duvall, J. Michael, and Julie Cary Nerad. "'Suddenly and Shockingly Black': The Atavistic Child in Turn-into-the-Twentieth-Century American Fiction." *African American Review.* 41, no. 1 (2007): 51–66. https://www.jstor.org/stable/40033765.

Freyre, Gilberto. *The Mansions and the Shanties.* Translated by Harriet de Onís. New York: Alfred A. Knopf, 1963.

Gilbert, David. "Meghan Markle Fake Pregnancy Conspiracies Are Flooding Twitter and YouTube." *Vice,* December 20, 2022. https://www.vice.com/en/article/akepvk/meghan-markle-fake-pregnancy-conspiracies.

Gilroy, Paul. *There Ain't No Black in the Union Jack.* Chicago: University of Chicago Press, 1987.

Green, Simon. "Meghan Markle's 'Trashy' Baby Shower for Archie 'Horrified' Royal Aides." *Daily Star,* May 20, 2021. https://www.dailystar.co.uk/news/latest-news/meghan-markles-trashy-baby-shower-24146444.

Handyside, Fiona. "It's All About the Poise: Meghan Markle, Doria Ragland, and Black Motherhood(s)." *Women's Studies in Communication* 44, no. 2 (2021): 198–214. https://doi.org/10.1080/07491409.2021.1912507.

Hartman, Saidiya. "Seduction and the Ruses of Power." *Callaloo* 19, no. 2 (1996): 537–60. https://www.jstor.org/stable/3299219.

Hernández, Tanya Katerí. *Multiracials and Civil Rights.* New York: New York University Press, 2018.

Hirsch, Afua. "Black Britons Know Why Meghan Markle Wants Out." *New York Times,* January 9, 2020. https://www.nytimes.com/2020/01/09/opinion/sunday/meghan-markle-prince-harry.html.

Hope, Hannah. "SUITS ME, SIR: Prince Harry Spent Two Years 'Lusting' Over Meghan Markle's Sexy Suits Character Rachel Zane Before Meeting Her." *The Sun*, October 27, 2017. https://www.thesun.co.uk/tvandshowbiz/4776680/prince-harry-meghan-markle-relationship-secrets/.

Knight, Marian, Kathryn Bunch, Derek Tuffnell, Roshni Patel, Judy Shakespeare, Rohit Kotnis, Sara Kenyon, and Jennifer J Kurinczuk. *Saving Lives, Improving Mothers' Care*. Oxford: MBRRACE-UK, 2018. https://www.npeu.ox.ac.uk/assets/downloads/mbrrace-uk/reports/maternal-report-2021/MBRRACE-UK_Maternal_Report_2021_-_FINAL_-_WEB_VERSION.pdf.

Jackson, Nicole M. "Imperial Suspect: Policing Colonies Within 'Post'-Imperial England." *Callaloo* 39, no. 1 (2016): 203–15. https://doi.org/10.1353/cal.2016.0003.

Johnson, Rachel. "Sorry Harry, but Your Beautiful Bolter Has Failed My Mum Test." *The Daily Mail*, November 5, 2016. https://www.dailymail.co.uk/debate/article-3909362/.

Johnston, Harriet. "Palace Aides 'Rolled Their Eyes' When Meghan Had 'Trashy and Common' $500,000 Baby Shower in New York When Pregnant with Archie, Friend Omid Scobie Claims." *Daily Mail*, May 20, 2021. https://www.dailymail.co.uk/femail/article-9596865/Palace-aide-rolled-eyes-Meghan-Markle-common-baby-shower-New-York.html.

Jones, Liz. "Why Can't Meghan Markle Keep Her Hands off Her Bump? Experts Tackle the Question That Has Got the Nation Talking: Is It Pride, Vanity, Acting—or a New Age Bonding Technique?" *Daily Mail*, January 26, 2019. https://www.dailymail.co.uk/news/article-6636233/Why-Meghan-Markle-hands-bump-Experts-tackle-question.html.

Manganelli, Kimberly Snyder. "The Tragic Mulatta Plays the Tragic Muse." *Victorian Literature and Culture* 37, no. 2 (2009): 501–22. https://doi.org/10.1017/S1060150309090317.

Markle, Meghan. "Meghan Markle: I'm More Than an 'Other.'" *Elle*, updated December 22, 2016. https://www.elle.com/uk/life-and-culture/news/a26855/more-than-an-other/.

Markle, Meghan. "The Duality of Diva with Mariah Carey." *Archetypes*, Podcast audio, August 30, 2022. https://open.spotify.com/episode/6S3Y5mKB9nJAk6wvZdbVo8.

Masters, N. Tatiana, Taryn P. Lindhorst, and Marcia K. Meyers. "Jezebel at the Welfare Office: How Racialized Stereotypes of Poor Women's Reproductive Decisions and Relationships Shape Policy Implementation." *Journal of Poverty* 18, no. 2 (2014): 109–29. https://doi.org/10.1080/10875549.2013.833159.

McGill, Mary. "A Question of Contrast: Unpacking the *Mail Online*'s Depiction of Meghan Markle's Royal Motherhood." *Women's Studies in*

*Communication*. 44, no. 2 (2021): 215–30. https://doi.org/10.1080/07491409.2021.1912516.

Miller, Adam. "Meghan Markle GYRATES with Suits Co-star in Outrageously Sexy Scene—Watch Out, Harry!" *Express*, June 27, 2017. https://www.express.co.uk/showbiz/tv-radio/820213/Meghan-Markle-gyartes-Suits-Patrick-J-Adams-sex-scene-Rachel-Zane-Prince-Harry.

Nardino, Meredith. "Meghan Markle's Half-Sister Samantha Markle Details Their Childhood, Last Conversation and More in 'The Diary of Princess Pushy's Sister Part 1." *US*, February 17, 2021. https://www.usmagazine.com/celebrity-news/pictures/meghan-markles-half-sister-tells-all-in-new-book-8-revelations/.

Neal, Jonathon. "Prince Harry Talks About Anti-Racism, Education, and Mental Fitness." *GQ*, October 26, 2020. https://www.gq-magazine.co.uk/gq-heroes/article/prince-harry-patrick-hutchinson-anti-racism.

Newton, Jennifer. "Royal Fans Amazed by Archie's Hair in New Snap—and Notice Familiar Feature in Lilibet." *The Mirror*, December 23, 2021. https://www.mirror.co.uk/news/us-news/royal-fans-amazed-archies-hair-25774244.

O'Connell, Oliver. "Thomas Markle Says He Blocked Doctor from Identifying Meghan as Black on Her Birth Certificate." *The Independent*, March 16, 2022. https://www.independent.co.uk/news/world/americas/thomas-markle-meghan-duchess-sussex-b2036322.html.

O'Toole, Scarlett. "Prince Harry Thought 'the Ginger Gene Wouldn't Stand Up' in Kids with Meghan Markle." *The Mirror*, January 11, 2023. https://www.mirror.co.uk/3am/us-celebrity-news/prince-harry-thought-the-ginger-28932949.

Orgad, Shani, and Kate Baldwin. "'How Any Woman Does What They Do Is Beyond Comprehension': Media Representations of Meghan Markle's Maternity." *Women's Studies in Communication* 44, no. 2 (2021): 177–97. https://doi.org/10.1080/07491409.2021.1912497.

Petersen, Emily E., Nicole L. Davis, David Goodman, Shanna Cox, Carla Syverson, Kristi Seed, Carrie Shapiro-Mendoza, William Callaghan, and Wanda Barfield. "Racial/Ethnic Disparities in Pregnancy-Related Deaths—United States, 2007–2016," *MMWR Morbidity and Mortality Weekly Report*. 68, no. 35 (2019): 762–65. https://www.cdc.gov/mmwr/volumes/68/wr/mm6835a3.htm.

Petter, Olivia. "'Snob' Prince William 'Wanted to Make Sure Harry Wasn't Blindsided by Lust' with Meghan." *The Independent*, July 26, 2020. https://www.independent.co.uk/life-style/royal-family/prince-william-harry-meghan-markle-finding-freedom-biography-a9638246.html.

Pimpare, Stephen. *Ghettos, Tramps, and Welfare Queens: Down and Out on the Silver Screen*. New York: Oxford University Press, 2017.

Platell, Amanda. "No Tears or Tantrums Here, 'Waity Katie' Middleton Has Become the Royals' Crown Jewel After a Torrid Week for Prince Harry and Meghan Markle." *Daily Mail*, January 10, 2020. https://www.dailymail.co.uk/debate/article-7874905/AMANDA-PLATELL-No-tears-tantrums-Kate-Middleton-Royals-crown-jewel.html.

Pramaggiore, Maria, and Páraic Kerrigan. "Brand Royal: Meghan Markle, Feuding Families, and Disruptive Duchessing in Brexit era Britain." *Feminist Media Studies* 22, no. 8 (2022): 2037–57. https://doi.org/10.1080/14680777.2021.1928258.

Ritschel, Chelsea. "Meghan Markle Discusses Being in an Interracial Relationship and Raising a Mixed-Race Child." *The Independent*, October 21, 2020. https://www.independent.co.uk/life-style/royal-family/meghan-markle-alexis-ohanian-reddit-interview-time100-talks-serena-williams-b1186205.html.

Ritschel, Chelsea. "Meghan Markle's Brother Writes Apology Letter After Previously Urging Prince Harry to Call Off Wedding." *The Independent*, November 8, 2021. https://www.the-independent.com/life-style/royal-family/meghan-markle-brother-thomas-letter-b1953642.html.

Roberts, Dorothy E. *Killing the Black Body: Race, Reproduction and the Meaning of Liberty*. New York: Vintage Books, 1997.

Rockquemore, Kerry Ann, and David L. Brunsma. "Socially Embedded Identities: Theories, Typologies, and Processes of Racial Identity Among Black/White Biracials." *Sociological Quarterly* 43, no. 3 (2002): 335–56. https://doi.org/10.1111/j.1533-8525.2002.tb00052.x.

Rodger, James. "Holly Willoughby Reacts as Royal Fans Say Same Thing About Lilibet Birthday Photo." *Birmingham Live*, June 8, 2022. https://www.birminghammail.co.uk/news/showbiz-tv/holly-willoughby-reacts-royal-fans-24171764.

Roth, Wendy D. "The End of the One-Drop Rule? Labeling of Multiracial Children in Black Intermarriages." *Sociological Forum* 20, no. 1 (2005): 35–67. https://doi.org/10.1007/s11206-005-1897-0.

Schwarcz, Lilia Moritz. *O Espetáculo das Raças—cientistas, instituições e questão racial no Brasil, 1870–1930*. São Paulo: Companhia das Letras, 1883.

Shome, Raka. *Diana and Beyond: White Femininity, National Identity, and Contemporary Media Culture*. Champaign: University of Illinois Press, 2014.

Simon, Carlisa. "The Role of Race and Ethnicity in Parental Ethnic-Racial Socialization: A Scoping Review of Research." *Journal of Child and Fam-*

*ily Studies* 30, no. 1 (2020): 182–95. https://psycnet.apa.org/doi/10.1007/s10826-020-01854-7.

Sims, Jennifer, and Chinelo Njaka. *Mixed-Race in the US and UK: Comparing the Past, Present, and Future.* Leeds, U.K.: Emerald Publishing, 2019.

Song, Miri. *Multiracial Parents: Mixed Families, Generational Change, and the Future of Race.* New York: New York University Press, 2017.

Styles, Ruth. "Harry's Girl Is (Almost) Straight Outta Compton: Gang-Scarred Home of Her Mother Revealed—so Will He Be Dropping By for Tea?" *Daily Mail,* November 2, 2016. https://www.dailymail.co.uk/news/article-3896180/Prince-Harry-s-girlfriend-actress-Meghan-Markles.html.

Sun Reporter. "Mark My Words: Meghan Markle Oprah Interview." *The Sun,* January 31, 2024. https://www.the-sun.com/news/2475583/meghan-markle-oprah-interview-full-transcript/.

Thompson, Dan. "Prince William 'Unimpressed' over Meghan's 'Prima Donna' Efforts to Hide Archie's Birth." *OK! Magazine,* December 6, 2022. https://www.ok.co.uk/royal/prince-william-meghan-harry-archie-28666935.

Twine, France Winddance. *A White Side of Black Britain: Interracial Intimacy and Racial Literacy.* Durhan, NC: Duke University Press, 2010.

Vonow, Brittany. "It's All for Archie." *The Sun,* February 22, 2020. https://www.thesun.co.uk/news/11018441/meghan-markle-reveals-archie-big-personality-like-prince-harry/.

Walter, Bronwen. *Outsiders Inside: Whiteness, Place and Irish Women.* London: Routledge, 2001.

Ward, Jonathan. "All." *Women's Studies in Communication* 44, no. 2 (2021). 231–51. https://doi.org/10.1080/07491409.2021.1912532.

Waterson, Jim. "All the World's a Stage: Thomas Markle and the Art of the Celebrity Photo." *The Guardian,* May 15, 2018. https://www.theguardian.com/uk-news/2018/may/15/all-the-worlds-a-stage-thomas-markle-and-the-art-of-the-celebrity-photo.

Weidhase, Nathalie. "The Feminist Politics of Meghan Markle: Brexit, Femininity, and the Nation in Crisis." *European Journal of Cultural Studies* 20, no. 3 (2022): 916–33. https://doi.org/10.1177/1367549420980010.

Wiggins, Benjamin. "Race and Place at the City Limits: Imaginative Geographies of South Central Los Angeles." *Ethnic and Racial Studies* 39, no. 14 (2016): 2583–600.

Wilson, Christopher. "Now That's Upwardly Mobile! How in 150 years, Meghan Markle's Family Went from Cotton Slaves to Royalty via Freedom in the U.S. Civil War . . . While Her Dad's Ancestors Included a Maid at Windsor Castle." *Daily Mail,* November 29, 2017. https://www

.dailymail.co.uk/femail/article-5130473/Meghan-Markles-upwardly-mobile-family.html.
Woldemikael, Eve, and Olivia Woldemikael. “From Suits to Royals: The Politics of Meghan Markle’s Racial Ambiguity.” *Women’s Studies International Forum* 85 (2021). https://doi.org/10.1016/j.wsif.2021.102439.
Zeigler, Hannah “Meghan Markle Addresses Black Lives Matter Protests in Speech to Alma Mater Grads.” *Elle*, June 4, 2020. https://www.ellecanada.com/culture/society/watch-meghan-markle-commencement-speech.

CHAPTER 9

# YOU'RE IN, BUT YOU'RE OUT

## *The Exile of Meghan Markle in the Age of the British Tabloids*

LILY TALMONT

Cinderella was abused in her own home and excluded from attending the ball. Mulan was abandoned on a snowy cliff by the army when they discovered she was a woman. Rapunzel and Sleeping Beauty grew up deep in the forest, away from their parents and kingdoms. They were all pushed out, forced to flee, and isolated from society. In effect, all these princesses were exiles. At the end of their stories, they manage to escape their exile, finding love, family, or both. These stories are fiction, but as a child, they shaped my idea of what makes someone a true princess. Now that I am a young adult, I can see how princess stories are really stories of women overcoming isolation and fighting for their happiness.

Being a royal in real life is more complicated than in animated movies. When Meghan Markle joined the royal family, the public celebrated the symbolic wedding between a Black American Meghan and white Prince Harry. In princess movies, the wedding is the end of the story, but it was only the beginning for Meghan. This essay explores her exile from British society and the strength she had to leave it all behind.

## Exile Is No Accident: Background on Exile

Edward Said's essay "Reflections on Exile" informs deeply this chapter's understanding of exile. Said writes that exile "is the unhealable rift forced between a human being and a native place, between the self and its true home: its essential sadness can never be surmounted." This suggests that exile is based on geographical change and can never be healed. If exile is truly "unhealable," then who would put that on themselves? This begs the question: Is exile always imposed? Said has an answer, noting that "exile originated in the age-old practice of banishment. Once banished, the exile lives an anomalous and miserable life, with the stigma of being an outsider." Banishment is a punitive measure, implying that the banished has committed some wrong that caused the banishment. It is the combination of being pushed away and living outside your native place that creates a sense of "otherness" in exile. Definitions of exile commonly mention being forced out of one's native country as punishment or for political reasons.[1] The purpose of this chapter is to investigate exile as being far more complex, through an exploration of Meghan Markle's experiences in the royal family.

Before we begin with Markle, I want to present two examples of exile that both illustrate points that will be fundamental to the understanding developed in this chapter. My first assertion is that exile does not have to be based on geographical displacement; rather, it is the exclusion of a people from their societal image. For this, I use the example of Tibetan communities in Nepal and India. Then I argue that the acceptance or rejection of an exile in their host country's society plays a significant role in cementing their status as an exile. For this point, I will share the story of my own family's immigration from Nazi-occupied Poland to the United States.

## Born an Exile: The Tibetan Community in Diaspora

Tibet is a large country that has been occupied by China since 1949. Since the violent occupation of Tibet began, thousands have fled the country to settle in Nepal or India. In the seventy-five-plus years since the invasion, three generations of Tibetans have lived in exile. The Tibetans born in Nepal or India are considered "born refugees," which means that even Tibetan children who were born and raised in there do not have citizenship of their birth countries. I have met little boys who are considered exiles, even though the last three generations of their families have lived in Nepal. Under a strict definition, these Tibetan children would not be considered as exiles because they live in their "home country." However, the connection they have to Tibet and the rights that they are not afforded because of that connection cannot be denied. Tibetans are forbidden from returning to their home, which is one reason why they call themselves exiles.

Furthermore, Tibetans in Nepal and India live in refugee settlements, which are situated in isolated locations and are an explicit attempt to keep Tibetans outside mainstream society. Due to their lack of statehood, Tibetans in Nepal and India cannot own property or businesses, which makes economic advancement nearly impossible. I can say from experience that Tibetan refugee camps are wonderful centers for the Tibetan community, but they are not without their issues. In many cases, the camps are on the edges of major cities and the land is not sufficient for farming or housing.

The Tibetan situation shows us how exile can be manufactured for a minority ethnic group. The Indian and Nepali governments created these systems to push Tibetans down and aside, exiling them from the rest of their societies. This is also an example of systematic racism. Global systematic racism is rooted in white supremacy, meaning the concept of exile is rooted in white supremacy as well. Said writes "that exile is irremediably secular and unbearably historical; that it is produced by human beings for other human beings; and that, like death but without death's ultimate mercy, it has torn millions of people from the nourishment of tradition, family, and geography."[2] While I wholeheartedly agree with Said, his language does leave something to be desired on one front. Exile was created by human beings for other human beings, but in recent history these creators were white colonial powers and those experiencing exile were people of color. Said adds the indispensable point that to exile is to remove someone from their family, culture, and place. Being forbidden from going home to Tibet, even a home that you, your father, and grandfather have never seen, is a form of exile. Moreover, being made an outsider in India and Nepal has cemented this exile for more than seventy-five years.

## Whiteness and Exile: Polish Immigrants in the United States

Any experience of exile is horrid; however, not all exiles are equal. Depending on the cause of exile, one's race, and the host country, an exile may be subject to insurmountable challenges or relative ease. I find no better example to investigate this point than my own family's history.

My grandfather escaped Nazi-occupied Poland during the early years of World War II. My great-grandfather was a member of the Polish Underground State, a resistance group whose goal was to end the Nazi occupation. Resistance members were targeted by the Nazis and my family was forced to abandon the country they had fought for or risk arrest or execution. They were exceedingly lucky and all eventually made it out of Warsaw by the early 1940s. They landed in northern New Jersey, which would become my grandfather's home and where he would spend the rest of his life. It is not my intention to brush off the experiences of World War II survivors; their exile was violent and deeply traumatic. However, even though my grandfather was an immigrant with a Polish name who did not speak any English, he was white. He could vote, own property, obtain U.S. citizenship, or open a business in the U.S. if he wanted to. Even if he never gained citizenship, he would still have had more basic human rights than any Black person in the U.S. at that time. When he had his three children, he decided to give them typical American names so they would be completely assimilated. Welcomed without reservation into American society, my family never lived in exile. I grew up knowing about Poland and my family's history there, but I would never call it my home because the U.S. had been our home ever since my grandfather arrived. If I ever did want to go to Poland, it would be incredibly unlikely that I would be denied a visa. The U.S. intervened in World War II on behalf of the occupied countries; in contrast, the U.S. did not intervene in Tibet, leading to the exile of thousands.

Whiteness is inseparable from the U.S. national identity. Nationalism, especially in the age of Donald Trump, has come to be synonymous with white supremacy. With this, I return to the words of Said, who defines "nationalism [as] an assertion of belonging in and to a place, a people, a heritage. It affirms the home created by a community of language, culture, and customs; and, by so doing, it fends off exile, fights to prevent its ravages."[3] My white grandfather, despite his foreignness, was welcomed into U.S. culture because he learned English, had white skin, was a man, was educated, and was not a communist. He fit into the mold of the nationalist image of an "American" and was therefore perceived as nonthreatening. Said points out that "all nationalisms in their early stages develop from a condition of estrangement."[4] U.S. nationalism was created based on a myth of white supremacy that supported the enslavement of Black people and the genocide of Indigenous people. Segregation and reservations were methods of exiling these communities to the outskirts of American society, just as the Tibetans were forced to live in refugee camps. What these two stories show is how exile is based on concepts of national identity and othering people who do not fit that national image.

## Meghan Markle in the Royal Family: Exile on the Global Stage

Characterizing Meghan Markle as an exile may seem ridiculous when you consider her designer clothes, Santa Barbara mansion, and royal title. She has access to money and power, and lives in her home country and home state. These arguments are answering the question: Is Meghan Markle an exile *now*? Markle was not always making podcasts in Southern California; she was once a resident of the U.K. and a working member of the royal family. For now, let us discuss Markle before her departure from the U.K. and her working royal role, answering the question: Was she an exile *in* the royal family?

## The Royal Family and Meghan Markle

When Markle married Prince Harry in May 2018, she also became the Duchess of Sussex. Her status as a senior working royal meant she was now obligated to serve the Crown and support its charitable endeavors. The royal family steers clear of political statements; however, they do make their position as a piece of the British identity extremely transparent. On the royal family's website it reads, "The Sovereign acts as a focus for national identity, unity and pride; gives a sense of stability and continuity; officially recognises success and excellence; and supports the ideal of voluntary service. In all these roles The Sovereign is supported by members of their immediate family."[5] The royal family is the source and protector of British nationalism. Therefore, whiteness, white supremacy, concentrated inherited wealth, patriarchy, anti-Blackness, and so much more that the royal family symbolizes are also inherent to British nationalism.

This symbolism extends to individual members of the family as well. Kate Middleton, the wife of Prince William, is characterized by the British media as an English rose, or the ideal British woman. Middleton is white, thin, conventionally beautiful, and educated. She was wealthy before her marriage to the prince, and she presents an ideal of motherhood as well. Obviously, Middleton is a human being, but what she represents on behalf of the monarchy makes her an insider in the royal family. Markle was eventually pitted against Middleton by the press, the symbolic weight being that Markle's Blackness was portrayed as lesser than Middleton's whiteness. Especially when Markle was pregnant with her first baby, the image of Black motherhood was ridiculed and scrutinized in favor of Middleton's idyllic white motherhood. This specific scenario, as well as others throughout Markle's career in the royal family, illustrate how her image was not congruent with the royal family's image of a model white family for the U.K. Moreover, the royal family *never* attempted to protect her from the media or make space for a vocal Black woman within their family and institution.

Another prime example of the royal family's image clashing with Markle's presence was in 2017, before her marriage to Prince Harry. At a Christmas luncheon that December, Princess Michael of Kent wore a brooch that consists of a small bust of a Black man. Called a Blackamoor figure, such items are derogatory, exoticized portrayals of African men that were popular in the seventeenth and eighteenth centuries. This particular brooch had been worn many times before. Princess Michael is a daughter of a major who served in the Nazi SS and a cousin to the late Queen Elizabeth II.[6] Meghan Markle was in attendance at the luncheon, as the only family member of color. Afua Hirsch, an accomplished journalist and author of the book *Brit(ish)*, appears in Markle and Prince Harry's Netflix documentary to discuss this incident. Hirsch, who is Black, notes that she was not surprised when the news broke, saying that "if you go into a palace or a stately home or anywhere that represents tradition, you are likely to be faced with racist imagery."[7] Here Markle was, at a party with her soon-to-be-in-laws, and she was faced with this brooch. Markle was set to join this institution that was built on the backs of enslaved people. Her marriage forever bound her to the royal family, but she would never uphold the white supremacist image the royal family seeks to perpetuate. What is critical to understand about this situation is that Markle's presence is what made the story newsworthy. Conservative outlets wrote headlines that criticized the "woke" Left for getting up in arms over a brooch. Left-leaning publications wrote articles critiquing the princess's choice to wear a racist piece of jewelry. Without Markle, it is doubtful anyone would be having a conversation about racist imagery in traditional British decor or jewelry. Furthermore, they would not be discussing how the monarchy protects thousands of racist artifacts among their numerous properties, which they would not own if not for their inherited wealth from slave labor.

After Markle's marriage to Harry, she became a full-fledged royal family member, but her presence continued to generate stories similar to the brooch incident. In an article titled "Unsettling Ways of Exile," Eddie Tay provides a framework to help understand an exile who is both a citizen and noncitizen. Tay echoes Said when he points out that "we cannot help but realise that the boundaries that affirm . . . national identity [have] the effect of privileging a particular group . . . at the expense of others."[8] Tay is describing someone like Markle, who finds themselves at a crossroads of belonging and a feeling of being pushed aside by the barriers of a national identity. Tay discusses Homi Bhabha's "notion of the 'unhomely' [as] a function of . . . exile. To be 'unhomely' . . . is to be caught in 'the condition of extra-territorial and cross-cultural initiations [where] . . . the borders between home and the world become confused.'"[9] This term, "unhomely," I feel aptly describes Markle during her time as a working royal. She was at home, living with her husband, and raising their son, Archie; however, she was systematically dehumanized by the British press for subverting the image they had of the monarchy.

Markle was treated horribly by the British media because she is a Black woman. No matter how Markle behaved, it is likely she would have been treated unfairly. Unlike the many articles that suggest she had abandoned herself for a prince, she was never silent. She could not and would not support the discretion that the monarchy loves. In an early 2018 panel (before the wedding) with Prince William, Duchess Catherine, and Prince Harry,

Markle supported the Me Too and the Time's Up movements. *Vanity Fair* noted the "Avengers, assemble!" vibe of the panel, but pointed out that Meghan's activist rhetoric stood in contrast to the participation of her fiancé and future in-laws.[10] Unlike the straightforward *Vanity Fair* article, many British tabloids like the *Daily Mail* published articles critiquing the future duchess for speaking out on issues deemed "too political" by royal family standards.

Besides this panel, there are countless examples of Markle speaking eloquently about basic human rights issues and supporting fellow women of color, only to be chastised by the British press. Unfortunately, even when she was doing nothing, the British media decided to publish dozens of stories critiquing her. Hirsch writes in defense of the duchess for *The Guardian*, "racism is a lucrative business. When it comes to Meghan Markle, the media's strategy is transparent. Tabloids pillory her with a range of mostly ludicrous allegations—her baby bump is too prominent, her avocados are not 'woke,' her earrings are 'drenched in blood.'"[11] Hirsch points out how Markle is seen as threatening by the predominantly white British press: "It's also not without context because—as numerous black women have attested of their experiences in white spaces—we are frequently perceived as threatening."[12] Markle, as a working royal, was not in a typical white space. She was in the white space that defines British nationalism; thus, whatever "threat" she posed was to the nation as a whole.

## They Thought She Would Be Quiet

Whether it was attending a party also attended by the daughter of a Nazi wearing a racist brooch, holding her baby bump, or speaking in support of Me Too, Markle's life was making waves in the British media. Her visibility as a Black woman in a white space, as well as how she used her voice to illuminate issues normally not spoken about by the royal family, posed a threat to the status quo. The famous bell hooks book *Talking Back: Thinking Feminist, Thinking Black* specifically discusses the concept of talking back. She writes, "Surely, the absence of a humane critical response has tremendous impact on the writer from any oppressed, colonized group who endeavors to speak. For us, true speaking is not solely an expression of creative power; it is an act of resistance, a political gesture that challenges politics of domination that would render us nameless and voiceless. As such, it is a courageous act—as such, it represents a threat. To those who wield oppressive power, that which is threatening must necessarily be wiped out, annihilated, silenced."[13] Applying hooks's framing, Markle needed to be silenced by the British press and the royal family so that they could maintain their power based on their white supremacy. Not adhering to the model of what the royal family wants to define as the British national identity exiled Markle from the country and the protection she deserved from the royal institution.

Another layer to Markle's image in the press and within the royal family is that she is mixed. A framing that might be helpful to understand how Meghan is viewed is that of the tragic mixed girl. The most famous example of this stereotype is the 1934 film *Imitation of Life*, a movie about a white-passing woman named Peola, whose mother is Black. Peola wants to marry a white man, and in order to fully join white society, she rejects her Black mother, who then dies of a broken heart.[14] Audiences reacted in several ways. "Audiences, black and white (and they were separate), hated what Peola did to her mother—and they hated Peola. She is often portrayed as the epitome of selfishness."[15] For white audiences, Peola was selfish because she did not respect the boundaries of white society. In other words, Peola didn't know her place. White audiences responded well to Peola's mother because she was the stereotypical mammy character who understood her position. There are many parallels between the white public's reaction to this character and their reaction to Meghan Markle. Markle is portrayed as calculating, conniving, and striving for money and power. Her estrangement from her father, a white man, is written as if Markle is entirely to blame. The white public and press express a sense of betrayal that Markle has joined the highest social rung in white society and has not abandoned her Blackness in the process.

It is no secret that Markle struggled immensely during her time as a working royal. In her article for *The Guardian*, Hirsch notes that the media "relentlessly bullied Meghan, including most intensely during two periods when she has been pregnant."[16] Shortly after having her first child, Markle filmed a now-famous interview for ITV that aired in October of 2019. The interview is as emotionally raw as it is understated, Markle nobly sharing that the pressures of being a new mom, new wife, and new royal have been challenging. Most importantly, Markle admits that she "hasn't been OK."[17] Watching that ITV interview, one cannot help but get the sense that Markle's life was deeply isolating. Said writes on the emotional toll of exile, "Nationalisms are about groups, but in a very acute sense exile is a solitude experienced outside the group: the deprivations felt at not being with others in the communal habitation."[18] Exile, at its core, is about separation, the separation from place, people, and community. The royal family never protected her from the media, which was well within their power to do, because she did not fit into their national mold. She had sacrificed so much to be a part of Prince Harry's family and country, and in return she was bullied and exiled.

## On Her Own: Meghan's Departure from Royal Life

Markle graduated from Northwestern University, where she studied international relations and theater. She has a warm, loving relationship with her mother, Doria, and had a successful career on the TV show *Suits*. Before her marriage to Prince Harry, Markle worked with the United Nations to promote women's rights. Not to mention, she is absolutely beautiful. Any logical family would jump for joy if someone like Markle was marrying their son. As was just outlined, however, the royal family was nothing short of hostile toward Markle, and the attacks the couple suffered culminated in Prince Harry and Markle leaving the U.K. in 2020 and announcing in February 2021 that they would be formally ending their time as working royals.[19] Does this move mean Markle was exiled again? Forced to flee her unhomely home in the U.K.? Or was she banished?

Banishment is typically a punishment, falling within the more punitive aspect of exile. The word "banish" can conjure images of fairy tales or medieval Europe, the scorned villain skulking into the dark forest. However, banishments occur regularly in the modern-day U.S. In Georgia and Mississippi, judges frequently add conditions to sentences, banishing someone from a certain town or county within their state. The decision to banish someone is not made lightly; as journalist Briana McGinnis puts it, "more even than other forms of punishment, [banishment] is fundamentally political. It controls community membership and reinforces existing ideas about what kind of a person is or is not eligible to belong to a given polity."[20] This is the same dynamic between nationalism and exile, the power to decide the image of a nation and who is excluded from that image.

Banishment has also been used to punish interracial couples. The Lovings, an interracial couple who fought for marriage rights in the U.S., were forced to leave the state of Virginia for twenty-five years or risk imprisonment because their marriage was considered illegal.[21] If the Lovings could be criminally charged and banished due to their marriage in 1959, could Markle and Prince Harry be banished in 2021 for theirs? These marriages symbolize a violation of the national identity of both the U.S. and the U.K. and therefore are a threat to power. However, Markle and Prince Harry do not perfectly fit the image of banishment. Neither committed a crime or spoke outwardly against the monarchy or the royal family. In fact, in their Netflix documentary the couple speak of their affection for the queen and her life's work protecting the Commonwealth. Moreover, they were definitely not content with their situation in the U.K.; someone who is banished is likely very unhappy to be forbidden from their home. That said, the reported ill will between the Sussexes and the royal family suggests that the royal family has apologized or is hoping for their return.

If we are to entertain the idea that Markle is an exile in 2026 then we must also consider the other possibility: that Prince Harry and Markle fled the royal family. We are in an age where mass exoduses are occurring all over the planet, due to economic insecurity, conflicts, and climate change. Returning to the example of the U.S., there has been a trend some sociologists are calling the "Big Sort." This is the phenomenon of people moving to zip codes that reflect their political views more than their previous area. The COVID-19 pandemic was a particular motivator for many families, who sought a new home based on whether their existing town or city had a vaccine and mask mandate. For one family, the Wootens, who moved from deeply conservative Indiana to Austin, Texas, a famously blue city in a red state, the move was prompted by much more than COVID. Tiffany Wooten told NPR that she fell out with conservative members of her family in Indiana over political disagreements and that the family felt increasingly "out of place" as Democrats. Her son, Cole, called his Indiana high school "a really threatening atmosphere" due to fervent Trumpism on campus. NPR reported that the family "discovered someone had put broken glass in their mailbox."[22] The Wootens are certainly not exiles in their adoptive city of Austin, where they enjoy life among people who share their values. It could be argued, however, that they are exiles *from* their hometown in Indiana, where it is clear the community was not hospitable. In other words, returning to Indiana might be out of the cards for the Wootens. Markle, like the Wootens, was living in a deeply threatening atmosphere in the U.K., so flight does seem like a motivator for her potential exile in the U.S.

Markle has returned to the U.K. twice since moving to California with her family, once for Queen Elizabeth II's jubilee and once for her funeral. In May 2023, she did not attend King Charles III's coronation with her husband, and if the couple were to decide to move back to the U.K., it would definitely not be to their previous home at Frogmore Cottage. The BBC reported that Prince Harry and Markle were "told to leave the [Frogmore] property by Buckingham Palace in January [2023], days after Harry published his explosive memoir, *Spare*."[23] (In a somewhat shocking turn of events, the palace reportedly offered the house to Prince Andrew, who "stepped down as a working royal in 2019 after a controversial Newsnight interview about allegations that he had sexually assaulted Virginia Giuffre,"[24] though Charles ultimately sent him to a privately owned estate outside Windsor.) These actions send the same message as the glass in the Wooten's mailbox: You are not welcome here. If the couple did want to return to the U.K., they could certainly do so. They have the connections and the financial means, but they choose not to.

Markle now lives in a gorgeous Santa Barbara mansion with her loving husband and two beautiful children in her home state of California. Markle took her family to a place where they were safe, and removed them from the obligation to the royal family and the British public. It is impossible to know the emotional roller coaster that those months must have been for Markle, but we may glean something through Said's words. "The pathos of exile is in the loss of contact with the solidity and the satisfaction of earth: homecoming is out of the question," Said writes of a character, Conrad, who is doomed to be obsessed with his exile, forever longing for his home and who tried but failed to build a new one.[25]

Markle does not fit this mold; she did find her homecoming in California and has built a life for herself. She has made successful business deals with Netflix and Spotify, making a podcast called *Archetypes* (2022–23), in which she discussed feminist issues with powerful women like Serena Williams. Markle is creating her own image of a family in the U.S., under her own control. She does not have to assimilate into the idea that the royal family has created, placating the British press. She can tell her own story. Of course, Markle does not fit the American nationalist image of the perfect white mother; there are still incredible amounts of anti-Blackness in this country. However, she is making her own picture of the American mother on the (inter)national stage, an attempt to create a more inclusive nationalism.

## The Implications of the End to Markle's Exile

Markle freed herself from exile, but this is not a textbook happy ending where all the loose ends are carefully tucked away. Let us return to Said's words, "exile originated in the age-old practice of banishment. Once banished, the exile lives an anomalous and miserable life, with the stigma of being an outsider."[26] We have already established that Markle was not banished, and although it is impossible to know what Markle is feeling behind closed doors, her life does not appear to be miserable. Markle has claimed her right to share her story as a Black member of the royal family. She took the right to raise her children away from the environment that scarred her husband. A Black woman protecting her mental health, her family, and her peace has clearly caused turbulence in the royal family and the British press, and it is important to understand why.

If one removes the context of the Sussexes being royal, Markle and Prince Harry's choice to leave seems like the most logical thing to do to protect the mental and physical health of their family. They are royal, however, which means that their rejection of their duties is also a rejection of their role in shaping the British national identity. On the royal family's website, there is a page for every member of the family. Prince Harry and Markle are at the very bottom of the page. At the time of this writing, The Sussexes' page reads, "the Duchess will continue to support a number of charitable causes and organizations which reflect the issues with which she has long been associated including the arts, access to education, support for women and animal welfare."[27] In contrast, Prince William is described by his many royal duties, including the support of organizations "which reflect his interest in their work, *their importance to the nation*, and issues he wishes to support" (emphasis mine).[28] Following the announcement of Markle's and Prince Harry's engagement and their wedding, dozens of news outlets declared that Markle was a "modern" princess, a clear reference to her race and what she could possibly mean for the longevity of the monarchy. Markle was, for a time, seen as an asset to the crown because she could align the royal family's image with the real Britain. Markle's leaving symbolizes how the royal family is inhospitable to Black people, and therefore, how U.K. nationalism is as well.

Many commentators have noted that it is ironic that the royal family pushed away what could have been their only chance at survival. Of course, it is in the interest of the royal family to continue collecting money from the British public and retain their status as royal. This family and the political structures that keep them afloat, however, are based on the legacy of white supremacy and slavery. It is antithetical to their existence to be antiracist; therefore, they wanted Markle to support their family without being too Black for their comfort. Again, we return to bell hooks, who characterizes assimilation as

> the strategy that has provided social legitimation for this shift in allegiance [toward white supremacy]. It is a strategy deeply rooted in the ideology of white supremacy and its advocates urge black people to negate blackness, to imitate racist white people so as to better absorb their values, their way of life. Ironically, many changes in social policy and social attitudes that were once seen as ways to end racial domination have served to reinforce and perpetuate white supremacy. This is especially true of social policy that has encouraged and promoted racial integration.[29]

Markle never assimilated. She never distanced herself from her Blackness or the antiracist causes she supported before becoming royal. Since leaving the royal family, she has spoken out in support of Black Lives Matter and against police brutality. In late 2022, she accepted an NAACP award in the most stunning blue dress designed by the Black designer Christopher John Rogers. *Vogue* reported on more than the duchess's fashion, writing that "in a short acceptance speech, the Duchess solidified the couple's commitment to racial justice and voter rights—'It's inspiring to think about the legacy surrounding the Image Awards, which began shortly after the Civil Rights Act of 1964 and Voting Rights Act of 1965 were passed into law,' she said. 'Today, we can continue that legacy by re-establishing federal voting protections in our country.'" Together with the duke, she also expressed their solidarity with the people of Ukraine and then reflected on the powerful memory of George Floyd.[30] By using her voice as an American Black woman to speak on salient issues, Markle is stepping back fully into her identity. No longer silenced, exiled, and bullied by the British press and the royal family, she has managed to begin creating her own image without their input. With every speech like this, she illustrates how unwelcome she was in the royal family. She is a living example of the racial reckoning that needs to happen in the U.K., which makes the royal family deeply uncomfortable.

After their departure from the U.K., Markle aligned herself with powerful Black people in Hollywood. Of course, Tyler Perry saved the Sussexes in early 2021 when he allowed them to stay at his home, but it was Prince Harry and Markle's choice to put him in the 2022 documentary and make him Lilibet's godfather. Selecting Oprah for their shocking 2021 interview was an explicit choice. After being exiled within the white institution of the royal family, Markle created her own coalition of powerful Black people who support her. This sends a clear message to the royal family: I am not alone anymore and the Black community is standing behind me.

## Conclusion

Unlike the other cases of exile I have written about, Markle's world was one I am completely unacquainted with on a personal level. I have spent no time with the duchess, unless you count the TV screen, and have only spent two days in London, en route to another destination. Despite this, I can see the same unbelievable strength and resilience in her that I have known firsthand in other exiles. Meghan Markle is a role model for young girls and women everywhere. She was isolated but she found her way back to love and family. Just like her Disney forebears, she is a true princess.

### Notes

1. Said, "Reflections on Exile," 173, 181.
2. Said, "Reflections on Exile," 174.
3. Said, "Reflections on Exile," 176.
4. Said, "Reflections on Exile," 176.
5. "The Role of the Monarchy," official website of the British royal family, Royal Household, accessed December 19, 2025, https://www.royal.uk/role-monarchy.
6. *BBC*, "Princess Michael of Kent Sorry."
7. Garbus and Sashin, *Harry & Meghan*, 3.
8. Tay, "Unsettling Ways of Exile."
9. Tay, "Unsettling Ways of Exile."
10. Duboff, "Meghan Markle Speaks Out in Support of #MeToo and Time's Up."
11. Devine, "Fans Are Claiming Meghan Markle's Baby Bump Is Bigger Than Six Months"; Read, "Meghan Markle's Beloved Avocado Linked to Human Rights Abuse"; Duell and English, "Revealed: Meghan's £500,000 Diamond Earrings"
12. Hirsch, "For Meghan Markle, Leaving Britain Must Seem . . . Like the Right Choice."
13. hooks, *Talking Back*, PAGE NUMBER.
14. Stahl, *Imitation of Life*.
15. "The Tragic Mulatto Myth," Jim Crow Museum, accessed December 19, 2025, https://jimcrowmuseum.ferris.edu/mulatto/homepage.htm.

16. Hirsch, "For Meghan Markle."
17. *ITV News*, "Meghan Says 'Not Many People Have Asked if I'm OK.'"
18. Said, "Reflections on Exile," 177.
19. Lawless and Pylas, "Harry and Meghan Won't Return."
20. McGinnis, "Analysis: This Is Shy Some U.S. Judges Banish Convicts."
21. McGinnis, "Analysis."
22. Burnett, "The 'Big Sort,' Again."
23. *BBC*, "Harry and Meghan Residence Frogmore Cottage Offered to Andrew."
24. *BBC*, "Harry and Meghan Residence Frogmore Cottage Offered to Andrew."
25. Said, "Reflections on Exile," 179.
26. Said, "Reflections on Exile," 181.
27. "About the Duchess of Sussex," the Royal Family, n.d., https://www.royal.uk/the-duchess-of-sussex. At the time of publication, the language quoted here no longer appears on the duchess's About page; most of the details of their charitable work have been removed from the royal family page and instead redirect readers to https://sussex.com/.
28. "The Prince of Wales," the Royal Family, n.d., https://www.royal.uk/the-prince-of-wales. At the time of publication, the language quoted here has been amended slightly.
29. hooks, *Talking Back*, PAGE NUMBER.
30. Taylor, "Meghan Markle Accepts NAACP Award."

## Works Referenced

*BBC*. "Harry and Meghan Residence Frogmore Cottage Offered to Andrew—Reports." March 1, 2023. https://www.bbc.com/news/uk-64812549.

*BBC*. "Prince Harry and Meghan: Where Do They Get Their Money?" December 8, 2022. https://www.bbc.com/news/explainers-51047186.

*BBC*. "Princess Michael of Kent Sorry for Wearing 'Racist' Brooch." December 23, 2017. https://www.bbc.com/news/uk-42462724.

Burnett, John. "The 'Big Sort,' Again: Americans Are Moving for Political Alignment." *NPR*, February 18, 2022. https://www.npr.org/2022/02/18/1081295373/the-big-sort-americans-move-to-areas-political-alignment.

Devine, Lucy. "Fans Are Claiming Meghan Markle's Baby Bump Is Bigger Than Six Months but Celebs from Kim Kardashian to Pippa Middleton Prove Even A-List Babies Come in All Shapes and Sizes." *The Sun*,

January 18, 2019. https://www.thesun.co.uk/fabulous/8217231/meghan-markle-baby-bump-more-than-ssix-months-other-celebrities/.

Duboff, Josh. "Meghan Markle Speaks Out in Support of #MeToo and Time's Up in First Official Appearance with William, Kate, and Harry." *Vanity Fair*, February 28, 2018. https://www.vanityfair.com/style/2018/02/meghan-markle-metoo-times-up-harry-william-kate-royal-foundation.

Duell, Mark, and Rebecca English. "Revealed: Meghan's £500,000 Diamond Earrings Were NOT Borrowed, but a 'Wedding Gift from Saudi Crown Prince'—and Worn by Duchess Three Weeks After He Approved the Assassination of Jamal Khashoggi in Consulate." *Daily Mail*, March 11, 2021. https://www.dailymail.co.uk/news/article-9320065/Meghan-Markles-earrings-wedding-gift-Saudi-Crown-Prince.html.

Garbus, Liz, and Erica Sashin, dirs. *Harry & Meghan*. Aired December 2022 on Netflix. https://www.netflix.com/watch/81478159.

Hirsch, Afua. "For Meghan Markle, Leaving Britain Must Seem More and More Like the Right Choice." *The Guardian*, March 5, 2021. https://www.theguardian.com/commentisfree/2021/mar/05/meghan-britain-duchess-of-sussex-media-palace.

hooks, bell. *Talking Back: Thinking Feminist, Thinking Black*. 2nd ed. New York: Routledge, 2015.

*ITV News*. "Meghan Says 'Not Many People Have Asked if I'm OK' amid Intense Media Spotlight | ITV News." October 18, 2019. YouTube video, 2:26. https://www.youtube.com/watch?v=Zo9G91QWMQs.

Lawless, Jill, and Pan Pylas. "Harry and Meghan Won't Return as Working Royals." *PBS*, February 19, 2018. https://www.pbs.org/newshour/world/harry-and-meghan-wont-return-as-working-royals.

McGinnis, Briana. "Analysis: This Is Why Some U.S. Judges Banish Convicts from Their Home Communities." *Washington Post*, March 16, 2017. https://www.washingtonpost.com/news/monkey-cage/wp/2017/03/16/this-is-why-some-u-s-judges-banish-convicts-from-their-home-communities/.

Read, Carly. "Meghan Markle's Beloved Avocado Linked to Human Rights Abuse and Drought, Millennial shame." *Express*, January 23, 2019. https://www.express.co.uk/news/world/1076626/meghan-markle-news-avocado-toast-vegan-instagram.

Said, Edward. "Reflections on Exile." In *Reflections on Exile & Other Literary and Cultural Essays*, 173–86. London: Granta Publications, 2000.

Stahl, John M., dir. *Imitation of Life*. Los Angeles: Universal Pictures, 1934.

Tay, Eddie. "Unsettling Ways of Exile." *Quarterly Literary Review Singapore* 1, no. 1 (2001). http://www.qlrs.com/issues/oct2001/essays/uwoe.html.
Taylor, Elise. "Meghan Markle Accepts NAACP Award in Christopher John Rogers." *Vogue*, February 26, 2022. https://www.vogue.com/article/meghan-markle-accepts-naacp-award-in-christopher-john-rogers.

CHAPTER 10

# BLACK MAMMY SAVIOR, UPPITY BLACK WOMAN, OR SUBJUGATED SISTER-IN-LAW

## *Hyper-Partisan Media Treatment of Meghan Markle Reinvigorates Outdated Racial, Monarchical, and Colonial Beliefs*

ELWOOD WATSON

It didn't take long for the right-wing media in the United States and in the United Kingdom to gin up their propaganda/outrage machine toward Meghan Markle, Duchess of Sussex. As it became increasingly likely Ms. Markle's relationship with Prince Harry was serious, and her entry into the British royal family imminent, vitriolic descriptors and tabloid titles began pervading the media: "unreasonable," "entitled," "uppity,"[1] "spoiled," "Liar! Fake Outrage," "Fights, Camera, Action," "Megxile," "So Who Is The Royal Racist?"[2] and so on. Tucker Carlson, Ben Shapiro, Charlie Kirk, Tomi Lahren, and other right-wing darlings eagerly weighed in on the drama surrounding the American biracial woman's marriage into the British royal family.[3] Perennial Meghan Markle antagonist and fierce critic Piers Morgan literally stomped off of the set and quit his own program, *Good Morning Britain*, when faced with criticism of one of many problematic accusations: his insinuations that Ms. Markle is a liar and that her claims, in the infamous 2021 Oprah Winfrey interview, of problematic racism directed at her from the royal family and the monarchy as an institution were lies.[4] It was a meltdown of epic proportions for all to see, revealing his deep emotional investment in using his platform against her. Later, U.K. academic, activist, and author Kehinde Andrews recounted a May 2018 debate on *Good Morning Britain* where he disagreed with Afua Hirsch as to whether the Sussexes' royal wedding signaled British progress (Hirsch felt hopeful; Andrews referred to it as "nothing more than a dream"), with Morgan retaliating by referring to Andrews as a "party pooper."[5]

Taking a step back: Two years prior to Morgan's meltdown, we look to 2019, as British columnist Celia Walden, wife of Morgan, insisted that as a member of the royal family (which she referred to as "that corporation") Ms. Markle had no right to privacy.[6] However, right around British Mother's Day in 2024, as press chattered about the manipulation of Kate Middleton's Mother's Day family photo, Walden became a fierce advocate for Middleton's privacy. "The Shameful Speculation About the Princess of Wales's Health," her article headline reads, "Has to Stop."[7] Well now, apparently, what's good for the goose is not good for the gander! Talk about a naked degree of hypocrisy!

To her online and various media detractors, when Ms. Markle became a member of the royal family, she entered political, social, and cultural territory that was supposedly "forbidden" to her and people like her. By their targeted commentary, language, and arguments, their rancidly bigoted minds clearly and unmistakably lamented, "How dare a Black woman, even a biracial one, become part of the one of the most distinguished Anglo-Saxon institutions in history?!" The ultra-right-wing press and hyper-partisan media continue to see even a drop of Black blood as "wholly distinct from whiteness [and] a legacy of the 'one drop rule.'"[8]

Furthermore, in their insistence in portraying her as a "Black woman," ultra-right-wing personalities and commentators sustain and continue a long history of "intersectional failure" as defined by Kimberlé Crenshaw. Crenshaw's use of intersectional failure explains one inequality offset by another: in Markle's case, working against her as both a woman and a "Black" person.[9] It can be further argued that Markle experiences a third thread of intersectional failure, in that she is American. Because she is a U.S. citizen, the press can also "treat her Blackness as a foreign body, drawing on well worked media tropes from the U.S., and ignoring U.K. experiences of racism and being Black."[10] In emphasizing this narrative, media personalities and other members of the press take away the potential power she may have possessed as a symbol for positive change and progress within the institution of the monarchy or society at large. Media commentary in the U.K. uses her U.S. origin to balance and justify their racist discourse while also masking the nation's terribly problematic racist history in their own colonial endeavors. As Markle herself states in her interview with Oprah Winfrey,

> It wasn't until Harry and I were together that we started to travel through the Commonwealth, I would say 60 percent, 70 percent of which is people of color . . . even grown women and men who, when I would meet them in our time in the Commonwealth, how much it meant to them to be able to see someone who looks like them . . . in this position. And I could never understand how it wouldn't be seen as an added benefit . . . and a reflection of the world today. At all times, but especially right now, to go—"how inclusive is that, that you can see someone who looks like you in this family, much less one [Archie] who's born into it?"[11]

Markle hits on the issue here, pointing out "how much it meant to them to be able to see someone who looks like them . . . in this position." Unfortunately, she fails to connect that idealistic and inspirational hope to its problematic potential for the monarchy—and the colonial U.K. as a whole—should the visual lines of their status be blurred by the fact that "someone who looks like them" could in fact rise to that status. (I want to note here that when I refer to the "monarchy" I mean the royal family, as well as their staff and advisors, often referred to as the Firm).

That ideal in visual likeness based on skin color Markle refers to could open an entire can of worms around reparation and reconciliation that would be catastrophic to deeply ingrained colonial social, cultural, and even economic systems in the U.K. Thus, to maintain that divisive—and, for many comfortable white citizens and organizations, nostalgic—status quo based on skin color, she must be symbolized and subjugated as a villain. Enter again the popular press.

In essence, as right-wing media personalities and publications utilize their platforms, they manipulate their audience to assume that Markle has "poisoned" and permanently soiled the monarchy. As Jonathan Ward explains in "Markle & Motherhood: Making Black Motherhood (In)Visible: The Importance of Race, Gender, and Nation in the Mediation of Meghan Markle on Instagram," Markle can serve one of two symbolic representations within the British royal family and the monarchy as an institution. We've seen this consistently play out in the tabloids and other news media in the U.S. and in the U.K. She is either "the Black woman who represents a threat to the racial purity of the British royal family (and thus the nation)," especially when she demonstrates her own individuality and power, or, as Ward suggests, her "production of a new royal offspring"—but only if placed in the control of Prince Harry and the monarchy—represents racialized ownership, once again diminishing Markle's potential as a symbol for progress.[12]

What makes Meghan Markle an especially pivotal study in the media's role in maintaining status quo by—even implicitly, although as we've seen play out, not so subtly—perpetuating racist mentality and other antiquated beliefs is the fact that she was already a celebrity coming into her relationship with Prince Harry and the royal family. As M. P. Marks and Z. M. Fischer note in "The King's New Bodies: Simulating Consent in the Age of Celebrity," "The investiture of authority in celebrities represents a continuation of the trend by which social bodies operate as the site where relations of power are played out, and by which the media serve as a means in which real democracy has been replaced by a simulated one." We can apply this sentiment to the media's treatment of Markle, as Marks and Fischer elaborate: "Society is incorporating a new language that deploys celebrities as chief vehicles for the simulation of political consent, thereby overcoming public apathy, and buttressing the existing political order."[13] Where have we seen this celebrity power relation simulation and excitability play out recently and so overtly that it's literally thrown in our face? The answer: President Trump's MAGA campaign and the retroactive progress it sparked and amplified, not only in terms of race but also other problematic outcomes.

This trend toward new celebrity simulation driving political consent also jumped across the pond to the land of the British monarchy. In "The Post-racial Princess: Delusions of Racial Progress and Intersectional Failures," Kehinde Andrews draws the connection between the MAGA campaign and the Brexit movement in their "political moment [as] an urge to reclaim a past" that includes a "Whiter nation."[14] Marks and Fischer further explain this phenomenon: "In recent years, the figurative face of politics in America often quite literally has become the face of a celebrity. This trend finds citizens in democratic society willing to yield up their political consciousness to media-created celebrities."[15] Placing this lens back on Markle, her celebrity, and the media's unrelenting obsession with her skin color and relationship to the royal family, it is understandable that the press caused a regression in progressive political consciousness that is clear to see when they focused so negatively on her race.

## Know Your Place: Media and Power Retention, a Nostalgic Return to an Outdated Status Quo

Before drawing in more closely on how the media's portrayals of the relationship between Meghan Markle and Catherine (Kate) Middleton punctuate their propagation of racist and colonialist attitudes, it's important to first examine the media's role in power relation and status quo normalization. To start, as racists see it and the far-right media continuously announce it, Markle is wealthy and privileged. Thus, she should have been "grateful," "appreciative," and "thankful" and should "count her blessings." After all, she inhabited a position and status that, indeed, many white women would have been eager and satisfied to have. Moreover, given the fact that she is a non-British, nonwhite woman, (biracial, but still Black in the eyes of many of her critics), she should possess and express an unalloyed feeling of gratitude for finding herself in such a situation. This largely anti-Markle group used (and still use)[16] their platforms to announce their expectations and spread their influence to others by declaring that Markle should engage in unadulterated mea culpas of thankfulness to Buckingham Palace and the larger British society, and she should definitely stop making those, in their estimation, "baseless and unfounded" charges of racism and racial nonsense. In essence, they felt, and still feel today, that Meghan Markle, Duchess of Sussex, should stay in her lane, know her place, and shut up.

In his 2013 book, *The Hybrid Media System: Politics and Power*, Andrew Chadwick discusses the political media's relationship to power and society, describing the "hybrid media" as "bundles of cultural, social, economic, and political practices" that create political, social, and media norms made up of journalists, politicians, activists, and others.[17] Furthermore, Chadwick argues that the new hybrid digital media era has blurred the lines between traditional and new media, thus allowing journalists, politicians, bloggers, and other media personalities to leverage their platforms in order to control information in the pursuit of power, which in turn flows into public influence, opinion, and attitudes. So, when someone like Brian Kilmeade uses his platform to argue against Markle's claims of racism in the monarchy, claiming instead that they cannot be racist thanks to "diversity" in the commonwealth, he (and the producers at Fox) absolutely influence public opinion in an attempt to sweep racist action and mentality under the rug.[18] They're working to maintain the status quo that white Americans and Britons are comfortable with and have benefited from for centuries.

The fact is that hyper-partisan news media—and, I would argue, those uncritically consuming it—undoubtedly factor into "the construction of mixed-race identity" in their development, dissemination, and perpetuation of racial narratives, thus shaping public opinion and attitudes.[19] Consider the obsession with race purposely woven into just a few U.K. tabloid headlines: "Harry's Girl Is (Almost) Straight Outta Compton: Gang-Scarred Home of Her Mother Revealed—so Will He Be Dropping By for Tea?"; "Now That's Upwardly Mobile! How in 150 years, Meghan Markle's Family Went from Cotton Slaves to Royalty via Freedom in the U.S. Civil War"; or "Prince Harry and Meghan Markle: The Royal Love Affair with Africa."[20] These types of tabloid stories and other media portrayals of Markle that so intently focus on racial biology disseminate implicit and explicit messages related to her race.[21] They negate her ability to define her identity on her own and they demolish the symbolic power she could have in the pursuit of racial progress.

It is important to note that Markle's unprecedented entry as a biracial woman into the royal family coincided with the rapid and incredible progress of new media, particularly in the digital realm. As Isabel Balteiro discusses in "From Kisstory to Megxile: Tabloids as Lexical Trendsetters," racism has been reignited and energized by digital media, as critical research has exhibited.[22] No longer are journalists the "gatekeepers" and broadcasters of unbiased facts. Rather, social media platforms have blurred the lines of integrity between what is the truth and what is completely made up. This development has allowed communications outlets to be used to deceive digital media consumers while promoting racism, a tactic coined as "platformed racism," which Farkas and Neumayer credit Ariadna Matamoros-Fernández for introducing. He explains it as the "amplification of racist discourses on digital platforms at the intersection of user practices, algorithms, interfaces, policies, and business models."[23] In that respect, digital media platforms can be rampant with dangerous messaging, confusing the consumer about what is fake, normal, pertinent, true, and/or outright trolling. In this way, the media has spent years legitimizing utterly inappropriate racist behavior when it comes to their attacks on Markle, ultimately functioning to influence readers to interpret their attitudes and behaviors as acceptable.

Again, it must be stressed that in their mission to reignite and reenergize racist attitudes and action, hyper-partisan media and news outlets strategically use intentional tactics to influence their audiences. This behavior could not be more obvious than if we look at all the racial stereotypes permeating headlines and content that focus on the Black portion of Ms. Markle's ancestry.[24] Clearly, these actors of the far-right wing press are employing stereotypes and negative Black-associated tropes to deflect from reality and disguise their objective to perpetuate racist beliefs and actions.[25]

In using these racial stereotypes, news and other media outlets attract great attention thanks to their "often simplified, speculative, negative, and provocative" nature, which then spreads like wildfire via social media. Farkas and Neumayer further explain the power within this function, stating, "Professional news media can amplify and legitimize harmful digital content by increasing its visibility and reach."[26] Sadly, truth is being sacrificed for clickbait, thus giving rise to "fake news" and "junk news."

## "If You Love Her, You Don't Need to Hate Me"

Since Markle's 2017 engagement to Prince Harry, the popular press has positioned Markle and Kate Middleton as each other's nemesis.[27] In Markle's own words in that pivotal Oprah Winfrey interview, "So much of what I have seen play out is this idea of polarity, where if you love me, you don't have to hate [Kate Middleton]. And if you love her, you don't need to hate me," to which Oprah Winfrey replies, "Mm-hmm. You know, there were several stories that compared headlines written about you to those written about Kate."[28] That dichotomy between the two women in the press and hyper-partisan media commentary continues today, despite the Sussexes' exit from the U.K., the monarchy, and the royal family.

Markle tends to be depicted on either one of two polarizing ends of a spectrum: one, more progressive, regal, and enticing; some have even had the nerve to backhandedly use the term "exotic."[29] Or, to the contrary, but just as problematic, bratty, demanding, and sinister—as Ward puts it, "the 'bad Black woman' who is simultaneously tainting the purity of the royal family."[30] Middleton, too, tends to be positioned at one end or the other, but notably, both portrayals are positive. One frames her as more conservative, down-to-earth, and pedestrian, while the other depicts her as royal and maternal. Since their meeting at the beginning of Markle's relationship with Prince Harry, the two women have always been intertwined, rarely seen as independent of each other, but rather contrasted against one another. Thus more recently, it is understandable that despite support from Buckingham Palace and the media in general, Middleton's absence from the public eye in light of medical challenges has tended toward tawdry gossip and scandal as Markle supporters have inquired why the royal family, the monarchy, and the media appeared so eager to grant special privileges—particularly protection within the popular press and tabloid publications—for Middleton that they were unwilling to grant for Markle and Prince Harry. Such a question is certainly fair game.

From the outset of her involvement with Prince Harry, Markle was the target of vicious and racially coded venom, with comments and headlines such as those mentioned earlier. Such acerbic commentary increased considerably once the couple got engaged. Drama broke out as the press published allegedly false stories that Markle drove Middleton to tears in preparation for the wedding, apparently over Princess Charlotte's flower girl dress. According to Markle, the truth in who made whom cry was the opposite, and there were several witnesses. "What was hard to get over was being blamed for something that not only I didn't do but that happened to me," she recounts to Oprah, adding, "and the people who were part of our wedding going to our comms team and saying, 'I know this didn't happen.' I don't have to tell them what actually happened." For months after the wedding, the press ran with the story as Markle's realization became increasingly clear that the monarchy (the family and their staff) who had promised her press protection and guidance were most certainly not protecting her. "Everyone in the institution knew it wasn't true," she explains to Oprah. "I think, a lot of it, that was fed into by the media. And I would hope that [Kate Middleton] would have wanted that corrected, and maybe in the same way that the Palace wouldn't let anybody else."[31] The scrutiny of Markle, particularly in a polar contrast with Middleton, only grew over the course of Markle's pregnancy, and if the inverted story about the flower girl dress tears wasn't enough of a sign of what was to come, this period solidified the dangerous scenario in which the Sussexes were existing. As Markle explains to Oprah, "We talked about when things really started to turn, when I knew we weren't being protected. And it was during that part of my pregnancy, especially, that I started to understand what our continued reality was going to look like. . . . I mean, they would go on the record and negate the most ridiculous story for anyone, right? . . . But the narrative about, you know, making Kate cry, I think was the beginning of a real character assassination. And they knew it wasn't true. And I thought, well, if they're not going to kill things like that, then what are we going to do?"[32] The earlier venomous coverage climaxed when the couple granted that interview to Oprah, during which they revealed all these details that shone a light on the racism, whether conscious or unconscious—because it is so deeply ingrained—that reeked among certain members of the royal family and the monarchical staff. Between the popular press and the monarchy, the abuse amplified, ramping up still more with the Sussexes' exit from the royal family and eventual relocation to California.

After the Oprah interview, most critics and outlets were savvy enough not to refer to Markle as "uppity" (although a Sean Hannity producer had the nerve to do so in early 2020),[33] a word reserved for Black people who anger racist white people by taking them out of their comfort zones. These "uppity types" are the Black folks who upset white bigots by "doing their own thing on their own terms" and, in essence, by signaling such white people to "go to hell!" It's not a stretch to assume some in the right-wing media would have liked to have called her a "n—— bitch," though at least they seemed to understand satisfying the impulse would have resulted in some negative consequences, even in our current climate of overt racial animus. Thus, they resorted to disguising their views underneath Black stereotypes and shady messaging of varying levels—at times disgusting—of explicitness.

In that 2021 Oprah Winfrey interview, millions of people around the world watched in shock, suspense, and stunned silence as Markle and Prince Harry passionately and emotionally detailed the bigotry and decay they endured at the hands of an antiquated monarchical and colonial institution. Indeed, racism and white privilege intersect at the highest realm of the monarchy, and as mentioned earlier, so, too do womanhood and American heritage. Let's not forget the way Wallis Simpson, Duchess of Windsor and an American socialite, was treated going all the way back to the 1930s, along with King Edward VIII's abdication in order to marry her.

Viewers of the interview were titillated, fascinated, and spellbound by what many heard as the demeaning demoralization and dehumanization that Markle and even her husband endured at the hands of "the Firm," all of which was exacerbated by the media's constant abuse. Viewers of the two-hour interview learned that the couple were told their children would not receive the title of prince or princess, and therefore, their right to security detail. According to Markle, "They were saying they didn't want him to be a prince or a princess—not knowing what the gender would be, which would be different from protocol—and that he wasn't going to receive security. . . . But if you're saying the title is what's going to affect their protection, *we haven't created this monster machine around us in terms of clickbait and tabloid fodder.* You've allowed that to happen, which means our son needs to be safe" (emphasis mine).[34] The couple were also interrogated about how dark their child's skin color would be, compounding the security/no title issue, as Markle points out: "The idea of our son not being safe, and also the idea of *the first member of color in this family not being titled in the same way that other grandchildren would be . . .*" (emphasis mine).[35] As they were asked questions seemingly never asked of other members of the royal family, the indignities continued. It was infuriating and heartbreaking to listen to.

What counters the heartbreak in listening to the Sussexes' account of their ordeal is their use of that interview to reclaim their truth and counter the media's treatment of them as subjects to reignite and sustain racial inequality, holding up outdated positions of power and status quo within the monarchy and traditional white British society. The Sussexes' clever use of that interview and Oprah's formidable platform calls up the wise words of bell hooks regarding subjectivity: "As subjects, people have the right to define their own reality, establish their own identities, name their history."[36] I could not agree more.

In an effort to exercise damage control post-interview, Buckingham Palace released a statement on March 9 that same year, with Queen Elizabeth II stating that the family was "saddened to learn the full extent of how challenging the last few years have been for Harry and Meghan." The queen further stated that while the accusations of racism were "concerning," it was possible that "some recollections may vary," implying that the interview was tainted by untruths.[37]

This was the same royal family that sat idly by and allowed (perhaps even aided and abetted, according to some sources) the level of racism directed toward the couple by the popular press and tabloids, which escalated to such a volatile point that the Sussexes felt no choice but to depart the U.K. As much as the royal family attempts to represent themselves as paragons of racial tolerance (critical minds would never accuse them of total acceptance) and receptive to diversity, recent events and Markle's answers to Oprah's questions confirm otherwise. For instance, when Oprah asks her about not taking the traditional royal birth photo with Archie, Markle explains, "We weren't asked to take a picture. That's also part of the spin, that was really damaging. I thought, 'Can you just tell them the truth? Can you say to the world you're not giving him a title, and we want to keep him safe, and that if he's not a prince, then it's not part of the tradition? Just tell people, and then they'll understand?"[38]

As we know, they could not, or more likely, would not. No surprise there. The Sussexes, and most pointedly Markle, are not alone in being figuratively fed to the press hounds by the monarchy. RIP, Princess Diana. In fact, many Markle supporters, notably Prince Harry himself, have made the connection between how the monarchy sacrificed Princess Diana to the press throughout the 1990s until her tragic death and how Markle is treated today and denied. That relationship between the press and the monarchy is central to the messaging filtered out to the public about Markle in order to protect the institution's colonial history. Again, when we discuss the "monarchy," it is important to realize it extends beyond the family to an influential team of advisors and staff. Oprah addresses this in the interview: "So, are you saying you did not feel supported by the powers that be, be that the Firm, the monarchy, all of them?" Meghan confirms, "It's hard for people to distinguish the two because . . . it's a family business, right? So, there's the family, and then there's the people that are running the institution. Those are two separate things."[39]

Then there's the royal rota, a forty-plus-year-old agreement providing "exclusive inside access to the official engagements of members of the Royal Family." Within this agreement, the *Daily Express, Daily Mail, Daily Mirror, Evening Standard, Telegraph, Times,* and *Sun* "will share factual material obtained with other members of their sector who request it," making these publications the principal source for content on the royal family, which they can then farm out to other outlets around the globe.[40] The arrangement controls the flow of information and influence, to the detriment of serious, unbiased traditional journalism.

## It's Still Meghan's Fault: The Instagram Photo Edit Debacle

As reaction to the Oprah interview fizzled out, it was only a matter of time before segments of the right-wing media, both in the U.S. and in the U.K., would reignite their propaganda/outrage machine and target it toward the Duchess of Sussex. Rabid followers of popular culture may have heard that Markle was urged to defend her sister-in-law, Kate Middleton, Princess of Wales, after she found herself at the center of a royal crisis, thanks to an edited family photograph published on Instagram on U.K. Mother's Day.[41] According to *Page Six,* the photo contained "at least 10 failures," which is to say, deliberate signs that the photo had been edited or manipulated.[42]

Middleton posed for the photograph with her three children and then posted the photograph to her own Instagram account. Things turned fast as fans quickly took to social media to point out numerous issues with the photo, such as Middleton's missing wedding ring and a missing part of Princess Charlotte's wrist. In response, several news platforms killed articles that included the edited image. Middleton conceded to altering parts of the "amateur" photo, which was reportedly taken by Prince William and faulted her own inexperience with photo editing, apologizing for the supposed "confusion."[43] Kensington Palace was under immediate pressure to explain which parts of the image were changed, while numerous royal sources declared the controversy as "exceptionally damaging" to the British royal family at a time when public trust in them seems to be constantly in question.[44] The monarchy scrambled to resolve the negative presentation of Middleton while clearly protecting her, which they had so disappointingly failed to do for Markle. Royal sources attempted to explain the manipulated photo as the couple's attempt to share an "informal" family photo with only "minor adjustments" attributed to Middleton. According to *Page Six*, "A Kensington Palace source added, 'The Wales family spent Mother's Day together and had a wonderful day.'"[45]

Also of interest: Now that the obviously favored daughter-in-law, Middleton, had suddenly come under such dissecting scrutiny, various public relations experts, journalists, and crisis managers expected Markle to swoop in, come to the rescue, and act as the Black "Mammy" savior or "BBFF (Black best female friend)" for the white Middleton.[46] In projecting that stereotyped slavery-era savior role expectation onto Markle, the popular press made a deliberate move to juxtapose the two women based on Markle's "Blackness," framing it as inferior to Middleton's elite white status.[47] In the traditional sense of this trope, the press cleverly suggested underneath their literal words that Markle should "[know] her place," a move that serves to maintain the outdated status quo when it comes to race,[48] thus oppressing Markle within the symbol she could potentially have been, and quite literally in real life as she is objectified and dehumanized in the media using the metaphor of the "Black mammy" savior.

While the choice to step in as a "savior" is obviously Markle's to make, she has so far remained mum on the entire sordid episode. Indeed, given her history with the tabloids and the demeaning, demoralizing dehumanization she and her husband endured at the hands of their fellow royals and the popular press, a neutral stance is probably the most sagacious course of action. Perhaps her silence is an ironic resonating retort to the silence she received when she wished so badly that Middleton, or at least a palace representative, would correct the inverted flower girl dress/Kate crying story. Given the major public relations disaster the incident morphed into, British public relations expert Ryan McCormick arrogantly and audaciously called on Markle to come to the aid of her sister-in-law, stating, "If I was advising Meghan, I would tell her to speak loud and passionate [*sic*] in defence of Kate. Meghan may not like being on the brunt of negative press, but she's definitely more familiar with it than Kate. The Duchess could help the Princess of Wales tremendously by guiding her through this crisis publicly and behind the scenes."[49] Meanwhile, an anonymous Sussex-supportive source told *Page Six*, "If Harry and Meghan had ever encountered the same issue, they would have been annihilated. . . . The same rules do not apply to both couples."[50] The truth was spoken here.

## Color Blindness Is Not Progress

Hearing Prince Harry espouse how he never understood or thought much about racism until he married Markle places him firmly into the camp of the vast majority of white people. All too often, they lack understanding, irrespective of gender, socioeconomic status, religion, geographic region, or other cultural determinants. They are frequently unable—and in many cases, unwilling—to understand, let alone recognize, the burdens that people of color experience regardless of their station in life. Thus, even being a member of the royal family does not allow immunity from such mistreatment. As Eve Woldemikael and Olivia Woldemikael explain, various dichotomies have been projected onto people of mixed race over time, using the "tragic mulatta" trope both in fictional characters and in real life. They write, "Representations of mixed Black and white people are often caught between negative depictions as tragic 'race traitors' and optimistic figures who promise color blindness, racial neutrality and racial transcendence."[51]

The false ideal that "color blindness" is an "optimistic" step forward is highly problematic. In fact, Markle's tendency to portray herself as racially ambiguous is most certainly not progressive, whether her performance and portrayal in the press are intentional and permitted by her or not. As Woldemikael and Woldemikael observe, "In Markle's refusal to claim neither whiteness nor Blackness in its entirety, she resides in the tension between her self-definition and an externally imposed racial identity."[52] That external imposition has, of course, been forcefully issued by the right-wing media.

Perhaps, as a biracial woman who identifies as such and toes the line very cautiously between her Blackness and whiteness, Markle was unaware of the fact that both here in America, and in the larger diaspora, she is seen simply as Black, just like Barack Obama, Kamala Harris, Tiger Woods, Bubba Wallace, Maya Rudolph, Halle Berry, and other biracial individuals, no matter the shade of their skin. The specter of racial ambiguity is something that is forfeited.

Moreover, for a woman of color, the impacts of the intersection of race and gender, the U.S. history of which Pauli Murray and Mary Eastwood trace in "Jane Crow and the Law," are all too often commonplace.[53] This bigotry was and is evident in the treatment Markle has endured from her detractors, especially the hyper-partisan media outlets that continue to barrage her and use her as a pawn in their quest for that nostalgic return to an outdated status quo and unequal power relations based on race. This is a critical move on their part to prevent racial progress. As Ward states, "As a light-skinned biracial woman, Markle demonstrates how Black identity can be mitigated—whether by the control of a national institution that works to contain behavior and identity or by cultural codings of her light skin and facial features as not disruptive to Eurocentric expectations or desires."[54] Clearly, far right-wing conservatives are not ready for such a correction, so instead, they maintain the outdated falsehood that race is fixed and comes solely down to simple biology.

## Reclaiming Her Own Reality

While the Black Lives Matter movement signaled progress in the struggle for racial correction in the U.S. (and hopefully in the U.K.), Markle's treatment by the popular press and hyperpartisan media reeks of intentional regression and, as Andrews puts it, "colonial nostalgia [that underpins] contemporary manifestations of racism."[55] The media's fascination, particularly in the U.K., with the Blackness within Markle's biracial lineage can only be explained by one of two scenarios: complete ignorance, or—the one I'd put money on—a strategic effort to maintain, justify, and even revert to, a nostalgic, colonial mentality that has absolutely served an elite, white, and colonial-minded class of people. Furthermore, the Black, female, and American part of her ancestry appears to serve as an excuse to employ Markle as a pawn to suit whichever agenda the media and/or the monarchy prefer at any given moment. As a celebrity symbol in the popular media, she, as Ward states, "allows us to see how she is both invoked to strengthen a narrative of progressive modernity when this benefits the royal family and larger perceptions of British identity, but equally that she is disavowed or effaced when it suits the larger imperial project of solidifying the boundaries of British racial identity."[56]

To her credit, the former actress, now duchess, has refused to buckle under pressure from the royal family, the monarchy as an institution, the scurrilous British tabloids, or the intensely bigoted right-wing American media. As Oprah Winfrey reminds her audience, since Markle's 2018 entry into the royal family, she "became the target of unrelenting, pervasive attacks . . . [with]

undeniable racist overtones" that contradicted any other royal coverage. In addition to the extremely critical force the British tabloids and "internet trolls" rained down on Markle, Oprah points out, Markle was subject to "blatant sexist and racist remarks" that media consumers watched "play out in real time."[57] As Andrews observes, "Far from Markle's inclusion changing the symbol, she is the exception that proves the rule. The ongoing press hostility she has been subjected to is evidence of the unease of her presence."[58] Yet she has made it clear that she intends to call things as she sees them and will not be bullied or cowed into submission or silence. Despite the missed opportunity to deliver more diversity and inclusion to the monarchy and colonial Britain, we must give credit where credit is due. As Woldemikael and Woldemikael write, "There are limits to the agency of multiracial individuals to change institutions like the monarchy and broader racial stereotypes, such as those characterizing Markle's coverage in the *Daily Mail*." As she is just one biracial American woman, it is unfair to place the expectation and responsibility on Markle that she should have symbolized progress, especially when she was up against the formidable monster that the hyper-partisan press continues to be. Despite the fact that the Sussexes have relocated over five thousand miles away to completely distance themselves from the monarchy, and have not lived in the U.K. for six years, online news brims with headlines that pit Markle against Middleton. As Woldemikael and Woldemikael explain, these "divergent perceptions" and media-created portrayals of each sister-in-law underscore the dire "need for a paradigmatic shift in the way race is discussed and represented in the media."[59]

Still, it is admirable that Markle has retained her strength and grace throughout all these years of abuse and trauma by the media and the monarchical institution. She clearly intends to "keep it real" going forward. One has to salute Oprah Winfrey for conducting such a savvy and superb interview. It was first-rate in every respect. And while extreme right-wing commentators seemed to be outraged (perhaps terrified?) by what Markle shared in that interview about how the monarchy and the media aggressively and ruthlessly subjugated her, I'll repeat those wise words of bell hooks on subjectivity that remind us, "As subjects, people have the right to define their own reality, establish their own identities, name their history."[60] Ward further credits hooks's explanation of "objectification," and examines Markle through it, whereby her "reality is defined by others" and her "identity created by others."[61] In that case, it seems an intelligent move to take back power and present her own identity using the massive platform that only Oprah could provide.

Whatever potential shenanigans the public relations team at Buckingham Palace attempted to execute to combat the Oprah interview, silence seemed a wise tactic following that interview. Here again, I believe Markle ironically and cleverly utilized such silence as a retort to the silence she was given by the monarchy in far too many cases when she asked them for help and protection. She clearly won the public relations battle with a touchdown; it was a drop-the-mic performance. In their defiant departure from the royal family and their brave honesty in their candid discussion with Oprah Winfrey, Markle and Prince Harry stood up to the multiheaded dragon of racism, colonialism, imperialism, white privilege, and other oppressive forces, delivering a much-needed bruising. They two of them shrewdly outmaneuvered the competition. As many a Black pastor would tell his congregation, "Let the church say, AMEN!"

## Notes

1. Dicker, "Sean Hannity Producer Calls Meghan Markle 'Very Uppity.'"
2. Moore, "Meghan Markle Acted Like a Demanding Entitled Princess."
3. Kane, "Hold On, Did Fox News Try to Use COLONIALISM?," Sky News Australia, "Fox News Host Tucker Carlson Says He Always Thought Meghan Markle Was 'Ridiculous,'" Facebook, October 19, 2022, https://www.facebook.com/watch/?v=5310282999083220; Sky News Australia, "'Really Terrible': Ben Shapiro Says Prince Harry and Meghan Markle Are 'the Worst,'" February 23, 2023, YouTube

video, 2:07, https://www.youtube.com/watch?v=dgGxLDYDVhs; Royal Family News, "Charlie Kirk FINISHES 'Woke Princess,'" Facebook, October 12, 2025, https://www.facebook.com/permalink.php?story_fbid=pfbid0rxhjyqQEc4V1wCTwAYKyxvs7Rs81PGHojUSv6XKbizVQAtr4N6zZ8DEcCjzed1hl&id=61557424807078; Sky News Australia, "Prince Harry and Meghan Markle Suffer Not Only from Wokeism but Narcissism and Laziness," Facebook, December 13, 2023, https://www.facebook.com/watch/?v=821152383387549.

4. Watson, "Meghan Markle, the Royal Family, Right Wing Media."
5. Andrews, "Post-racial Princess."
6. Walden, "Meghan Can't Demand Privacy for Baby Archie."
7. Walden, "Shameful Speculation About the Princess of Wales."
8. Woldemikael and Woldemikael, "From Suits to Royals."
9. Cited in Andrews, "Post-racial Princess."
10. Andrews, "Post-racial Princess."
11. Sun Reporter, "Mark My Words."
12. Ward, "Making Black Motherhood (In)Visible," 241.
13. Marks and Fischer. "The King's New Bodies," PAGE NUMBER.
14. Andrews, "Post-racial Princess."
15. Marks and Fischer. "The King's New Bodies," PAGE NUMBER.
16. For example, Carlson, "Tucker Carlson: Meghan Markle Latest Example."
17. Quoted in Gainous and Wagner, "Book Review."
18. Kane, "Hold On, Did Fox News Try to Use COLONIALISM?"
19. Woldemikael and Woldemikael, "From Suits to Royals."
20. Styles, "Harry's Girl Is (Almost) Straight Outta Compton"; Wilson, "Now That's Upwardly Mobile!"; Drury, "Prince Harry and Meghan Markle."
21. Woldemikael and Woldemikael, "From Suits to Royals."
22. Balteiro, "From *Kisstory* to *Megxile*."
23. Farkas and Neumayer, "Mimicking News," 3.
24. McGarry, "Meghan Markle's Great-Great-Great Grandmother."
25. Ward, "Making Black Motherhood (In)Visible."
26. Farkas and Neumayer, "Mimicking News," 3.
27. Newton, "Kate Middleton and Meghan Markle's Tense Wimbledon Outing."
28. Sun Reporter, "Mark My Words."
29. Goodfellow, "UK Media's Coverage of Meghan Markle Really Is Racist."
30. Ward, "Making Black Motherhood (In)Visible," 246.
31. Sun Reporter, "Mark My Words."

32. Sun Reporter, "Mark My Words."
33. Dicker, "Sean Hannity Producer Calls Meghan Markle 'Very Uppity.'"
34. Sun Reporter, "Mark My Words."
35. Sun Reporter, "Mark My Words."
36. hooks, *Talking Back*, 42.
37. Linton, "Buckingham Palace Issues First Statement."
38. Sun Reporter, "Mark My Words."
39. Sun Reporter, "Mark My Words."
40. "Royal Rota," News Media Association, accessed December 19, 2025, https://newsmediauk.org/industry-services/royal-rota/.
41. Myers, "Inside Palace Chaos."
42. Nathan, "Kate Middleton's Photoshop Fail."
43. Clements-Thrower, "Exact Times Kate Middleton Edited Mother's Day Picture."
44. Myers, "Inside Palace Chaos."
45. Nathan, "Kate Middleton's Photoshop Fail."
46. Henderson, "'The Help' Isn't a Helpful Resource on Racism"; Bennett, "10 Examples of the 'Black Best Friend' Trope."
47. Ward, "Making Black Motherhood (In)Visible."
48. Ward, "Making Black Motherhood (In)Visible," 246.
49. Quoted in O'Toole, "Meghan Markle Needs to 'Speak Loud.'"
50. Nathan, "Kate Middleton's Photoshop Fail."
51. Woldemikael and Woldemikael, "From Suits to Royals."
52. Woldemikael and Woldemikael, "From Suits to Royals."
53. Murray and Eastwood, "Jane Crow and the Law."
54. Ward, "Making Black Motherhood (In)Visible," 235.
55. Andrews, "Post-racial Princess."
56. Ward, "Making Black Motherhood (In)Visible," 247.
57. Sun Reporter, "Mark My Words."
58. Andrews, "Post-racial Princess."
59. Woldemikael and Woldemikael, "From Suits to Royals."
60. Quoted in Ward, "Making Black Motherhood (In)Visible," 238.
61. Quoted in Ward, "Making Black Motherhood (In)Visible," 238.

## Works Referenced

Andrews, Kehinde. "The Post-racial Princess: Delusions of Racial Progress and Intersectional Failures." *Women's Studies International Forum* 84 (2021): https://doi.org/10.1016/j.wsif.2020.102432.

Balteiro, Isabel. "From *Kisstory* to *Megxile*: Tabloids as Lexical Trendsetters." *English Today* 39, no. 1 (2023): 35–40. https://doi.org/10.1017/S0266078422000025.

Bennett, Jessica. "10 Examples of the 'Black Best Friend' Trope Kerry Washington Now Rejects." *Vibe*, September 28, 2023. https://www.vibe.com/lists/examples-black-best-friend-trope/.

Carlson, Tucker. "Tucker Carlson: Meghan Markle Latest Example of Elites' Unseemly Victimhood." *Fox News*, 2021. https://www.foxnews.com/opinion/tucker-carlson-meghan-markle-elite-victimhood.

Clements-Thrower, Antony. "Exact Times Kate Middleton Edited Mother's Day Picture on Photoshop—and What She Used." *Mirror*, March 11, 2024. https://www.co.uk/news/royals/exact-times-kate-middleton-edited-32330121.

Dicker, Ron. "Sean Hannity Producer Calls Meghan Markle 'Very Uppity.'" *HuffPost*, January 15, 2020. https://www.huffpost.com/entry/sean-hannity-producer-Meghan-markle-uppity_n_5e1ee747c5b673621f6dff64.

Drury, Flora. "Prince Harry and Meghan Markle: The Royal Love Affair with Africa." *BBC*, November 28, 2017. https://www.bbc.com/news/world-africa-42153317.

Farkas, Johan, and Christina Neumayer. "Mimicking News: How the Credibility of an Established Tabloid Is Used When Disseminating Racism." *Nordicom Review* 41, no. 1 (2020): https://reference-global.com/article/10.2478/nor-2020-0001.

Gainous, Jason, and Kevin M. Wagner. "Book Review: *The Hybrid Media System Politics and Power*, by Andrew Chadwick." *Journal of Politics* 77, no. 2 (2015): e7–e8. https://www.jstor.org/stable/10.1086/678356.

Goodfellow, Maya. 2020. "Yes, the UK Media's Coverage of Meghan Markle Really Is Racist." *Vox*, January 17, 2020. https://www.com/first-person/2020/1/17/21070351/meghan-markle-prince-harry-leaving-royal-family-uk-racism.

Henderson, Cydney. "'The Help' Isn't a Helpful Resource on Racism: Here's Why Twitter Is Mad the Film Is Trending." *USA Today*, June 8, 2020. https://www.usatoday.com/story/entertainment/movies/2020/06/08/the-help-isnt-helpful-resource-racism-heres-why/5322569002/.

hooks, bell. *Talking Back: Thinking Feminist, Thinking Black*. Boston: South End Press, 1989.

Kane, Vivian. "Hold On, Did Fox News Try to Use COLONIALISM as Proof That the British Monarchy Isn't Racist?" *The Mary Sue*, March 11, 2021. https://www.themarysue.com/fox-news-kilmeade-meghan-markle-response/.

Linton, Caroline. "Buckingham Palace Issues First Statement Since Harry and Meghan Interview." *CBS News*, March 10, 2021. https://www.cbsnews.com/news/Buckingham-palace-statement-meghan-markle-prince-harry-interview-royal-family/.

Marks, M. P., and Z. M. Fischer. "The King's New Bodies: Simulating Consent in the Age of Celebrity." *New Political Science* 24, no. 3 (2002): 371–94.

McGarry, Patsy. "Meghan Markle's Great-Great-Great Grandmother Was a Belfast Catholic." *Irish Times*, January 23, 2019. https://www.irishtimes.com/culture/heritage/meghan-markle-s-great-great-great-grandmother-was-a-belfast-catholic-1.3767214.

Moore, Carissa. "Meghan Markle Acted Like a Demanding Entitled Princess During NYC Outing with Prince Harry, Claim Sources." *The Overtimer*, July 22, 2002. https://theovertimer.com/2022/07/meghan-markle-acted-like-a-demanding-entitled-princess-during-nyc-outing-with-prince-harry-claim-sources/.

Murray, Pauli, and Mary Eastwood. "Jane Crow and the Law: Sex Discrimination and Title VII." *George Washington Law Review* 34, no. 2 (1965): 232–56.

Myers, Russell. "Inside Palace Chaos After Kate Middleton Admits She Edited Mother's Day Photo." *Mirror*, March 12, 2024. https://www.mirror.co.uk/news/royals/Inside-palace-chaos-after-kate-32330133.

Nathan, Sara. "Kate Middleton's Photoshop Fail Mocked by Sources Close to Meghan Markle, Prince Harry: 'Would Never Make That Mistake.'" *Page Six*, March 11, 2024. https://pagesix.com/2024/03/11/royal-family/sources-close-to-meghan-markle-mock-kate-middleton-photoshop-fail/.

Newton, Jennifer. "Kate Middleton and Meghan Markle's Tense Wimbledon Outing Hinted at 'Rocky Road Ahead.'" *Mirror*, July 13, 2024. https://www.mirror.co.uk/news/royals/Kate-middleton-meghan-markles-tense-33219452.

O'Toole, Scarlett. "Meghan Markle Needs to 'Speak Loud' in Defence of Kate Middleton After Family Photo Crisis." *Mirror*, March 12, 2024. https://www.mirror.co.uk/3am/us-celebrity-news/meghan-markle-needs-speak-loud-32331518.

Styles, Ruth. "Harry's Girl Is (Almost) Straight Outta Compton: Gang-Scarred Home of Her Mother Revealed—so Will He Be Dropping By for Tea?" *Daily Mail*, November 2, 2016. https://www.dailymail.co.uk/news/article-3896180/Prince-Harry-s-girlfriend-actress-Meghan-Markles.html.

Sun Reporter. "Mark My Words: Meghan Markle Oprah Interview." *The Sun*, January 31, 2024. https://www.the-sun.com/news/2475583/meghan-markle-oprah-interview-full-transcript/.

Walden, Celia. "Meghan Can't Demand Privacy for Baby Archie While Asking the Public to Fund Her Family's Lifestyle." *The Telegraph*, July 1,

2019. https://www.telegraph.co.uk/women/life/meghan-cant-keep-baby-archie-away-public-still-expect-foot-bill/.

Walden, Celia. "The Shameful Speculation About the Princess of Wales's Health Has to Stop." *The Telegraph*, March 11, 2024. https://www.telegraph.co.uk/columnists/2024/03/11/princess-of-wales-kate-health-photo-mothers-day-privacy/.

Ward, Jonathan. "Making Black Motherhood (In)Visible: The Importance of Race, Gender, and Nation in the Mediation of Meghan Markle on Instagram." *Women's Studies in Communication* 44, no. 2 (2021). 231–51. https://doi.org/10.1080/07491409.2021.1912532.

Watson, Elwood. "Meghan Markle, the Royal Family, Right Wing Media Animus and the Specter of Deeply Entrenched Racism!" *Medium*, March 12, 2021. https://medium.com/the-polis/meghan-markle-the-royal-family-right-wing-media-animus-and-the-specter-of-deeply-entrenched-38e829ba3bd9?sk=33ae6dfbb8a6aa27e113da80abb08889.

Wilson, Christopher. "Now That's Upwardly Mobile! How in 150 years, Meghan Markle's Family Went from Cotton Slaves to Royalty via Freedom in the U.S. Civil War . . . While Her Dad's Ancestors Included a Maid at Windsor Castle." *Daily Mail*, November 29, 2017. https://www.dailymail.co.uk/femail/article-5130473/Meghan-Markles-upwardly-mobile-family.html.

Woldemikael, Eve, and Olivia Woldemikael. "From Suits to Royals: The Politics of Meghan Markle's Racial Ambiguity." *Women's Studies International Forum* 85 (2021). https://doi.org/10.1016/j.wsif.2021.102439.

# CONCLUSION

JULIE SCHWIETERT COLLAZO

Like Duchess, I was not a royals watcher before we began work on this collection.

My earliest memory of anyone in my ambit being interested in royals (indeed, obsessed with them) is of my godmother, whose living room walls featured portraits of the royal family—Princess Diana, especially—and other royal memorabilia, interspersed with curios that housed spoons and thimbles collected from her travels, most of which, I'd learn as I grew into adulthood, were to places seized by long-simmering imperialist fevers. They were places she'd write about in her annual Christmas letters, seemingly oblivious to the fact that everything she enjoyed in these countries was acquired through the objectification and exploitation of others, people who were entirely invisible to her.

To my young eyes, the people and world depicted on my godmother's walls looked dreadfully boring. As yet naïve to the politics of pain inflicted by royalty—a subject that has come to both fascinate and horrify me in the years since, especially while working on this book—what bewildered me at that age was why no one ever looked happy, why they never seemed to broadcast *any* emotion. And as a girl who detested lace and dresses, who wasn't the least bit interested in makeup and had very little interest in "accessories" of any sort, I wondered why anyone would ever willingly dress up in clothes and pin on brooches that appeared terribly uncomfortable, why they would subject themselves to the tiresome, antiquated protocols of a politeness so formal and so extreme (and, as I matured, I came to understand, so ironic and hypocritical) as to appear disconnected entirely from the world in which I lived.

Eventually, I'd stray far from my hometown in the American South and those walls covered with tributes to royalty, living first in Puerto Rico and then Mexico with my husband, who was Cuban. While it was Spain (and the United States) whose colonialist practices impacted these places more than England, the practices of imperialism and, crucially, their long-term effects, reverberating across generations, became visible to me and rendered themselves legible as part of a larger enterprise—and, indeed, it *was* and *remains* an enterprise—whose horrors could not be obscured by all the finery and formality the Western world or Global North could muster as distraction.

Duchess and I have worked on a number of projects together over the past two decades, and I daresay neither of us would have predicted when we began collaborating that we would end up working on a book about royalty. We are alike in so many ways, most of all in our relationship to The Academy (yes, capital *T*, capital *A*). Above all, we are both "in the trenches, with the people" scholars, thinkers who want our work to have practical meaning and application. We don't think for the sake of thinking. We think for the sake of provoking critical conversations, which, in turn, we hope will stimulate profound social change.

When she proposed we edit a collection of essays about Meghan Markle and the royal family, I hesitated. I was certainly no expert on either subject, and perhaps brought no real credentials to the project other than my undergraduate degree in women's studies, my background as a former psychotherapist, and a wide-ranging curiosity about how we harm one another, how we might heal ourselves and one another, and how we become free (or not) of circumstances and relationships that constrain us. I am grateful to her, and to the authors who contributed to this volume, for their confidence and trust.

As the authors of this collection have established, Meghan Markle offers a most compelling figure through which we can witness and process how colonialist powers are—and, mostly, are not—grappling with their imperialist legacies and white anxieties that perpetuate racialized power dynamics harming people of color the world over. Markle, through her marriage to Prince Harry, became the blank screen onto which so many white fears and fantasies were projected. Perhaps her most radical act has been one that has been read primarily as an act of self-preservation, but which is also a profound gesture of resistance. By deserting the royal family and physically removing herself from the empire, she has refused to assume the role of teaching the royal family how to do or be better, indeed insisting that they will not be let off the hook for past or present offenses. They are left to figure this out on their own . . . or not.

And mostly, to no one's surprise, they have not.

While we worked on compiling and editing this book, Duchess and I traded royal news, analyzing every story about reparations (a concept that "moved from a fringe idea to a thing everyone is talking about," in the words of *Time* journalist Janell Ross[1]) and sitting with the immense, if not surprising, horror of the discovery by historian Nicholas Radburn of a "highly unusual" symbol that was branded on slaves that "[established] a vivid link between the British monarchy and the slave trade": "A crown resembling the iconic St. Edward's headpiece from British coronations sat atop the letters S and C, apparently a stylized reference to the slave-trading South Sea Company. The accompanying text, written in 1715, declared that this was 'the Mark henceforward, to be put upon the Bodys of the Negros to be sold & Dipos'd of in the Spanish West Indies,' under a contract between Britain's late Queen Anne and Spain's King Philip V."[2]

New investigations and growing social movements led by people of color subjected to the Crown (most notably, Barbadian prime minister Mia Mottley) are allowing us to see and contest empire and royalty in new or deeper ways. And, of course, Meghan Markle, in her role as both insider and outsider, helps us interrogate the empire as well, not in spite of her departure but because of it.

As we conclude the editing of this volume, Meghan Markle and her family have continued to be a subject of interest and attention—and, in some (mostly white, mostly imperialist, neocolonialist) circles, of derision—in the media. This is true of both conventional outlets and social media, which, Elwood Watson so rightly points out in this collection, is an array of largely unmoderated, unfiltered, and unmitigated armchair commentary, often vicious. *Fox News* journalists reported with gossipy glee on the Spotify staffers who leaked their catty "secret" nickname for Markle to the press.[3] The headline—"Meghan Markle Earns Stinging Secret Nickname from Spotify Podcast Co-workers: Expert"—skillfully leverages the words "earns" and "expert" to underscore a particular position, one that continues to savage the princess.

The sordid "reportage" isn't limited to the English language. Robert Rodríguez, writing for Catalonia's *El Nacional,* let it slip that the couple is experiencing financial strain because they are living beyond their means—this despite Markle's newish orchard venture, Prince Harry's best-selling memoir, their lucrative Spotify deal (recently canceled), and Netflix deals—yes, plural.[4] As we approached the publication of this collection, Netflix announced a *new* show, *With Love, Meghan,* featuring Markle in an "inspiring series [that] reimagines the genre of lifestyle programming, blending practical how-to's and candid conversation with friends, new and old." The platform teased that the series will feature Meghan "shar[ing] personal tips and tricks, embracing playfulness over perfection and highlight[ing] how easy it can be to create beauty, even in the unexpected."[5] No doubt, critics will see the series as yet another Markle middle finger to the perfection-seeking, not playful royal family.

Meanwhile, Leonor Reyes, writing for Mexico's *Revista Clase,* authored a tabloid-esque piece that, translated, is headlined "Meghan Markle planned to write a book about her divorce from Prince Harry, [sources] reveal." If it comes as a surprise that Markle and the prince are getting divorced, it should. The author of the article even admits that, well, the pair haven't even announced plans to separate, much less divorce.[6] While one article—Rodríguez's—seems to suggest, though does not outright state, that the couple's economic precarity could, and perhaps, should, force them back into the royal fold and their attendant duties, the only safe and economically sure harbor available to them, the other, Reyes's, seems to suggest, as Lily Talmont explores in her chapter in this volume, that no princess can expect to have a happy ending. Markle's ultimate, eternal punishment for contesting—indeed, outright rejecting—royal protocol, can only be divorce, an outcome that would allow her narrative and her narration to be seized from her once again. In fact, Rodríguez, in his article, attempts to jump the gun by capturing the narrative reins before anyone else can do so, once again painting Markle as an opportunist and a gold digger, saying that it's rumored she'd ask for up to $80 million USD as part of a divorce settlement.

It is a challenging task to close this collection of essays. Markle's story is still very much in the process of being written. She—and the decisions she makes—will continue to influence vital, long-overdue discourses about race and monarchy, about the responsibilities of the latter to provide restitution and issue apologies for centuries of abuse, as well as to interrogate the continuation of its very existence. To be clear, Markle is not *responsible* for these conversations or decisions, nor the outcomes that result from them, especially given that the royal family did not take advantage of her arrival in their ranks to go inward and do the soul-searching work required to confront such painful, difficult matters. Nonetheless, the fact that she remains a public figure whose every decision is scrutinized endlessly in the court of public opinion means that she will continue to exert influence, even as she asserts her right to privacy and distance from the royal family.

## Notes

1. Ross, "Inside Barbados' Historic Push."
2. Adam, "A Crown Branded onto Bodies."
3. Nolasco and Papa, "Meghan Markle Earns Stinging Secret Nickname."
4. Rodríguez, "Meghan Markle y Harry empiezan a tener graves problemas."
5. Netflix, "With Love, Meghan."
6. Reyes, "Meghan Markle planeaba escribir un libro sobre su divorcio."

## Works Referenced

Adam, Karla. "A Crown Branded onto Bodies Links British Monarch to Slave Trade." *Washington Post*, September 28, 2023. https://www.washingtonpost.com/world/2023/09/28/slave-trade-monarchy-uk-archives/.

Netflix. "With Love, Meghan: Official Trailer." January 2, 2025. YouTube video, 1:49. https://www.youtube.com/watch?v=Vdro1p53LYQ.

Nolasco, Stephanie, and Ashley Papa. "Meghan Markle Earns Stinging Secret Nickname from Spotify Podcast Co-workers: Expert." *Fox News*, January 23, 2025. https://www.foxnews.com/entertainment/meghan-markle-earns-stinging-secret-nickname-spotify-podcast-coworkers-expert.

Reyes, Leonor. "Meghan Markle planeaba escribir un libro sobre su divorcio del príncipe Harry, revelan." *Revista Clase*, January 21, 2025. https://www.revistaclase.mx/realeza/meghan-markle-planeaba-escribir-un-libro-sobre-su-divorcio-del-principe-harry-revelan/.

Rodríguez, Robert. "Meghan Markle y Harry empiezan a tener graves problemas porque sus ingresos no cubren su alto nivel de vida." *El Nacional*, January 22, 2025. https://www.elnacional.cat/enblau/es/casa-real/meghan-Markle-harry-empiezan-tener-graves-problemas-porque-sus-ingresos-no-cubren-Su-alto-nivel-vida_1350277_102.html.

Ross, Janell. 2023. "Inside Barbados' Historic Push for Reparations." *Time*, July 6, 2023. https://time.com/magazine/europe/6294871/july-24th-2023-vol-202-no-3-u-s/.

# CONTRIBUTORS

**Lucca Ramone Carlson** is a graduate of the University of Florida, where he served as a research fellow for Dr. Sharon Austin.

**Duchess Harris** is a professor of political science and American studies at Macalester College in Saint Paul, Minnesota, and a nationally recognized expert on Black feminist politics and history. A governor-appointed member of Minnesota's Board of Public Defense and a founding member of the Kamala Harris Project, she regularly appears in national and international media to discuss race, feminism, and American politics and policing.

**Marissa Kessenich** is a doctoral candidate in the English department at the University of Virginia. Her research centers on contemporary African American literature with a particular focus on issues of historical recovery and the archive.

**Jasmine Mitchell** is an associate professor of Puerto Rican and Latinx studies at Brooklyn College.

**Sarah Olutola** is an assistant professor of writing at Lakehead University in Ontario, Canada.

**Portia Owusu** is a scholar of African and diaspora literature with a focus on twentieth- and twenty-first-century West African and African American narrative. She is interested in slavery, cultural philosophies, and history. She is an assistant professor of English at Texas A&M University.

**Therí A. Pickens** is a professor of English at Bates College, specializing in African American, Arab American, and disability literatures and theories. She is the author of two books: *New Body Politics* (Routledge, 2014) and *Black Madness :: Mad Blackness* (Duke, 2019). You can find her public scholarship in *Ms. Magazine, The Root,* and Medium (@tpickens). Learn more about her at www.tpickens.org.

**Amelia Ryan** is a graduate of Macalester College with a degree in psychology and French and Francophone studies. She is pursuing a master's degree in French at Middlebury College.

**Julie Schwietert Collazo** is a writer, editor, fact-checker, and translator. Along with Rosayra Pablo Cruz, she is the co-author of *The Book of Rosy*, the first memoir to be published by a parent affected by the 2018 family separation policy. The book was named by Kirkus Reviews as one of the best nonfiction titles of 2020. She specializes in subjects related to Latin America, migration, and women's roles in global social justice movements.

**Lily Talmont** is a graduate of Macalester College with a degree in international studies. She is a Peace Corps volunteer serving in Samoa teaching English literacy.

**Ariane Tulloch** is interested in the African diaspora. She has a doctorate in American studies from the University of Kansas and is a lecturer for American studies at the University of Kansas.

**Elwood Watson** is a professor of history, Black studies, and gender and sexuality studies at East Tennessee State University. He is a syndicated columnist and the author of four books: *Outsiders Within: Black Women in the Legal Academy After Brown v. Board*; *Understanding the Humanities*; *Keepin' It Real: Essays on Race in Contemporary America*; and *Talkin' to You, Bro! Liberating Yourself from the Confusing, Ambiguous Messages of Contemporary Masculinity*. He is currently working on a book about men who are members of Generation X—that is, men who were born between 1965 and 1980.

**Stephanie L. Williams** is an instructor of political science at the University of South Florida.

**Sharon D. Wright Austin** is a professor of political science at the University of Florida.

# INDEX